WILLIAM CAREY

PAINTED BY HOME. ENGRAVED BY SARTAIN.

WILLIAM CAREY,

AND MRITYUNJAYA HIS PUNDIT.

WILLIAM CAREY.

A Biography.

Birth Place and Early Residence.

WILLIAM CAREY:

A BIOGRAPHY.

BY JOSEPH BELCHER, D.D.,

AUTHOR OF "BAPTISMS OF THE NEW TESTAMENT," EDITOR OF "COMPLETE WORKS OF ANDREW FULLER," "WORKS OF ROBERT HALL," ETC., ETC., ETC.

PHILADELPHIA:
AMERICAN BAPTIST PUBLICATION SOCIETY.
118 ARCH STREET.

PHILADELPHIA:
STEREOTYPED BY GEORGE CHARLES

PREFACE.

THE question may, probably, be asked by some who take up this volume, Why publish a new life of a man who has been dead nearly twenty years? And especially, when a former Memoir, written by an able ex-missionary, a near relative of its subject, and personally acquainted with him, has been extensively circulated? Allow me, gentle reader, to write a few words in reply.

WILLIAM CAREY is one of the names which no section of the Christian church will ever permit to die. The pioneer of modern missionaries, he strikingly illustrates the grace of God in his own personal history, and shows us the kind of agency which God usually employs in accomplishing the designs of his mercy to our fallen world. His example presents great encouragement to Christians of every class to labor for God, while it exhibits the spirit and temper in which all services for the highest interests of the world must be accomplished. The life of CAREY will always be kept before the church of Christ; and no objection to two biographies of this extraordinary man can be made, so long as we have more than one of the illustrious MILTON, of the never-dying BUNYAN, of the zealous WHITEFIELD, or of the immortal WASHINGTON.

If the question be again asked, Why a new life should be written, rather than the former one be reprinted; our general answer is, that books are usually written for a particular country, and for a particular day; so that because a volume was written in England twenty years ago, and was so acceptable as to call for two editions in that country and four or five others in this, it by no means follows that a new work, constructed partly on the basis of the old one, but embodying a mass of new materials, and more clearly arranged, will not be far more acceptable. The fact is, that the Rev. Eustace Carey, the valued nephew of Dr. CAREY, and his first biographer, was a far better missionary, preacher, and missionary agent, than biographer. God has given him eminent gifts, but not of a *literary* character. Dr. Wayland, in his excellent Introduction to one of the

American editions of Mr. Carey's memoir of his venerated uncle, says, "In many parts we could wish that it had been more copious and specific, and had been more richly stored with domestic and daily incident, and illustrative anecdote." But the tact of collecting materials from all and every source, of condensing them into a small compass, and of presenting them before the reader in the most attractive form, never was possessed by the worthy biographer. Hence, though the Memoir has always been read with interest, it has been complained of that the book was, in technical phrase, *heavy;* and many worthy persons have lamented that the life of a man presenting so fine a subject to encourage the friends of Christian Missions, and to inspire our ardent and pious young men with a spirit of persevering labor in the Cause of Christ, was not more generally known. Again and again, since the author of this volume has resided in the United States, has the subject been urged upon him; and now—laid aside for a season from the pastorate, by impaired health—he has given a portion of his time to the production of a book which he hopes may interest many of the families of which our churches are composed, and diffuse that spirit of piety and zeal which is essential alike to personal and social Christian prosperity.

It is quite probable that my attention would have been practically directed to this subject several years ago, but that till recently there lived a gentleman—the Rev. Christopher Anderson, of Edinburgh—who was very generally looked to for a work of this character.* His fine talents and learning, his extensive correspondence with CAREY and his colleagues, and his enthusiasm in the subject, encouraged the hopes of many; and more than once, and by more than one method, did I urge the labor on that eminent servant of God. He never seemed unwilling to engage in it; but his hands were full of other work, and now, alas, he has been called to his reward, leaving the task undone.

It was my happiness, even from my infancy, to be well acquainted with the leading active persons of the English Baptist Missionary Society. I knew nearly every one of its Fathers and Founders, and have often heard the enchanting tales of their early labors, trials, and encouragements, from their own lips. Moreover, it was my happiness to serve the Society during its

Jubilee Year, in an office which delightfully compelled me to study its early history, and to become acquainted with its friends. And now, removed far from its scenes of action, I rejoice in what I have done, assured that I have had no temptation to take any other than an impartial view of whatever facts were important to introduce into this volume.

It would be injustice to Mr. Eustace Carey, if I did not acknowledge that for a large portion of the materials of this work I am indebted to him. I have endeavored to give every fact which I deemed important, especially to the American reader; but, as far as possible, without repetition. From the various publications also, connected with the JUBILEE of the Society, in 1842—3, including Dr. Cox's admirable history, sermons, lectures, magazines, etc.,—from periodical publications and other sources in this country, especially from a number of important denominational works in the Library of the AMERICAN BAPTIST PUBLICATION SOCIETY, to which I have been privileged with free access—I have collected, as well as from private sources, *many highly interesting facts, which have hitherto been nearly if not quite unknown.* I have sought to make the volume interesting to the general reader, rather than to the mere scholar, though the most enlightened man will most correctly appreciate the literary talents and attainments of the distinguished CAREY. The insertion or omission of PROFESSOR WILSON'S estimate of the mind and labors of the Translator at Serampore, at one time was a matter of question; but deliberation at length induced me to place it in the APPENDIX, as containing much matter that is highly interesting to the Linguist and the Missionary.

Commending the volume to the examination and candor of the reader, and to the blessing of the God of Missions, I withdraw from the audience-chamber of my friends, with the hope of having rendered some small service in the field of Missionary Biography.

J. B.

Philadelphia, May 1853.

CONTENTS.

CHAPTER I.

CHAPTER II.

CHAPTER III.

CHAPTER IV.

CHAPTER VII.

CHAPTER VIII.

CHAPTER IX.

APPENDIX.

ENGRAVINGS.

WILLIAM CAREY.

CHAPTER I.

Glance at Northampton—Meeting at the Baptist Church in 1787—Carey's first public introduction of Missions—Repulse—Early history—Conversion—Baptism—Call to the Ministry—Ordination at Moulton—Labors—Learning.

PERHAPS most readers of this volume have heard of the old quiet town of Northampton, situated nearly in the centre of England. It is now chiefly occupied by manufacturers of shoes, and commands a large trade; but little more than a century since, it was composed principally of residences of persons of moderate fortunes, who had retired from business. This town is celebrated as having been the birth-place of Robert Brown, the founder of Independency, or Congregationalism, the scene of the ministry of the learned and amiable Dr. Doddridge, the excellent expositor of the New Testament, and President of a dissenting college; and since his day as the residence of several other eminent men.

In the early part of the ministry of Dr. Doddridge, a few Baptist members of his church united with several other persons, in forming a small Baptist church in the town, which has since risen to very considerable eminence. In the autumn of 1787, a company of several neighboring ministers assembled for religious services with this church; and in the evening, when the public engagements were ended, and the ministers were occupied in the then common practice of smoking their pipes, John Ryland, the venerable and excellent, but eccentric ex-pastor of the church, entered the room where they were sitting, and with a tone of authority, required the two youngest ministers present, each to propose a question for discussion. One of these young pastors was John Webster Morris, afterwards the ablest biographer of Andrew Fuller; he suggested 2 Peter, ii. 1, as a topic of conversation, and was somewhat ludicrously told by the old gentleman to go home and read Gill and Brine, and other commentators, and not to come there with his Arminian questions! So was silence imposed on John W. Morris.

The other young pastor was of small stature, some twenty-five years of age; in the usual sense of the term, he was uneducated, and had lately been ordained pastor of a neighboring village church. He was very plainly dressed, and of quite unpolished manners. Nor will our readers wonder at these things when they are told that the salary received from his people was little more than fifty dollars a year; and the proceeds of a school, which he had commenced, that he might add to his income, was less than forty dollars in addition. The plough-boys around him loved him on account of the regard he showed to them, and for the little lectures he had been used to give them in the evening on the map of the world, and on the general religious ignorance of mankind. Beyond this little circle he was by no means popular. This diffident young man, after a long silence, rose to propose the question—"Have the churches of Christ done all they ought to have done for heathen nations?" The question somewhat startled the brethren; and the old minister of whom we have already spoken, without asking any of the company to express an opinion,—awfully afraid of some new-fangled fanaticism,—sprang on his feet, and with eyes flashing like lightning, and in tones resembling thunder, cried out, "Young man, sit down; when God pleases to convert the heathen world, he will do it without your help or mine either." For *that time* the question was settled. This young minister was William Carey; let us inquire into his previous history.

Edmund Carey, the father of William, was the parish clerk and parish school-master, at Paulerspury, a few miles from Northampton, where he succeeded his father we believe, in both these offices, and occupied a thatched cottage, built for his father, which is represented, with the school-room, in our Vignette.

In this cottage William Carey, the eldest child of his parents, was born August 17, 1761, and here he resided until he was fourteen years of age. From his very earliest days he was intent on the acquirement of knowledge. His mother was accustomed to hear him, when not more than six years old, repeat sums in arithmetic, which he had mentally wrought out. Whatever he began he finished; no difficulties ever discouraged him, and the more his mind expanded, the more intent was he on filling it. The room wholly appropriated to his use was filled with insects, placed in every corner, that so he might trace all their movements and growth. He was very fond of drawing and painting, as well as of collecting birds, flies, and the smaller animals. In his walks he observed every hedge, and carefully watched every plant. All this while, he was one of the most active in the amusements of the boys in the neighborhood, and was greatly beloved by the lads about his own age. Though his manners were awkward, and there was nothing in his person which to a stranger would be prepossessing, the more intelligent, even then, could see indications of talent and genius. A man who was held in high reputation for good sense and moral worth, used to say that if WILLIAM CAREY lived even to be old, he would never cease to be a learner, and would always be in pursuit of something farther. Fully, indeed, was the good man's opinion verified.

During these fourteen years, the subject of our memoir was without real religion. His parents, though highly moral, do not seem to have been the subjects of heartfelt piety. He himself says: "My education was that which is generally considered good in country villages, and my father being schoolmaster, I had some advantages which the other children of my age had not. In the first fourteen years of my life I had many advantages of a religious nature, but was wholly unacquainted with the way of salvation by Christ. During this time I had many stirrings of mind, occasioned by my being often obliged to read books of a religious character; and having been accustomed from my infancy, to read the Scriptures, I had a considerable acquaintance therewith, especially with the historical parts. I also have no doubt but the constant reading of the Psalms and Lessons in the parish church, which I was obliged to attend regularly, tended to furnish my mind with a general Scripture knowledge.

"Of real experimental religion, I scarcely heard any thing till I was fourteen years of age; nor was the formal attendance upon outward ceremonies, to which I was compelled, the matter of my choice. I chose to read books of science, history, voyages, etc., more than any others. Novels and plays always disgusted me, and I avoided them as much as I did books of religion, and perhaps from the same motive. I was better pleased with romances; and this circumstance made me read the "*Pilgrim's Progress*" with eagerness, though to no purpose."

About this time he became increasingly the subject of a cutaneous disease, with which he had been afflicted from childhood. Though it seldom appeared in the form of an eruption, it made the rays of the sun almost insupportable, and rendered it impossible that he should obtain a living by labor in the field. This fact led to a change of circumstances which in the good Providence of God placed him under sound evangelical preaching, and prepared the way for the great events of his future life. Intending as we do, to make CAREY, as much as possible, his own biographer, we copy from a letter to Dr. Ryland, the events of this period:—

"At about fourteen years of age, I was bound apprentice to Clark Nichols, of Hackleton, a shoemaker. He died when I had been with him about two years. I engaged to pay his widow a certain sum for the remainder of the time for which I was bound, and from that time worked as a journeyman with Mr. T. Old, of Hackleton, till his death. The childish story of my shortening a shoe to make it longer, is entitled to no credit, though it would be very silly in me to pretend to recollect all the shoes I made. I was accounted a very good workman, and recollect Mr. Old keeping a pair of shoes which I had made in his shop as a specimen of good workmanship. But the best workmen sometimes, from various causes, put bad work out of their hands, and I have no doubt but I did so too.

"My master was a strict churchman, and what I thought a very moral man. It is true, he sometimes drank rather freely, and generally employed me in carrying out goods on the Lord's day morning, till near church time; but he was an inveterate enemy to lying, a vice to which I was awfully addicted; he also possessed the qualification of commenting upon a fault, till I could scarcely endure his reflections, and sometimes actually transgressed the bounds of propriety. A fellow servant was the son of a dissenter; and though not at that time under religious impressions, yet frequently engaged with me in disputes upon religious subjects, in which my master frequently joined. I was a churchman; had read "*Jeremy Taylor's Sermons*," *Spinker's Sick Man Visited*," and other books; and had always looked upon dissenters with contempt. I had, moreover, a share of pride, sufficient for a thousand times my knowledge: I therefore always scorned to have the worst in an argument, and the last word was assuredly mine. I also made up in positive assertion what was wanting in argument, and generally came off with triumph. But I was often convinced afterwards that, though I had the last word, my antagonist had the better of the argument, and on that account felt a growing uneasiness, and stings of conscience gradually increasing. The frequent comments of my master upon certain parts of my conduct, and other causes, increased my uneasiness. I wanted something, but had no idea that nothing but an entire change of heart could do me good.

"There was a place of worship, and a small body of dissenters in the village; but I never attended it, and thought myself to have enmity enough in my heart to destroy it. As my uneasiness increased, my fellow-servant, who was about this time brought under serious concern for his soul, became more importunate with me. I was furnished by him, now and then, with a religious book, and my opinions insensibly underwent a change, so that I relished evangelical sentiments more and more, and my inward uneasiness increased. Under these circumstances, I resolved to attend regularly three churches in the day, and go to a prayer-meeting at the dissenting place of worship in the evening; not doubting but this would produce ease of mind, and make me acceptable to God. I also resolved to leave off lying, swearing, and the sins to which I was addicted, and sometimes when alone, I tried to pray; but was at present unacquainted with the wickedness of my heart, and the necessity of a Saviour.

"A circumstance which I always reflect on with a mixture of horror and gratitude, occurred about this time, which, though greatly to my dishonor, I must relate. It being customary in that part of the country, for apprentices to collect Christmas boxes [donations] from the tradesmen with whom their masters have dealings, I was permitted to collect these little sums. When I applied to an ironmonger, he gave me the choice of a shilling or a sixpence; I of course chose the shilling, and putting it in my pocket, went away. When I had got a few shillings, my next care was to purchase some little articles for myself; I have forgotten what. But then, to my sorrow, I found that my shilling was a brass one. I paid for the things which I bought, by using a shilling of my master's. I now found that I had exceeded my stock by a few pence. I expected severe reproaches from my master, and therefore came to the resolution to declare strenuously that the bad money was his. I well remember the struggles of mind which I had on this occasion, and that I made this deliberate sin a matter of prayer to God, as I passed over the fields towards home! I there promised, that if God would but get me clearly over this, or, in other words, help me through with the theft, I would certainly for the future leave off all evil practices; but this theft and consequent lying appeared to me so necessary, that they could not be dispensed with.

"A gracious God did *not* get me safe through. My master sent the other apprentice to investigate the matter. The ironmonger acknowledged the giving me the shilling, and I was therefore exposed to shame, reproach, and inward remorse, which preyed upon my mind for a considerable time. I at this time sought the Lord, perhaps much more earnestly than ever, but with shame and fear. I was quite ashamed to go out; and never, till I was assured that my conduct was not spread over the town, did I attend a place of worship.

"I trust, that under these circumstances, I was led to see much more of myself than I had ever done before, and to seek for mercy with greater earnestness. I attended prayer-meetings, only, however, till February 10, 1779, which being appointed a day of fasting and prayer, I attended worship on that day. Mr. Chater, [Congregationalist minister,] of Olney, preached, but from what text I have forgotten. He insisted much on following Christ entirely; and enforced his exhortation with that passage, 'Let us therefore go out unto him without the camp bearing his reproach.' Heb. xiii. 13. I think I had a desire to follow Christ; but one idea occurred to my mind on hearing those words which broke me off from the Church of England. The idea was certainly very crude, but useful in bringing me from attending a lifeless, carnal ministry, to one more evangelical. I concluded that the Church of England, as established by law, was the camp in which all were protected from the scandal of the cross, and that I ought to bear the reproach of Christ among the dissenters; and accord ingly I always afterwards attended divine worship among them.

"In a village near that in which I lived, were a number of people who had drank deeply into the opinions of *Law*, and other mystics. I had heard of these people, but knew none of them. After some time, and after, by reading some few books, I had formed to myself what I thought a consistent creed, one of these persons, the clerk of that parish, sent me word that he wished to have some conversation with me upon religious subjects. I had been informed that he was a great disputant, and violent in his temper; but I at that time thought every thing in the gospel system, as I had received it, so clear, that I had no hesitation about meeting him; I had also a stock of vanity, which, though then unperceived, prompted me to dispute with any one who would dispute with me. I therefore promised to meet him. At the appointed time a heavy rain prevented our meeting; but this only made me the more anxious to embrace another opportunity, which soon occurred. In about six hours' warm disputes upon various subjects, in which he frequently addressed me with tears in his eyes, in a manner to which I had been unaccustomed, and controverted all my received opinions, which I still think were, in the main, the doctrines of the gospel, I was affected in a manner which to me was new. He proved to my conviction, that my conduct was not such as became the gospel, and I felt ruined and helpless. I could neither believe his system of doctrines, nor defend my own. The conversation filled me with anxiety; and when I was alone, this anxiety increased. I was by these means, I trust, brought to depend on a crucified Saviour for pardon and salvation; and to seek a system of doctrines in the word of God. This man and I frequently met, and he generally left with me some of *Law's* writings, or something in that strain. I have always thought that this man was really possessed of divine grace, and still think so.

"Some old Christians in the village where I lived, had frequently taken me by the hand, and communicated their own experience and feelings to me, which had much encouraged me. But after I had conversed with this man once or twice, and they knew that I read books which he lent me, all began to suspect that I leaned to erroneous opinions, and for a long time said but little to me.

"The minister whose preaching I attended [Mr. Luck, a Congregationalist,] was but ill qualified to relieve my spirit, or to clear up my doubts; I therefore sometimes attended at Northampton; sometimes on Mr. Deacon, [Baptist,] at Road; and sometimes on Mr. Scott, afterwards the distinguished commentator, at Ravenstone; but was always in an inquisitive and unsatisfied state. During this time the people at Hackleton formed themselves into a [Congregational] church, and I was one of the members who joined it at that time; but I never was witness to the ordinances being administered there, except the sprinkling of an infant by Mr. Horsey, of Northampton [the successor of Dr. Doddridge,] might be so called. About the time of that church being formed, there was a considerable awakening, and prayer-meetings were more than ordinarily attended. A sort of conference was also begun, and I was sometimes invited to speak my thoughts on a passage of Scripture, which the people, being ignorant, sometimes applauded, to my great injury.

"When I had been apprenticed about two years, my master died. This involved me in some pecuniary difficulties, as I purchased the remainder of my time, and was obliged to work for lower wages than usual, on account of my imperfect knowledge of the business. This occasioned me to labor very hard, and kept me very poor. Some circumstances relating to my temporal concerns are so impressed on my mind, and the spiritual experience they gave rise to so imprinted on my soul, that I can never long lose sight of them; they produce in me a mixture of trembling and thankfulness. I thought those seasons very painful then; but it was better with me than it is now.

"One circumstance I may mention, because it was the introduction to others which I must not pass over. Not having the circular letter [Minutes,] to refer to, I cannot say in what year it was, [1782,] but you will recollect. At the [Baptist] Association at Olney, when Mr. Guy [of Sheepshead,] preached from 'Grow in grace,' etc., and you in the evening, the very first time that I heard you, from 'Be not children in understanding;' I, not possessed of a penny, that I recollect, went to Olney. I fasted all day because I could not purchase a dinner; but towards evening, Mr. Chater, in company with some friends from Earl's Barton, saw me, and asked me to go with them, where

I remember I got a glass of wine. These people had been supplied once a fortnight by Messrs. Perry, Chater, and Raban, [Congregational ministers,] in rotation. Mr. Chater advised them to ask me to preach to them; in consequence of which, about a fortnight afterwards, three persons came to ask me to preach at Barton. I cannot tell why I complied, but believe it was because I had not a sufficient degree of confidence to refuse; this has occasioned me to comply with many things which I would have been gladly excused from. I went to Barton; and the friends asked me to go again. Having thus begun, I continued to go to that place for three years and a half. I generally went on the Lord's day morning, and returned at night, as the distance was but about six miles. Soon after this was known, the few people at Paulerspury, my native village, asked me to preach to them once a month. This was [at the distance of] ten miles; but as I had the pleasure of seeing my parents, I went. On this occasion I frequently went to Towcester in the day, to attend Mr. Ready, and afterwards Mr. Skinner, [Baptist ministers,] who often gave me much encouragement, and the latter sometimes asked me to preach for him.

"I had remained in the state of uncertainty and anxiety about gospel doctrines already mentioned, till this time; and having so slight an acquaintance with ministers, I was obliged to draw all from the Bible alone. Mr. Skinner one day made me a present of Mr. Hall's [father of the celebrated Robert Hall,] "*Help to Zion's Travellers;*"* in which I

* Published by the AMERICAN BAPTIST PUBLICATION SOCIETY.

found all that arranged and illustrated which I had been so long picking up by scraps. I do not remember ever to have read any book with such raptures as I did that. If it was poison, as some [Antinomians,] then said, it was so sweet to me that I drank it greedily to the bottom of the cup; and I rejoice to say, that those doctrines are the choice of my heart to this day.

"A sermon preached by Mr. Horsey, of Northampton, at the *rantism* of an infant, and some conversation with Mr. Hunne, then on probation at Road, had drawn my mind to the subject of baptism; but I do not recollect having read any thing on the subject till I applied to Mr. Ryland, senior, to baptize me. He lent me a pamphlet, and turned me over to his son, who, after some time, baptized me at Northampton."

Let us stay a moment here, to listen to the statement made by the excellent Dr. Ryland, nearly thirty years after this event, at the first public meeting of the Baptist Missionary Society, held in London, June 1812:—"October 5th, 1783, I baptized in the river Nen, a little beyond Dr. Doddridge's meeting-house at Northampton, a poor journeyman shoemaker, little thinking that before nine years had elapsed, he would prove the first instrument of forming a society for sending missionaries from England to preach the gospel to the heathen. Such, however, as the event has proved, was the purpose of the Most High; who selected for this work not the son of one of our most learned ministers, nor of one of the most opulent of our dissenting gentlemen, but the son of a parish clerk, at Paulerspury, Northamptonshire."

If it were not occupying too much space in our volume, it would here be easy to afford high testimonials of the esteem in which WILLIAM CAREY was then held among all who knew him. We have before us a very interesting letter from Dr. Scott, the commentator, describing him in early youth, and rejoicing in the success of his after life. Of this excellent clergyman, CAREY wrote many years afterwards to Dr. Ryland: "If there be any thing of the work of God in my soul, I owe much of it to his preaching, when I first set out in the ways of the Lord."

We must now, however, proceed to speak of him as entering on the duties of the ministry. On the principle of allowing him to tell his own tale, we transcribe the larger part of a letter to Mr. Sutcliff, dated December 30, 1785, when he was at the age of twenty-four, simply premising that previously to writing it he had become a member of the church at Olney:—

"The people at Barton remain in a divided situation, and there is but little probability of my being useful amongst them. The little that they collect for me does not pay for the clothes which I wear out in serving them, and, which affects me most, those that are just setting out at Moulton, are left like sheep without a shepherd.

"The cause seems to increase at Moulton, and I have the pleasure to see most who have begun, hold on, and manifest a truly Christian spirit. It will be easy to settle the church upon evangelical principles, but I do not choose to attempt such a thing without your advice and concurrence. If you approve of it, I should be glad if you would send me word, and likewise the outlines of a covenant, which if strict in practical, and not too high in doctrinal points, will, I believe, be unanimously subscribed by all the old members of the church, and I think about eight or ten more would join in a little time. The friends are desirous to be in order, and things have a pleasing aspect at present. * * * Now I wish you to advise me to leave Barton, or not, and what steps to pursue at Moulton, whether to do any thing immediately, or wait longer, till I am completely sent out [into the ministry,] by your church. I should be glad, likewise, if the church would take my affair into consideration. If they want more trial of my gifts, I shall be willing to wait till they are satisfied; if they are satisfied already, I should be glad if they would avoid delay; I wish, however, to leave it to their discretion."

It will have occurred to the reader that Mr. CAREY had been already preaching several years, without the direct sanction of any church; and tradition says, that the difficulty half hinted at by CAREY himself, in the letter we have just quoted, did really exist at Olney; some of the brethren hesitated as to whether he possessed talents promising a useful ministry; and the same authority asserts that the only matter in which Mr. Sutcliff, during a very long pastorate, was disposed to stretch his influence to the utmost, was in connexion with calling Mr. CAREY to the ministry. At length, however, the church encouraged him to enter on the work, "and," says CAREY to Dr. Ryland, many years afterwards, "what I still *wonder* at, I was appointed to the ministry. I perfectly recollect that the sermon which I preached before the church, and on hearing of which they sent me out, was as weak and crude as any thing could be, which is or has been called a sermon."

As might have been expected, Mr. CAREY removed to Moulton. On February 13, 1787, he writes to the Rev. J. Stanger, more than fifty years the pastor of the church at Bessel's Green Kent:—"You desire that I would write an account of every thing that is worth writing, respecting the state of affairs at Moulton. I think I wrote you word that we had begun a gospel discipline in the church. Through the good hand of our God upon us, I trust that it has been useful; and our people, who knew little or nothing of its utility, begin to see both its necessity and usefulness. Seven have been added to the church, and affairs seem in a desirable train. The church and congregation have joined in inviting me to take upon me the pastoral office. I have not the least objection, except for fear about temporal supplies. Yet, after prayer to God, and advising with neighboring ministers, I am disposed to trust these things in the hand of God, who has helped me hitherto; and have accordingly signified my assent to the church." His ordination took place on August 1, following, when Andrew Fuller preached to the church; the sketch of his sermon may be found in the first volume of his works, as issued by the American Baptist Publication Society.

A reference to two matters connected with CAREY while residing at Moulton shall close this chapter. We have already said that his salary from his ministry was small, never exceeding at Moulton seventy-five dollars a year; and the question may well be asked, how did he live? for be it remembered that he had married in his twentieth year, and had now two or three children. He expected to raise a school; but a popular teacher, who had left the village, returned, and blighted this prospect; besides which, he had much less talent for teaching than for acquiring; and, in addition to all this, he could never assume the carriage, nor utter the tones, nor wield the sceptre of a schoolmaster. He would frequently smile at his incompetency in these respects, and facetiously say, "When I kept school, the boys kept me."

Mr. Morris, of whom we have already spoken as one of his earliest and most intimate friends, represents him at Moulton adding to his income by resorting to his trade as a shoemaker; and having told us that he was employed by a contractor with government, residing at Northampton, he says, "Once in a fortnight or three weeks CAREY might be seen walking eight or ten miles, with a wallet full of shoes upon his shoulder, and then returning home the same day with a fresh supply of leather to fulfil his future engagements."

But another subject is still of greater interest to us than this:—what was he now doing towards the acquirement of intellectual furniture? The bench was his seat of literature, and the shoemaker's stall, where the voice of a tutor was never heard, the hall in which he acquired all his early learning. To his friend and pastor, Mr. Sutcliff, he says in a letter at the close of 1785, from which we have already quoted:—"I have received the four volumes of '*Nature displayed*,' and '*Corderii Colloquiorum Centuria selecta*;' am much obliged to you and my unknown friend for the latter, and will pay, when I come to Olney, or see you elsewhere, for the former. I have written out great part of '*Ruddiman's Grammar*,' and intend to write the rest as soon as possible." Mr. Sutcliff often, in after life, congratulated himself that he lent him a Latin grammar, which he believed to be the first elementary book he had ever perused in that language or any other. Dr. Ryland used to tell with delight how the shoemaker visited his study at the end of six weeks master of Latin, and how, in an almost incredible short period, he acquired the Dutch language, just for the sake of furnishing the translation of a sermon which had been spoken of to the Doctor as a very excellent performance. Greek and Hebrew were both acquired without a living teacher, and within seven years he could read his Bible in six or seven languages! He one day purchased for a few pence an old book in the French language—"*Ditton on the Resurrection*," and in the course of three weeks made himself so far master of it, that he could read it with great satisfaction. To him the acquirement of a language seemed so easy that he had but to lay a book before him, while engaged in some laborious employment, and study it as a mere matter of amusement. Besides all this, "*Guthrie's Geography*," and "*Cook's*

Voyages round the World," together with his English Bible were very carefully studied. He always sat at work with a book before him, and when an hour's recreation was imperative, the hour was employed in cultivating a garden, of which labor he was passionately fond throughout life. In this happy and delightfully innocent engagement we will for the present leave him.

CHAPTER II.

Mr. Carey's view of his own character—His person and manners described by Mr. Gotch—His conduct at a minister's meeting—Advantages derived from neighboring ministers—Mr. Hall, senior—Mr. Fuller—Difficulties at Moulton—Invitation to Leicester—Removal—Interview with Mr. Robinson—Difficulties—Wise conduct—Labors—Division of time—Pains of separation.

HAVING seen MR. CAREY ordained at Moulton, and admired the ardor with which he conducted his "pursuit of knowledge under difficulties," it may not be improper to see what manner of man he was. His own account of himself at this time is thus given to his friend Dr. Ryland in 1804:—"I am convinced that some sins have always attended me, as if they made a part of my constitution; among these I reckon pride, or rather vanity,—an evil which I have detected frequently, but have never been free from to this day. Indolence in Divine things is constitutional: few people can think what necessity I am constantly under of summoning all my resolution to engage in any thing which God has commanded. This makes me peculiarly unfit for the ministry, and much more for the office of a missionary. I now doubt seriously, whether persons of such a constitution should be engaged in the Christian ministry. This, and what I am going to mention, fill me with continued guilt. A want of character and firmness has always predominated in me. I have not resolution enough to reprove sin, to introduce serious and evangelical conversation in carnal company, especially among the great, to whom I have sometimes access. I sometimes labor with myself long, and at last prevail sufficiently to break silence ; or, if I introduce a subject, want resolution to keep it up, if the company do not show a readiness thereto." It is true, that this account was given by CAREY some years after the time of which we are writing, but it was given in its special connexion with the account of his early life, and certainly was the view he always took of himself. Never was any eminent man more distinguished for Christian humility than WILLIAM CAREY, hence he closes this very letter with saying to his friend, "I have now only to desire of you that the above [his autobiographical sketch, from which we have so largely quoted,] may not be published ; though I have no objection to your publishing any parts thereof, provided you so conceal names and other allusions, as that it may never be known that it is an account of me. Every publication of this kind if the author be known, makes him more public ; and as it is very uncertain whether I shall not dishonor the gospel before I die, so as to bring a public scandal thereupon, the less is said about me the better."

The *external* man, CAREY, at this time was described more than fifty years afterwards, by Mr. Gotch, an eminent banker at Kettering, and deacon of the first Baptist church in that town. That gentleman presided at the London JUBILEE of the Baptist Missionary Society, in 1842, when he said—

"It was my happiness, when a boy, to be acquainted with the founders of the institution. I well remember that illustrious man, whose character, as a missionary, stands pre-eminent, and who, as a scholar, attained the highest distinctions; I remember a meeting, held in my father's house, at which were present the leading ministers of the denomination, among whom were Mr. Hall, of Arnsby,—the father of the late Robert Hall, Dr. Ryland, Mr. Fuller, and Mr. Sutcliff. In one corner of the room, sat a man mean in his appearance and unpolished in his manners; that man was CAREY. A circumstance occurred which called forth his geographical knowledge. A question arose respecting an island in the Indian Archipelago, and, with great modesty, he presumed to give his opinion upon the latitude, the longitude, the number of inhabitants, and the extent of that then comparatively unknown island. I remember the astonishment with which some regarded him, as much as to say, 'Who are you?'"

Possibly no blessing which Mr. CAREY enjoyed at Moulton was greater than his introduction to the ministers we have just named, together with Morris, of Clipstone, and the seraphic Samuel Pearce, of Birmingham. Mr. Hall, especially, was among his very first and warmest friends. This eminent minister was then venerable for age, and admired through the denomination to which he belonged, for the greatness of his talents, but still more for his elevated piety and the condescension of his deportment. The last feature of his character especially endeared him to his junior brethren, and most of all to CAREY and Morris. These young men, neither of whom had passed through a college, used to meet at fixed times in the study of the venerated divine, to benefit by his conversation, and to submit to his criticisms their pulpit exercises, the outlines of which they rehearsed to him. The instructions which they thus received were beyond all value in the prosecution of their ministry; CAREY especially, was never heard to speak of his intercourse with Mr. Hall, without the deepest emotion, such indeed as often impeded his utterance; and when the venerable patriarch was, soon afterwards suddenly called to his rest, the grief of CAREY was indescribably great.

But among all the men with whom the subject of our volume was now brought into connexion, there was no one with whom he so entirely assimilated as Andrew Fuller. In decision, simplicity, and native mental vigor, they were, perhaps, equal; though in other respects, their endowments were sufficiently dissimilar to mark out each one for eminence in a very distinct department. The intimate union between them, which proved of such important moment to the cause in which they exerted so mighty an influence, and which continued for nearly thirty years, without abatement, and without alloy, commenced at Northampton, at an annual meeting of ministers. The clergyman who was expected to occupy the pulpit failed to fulfil his engagement, and Mr. CAREY was requested to supply his place. He discoursed from the text, "Be ye perfect, as your Father in Heaven is perfect." Matt. v. 48. On his descending from the pulpit, Mr. Fuller took him by the hand,

and expressed the pleasure he felt in finding that their sentiments so closely corresponded, and hoped that they should know each other more intimately.

Two subjects at this time engrossed the attention and drew forth the energies of Mr. Fuller and Mr. CAREY. The first was the duty of all men to whom the gospel is made known to believe it; the other the duty of the Christian Church to publish the gospel throughout the world. A spurious system of Calvinism at that time extensively prevailed in the Baptist churches of England, which made obdurate the consciences of the unconverted, while it chilled the sympathies and paralyzed the efforts of professing Christians. The broad common-sense principle, that every man, when he hears the gospel is bound to believe it, and that he is welcome to its blessings was then but dimly seen, even by many ministers, and seldom fully announced. The entire denial of this doctrine by some, and the partial admission and timid avowal of it by others, was extremely disastrous, so that the whole history of the controversy may well impress the preachers of Christ with the importance of attaining clear, consistent, and comprehensive views of divine truth, and of making them known without hesitation or reserve.

Possibly the reader is scarcely prepared to hear that CAREY, after only some three or four years' residence at Moulton, was seriously entertaining the question of removal. At that period, removals among Baptist pastors in England were very rare; and when they did occur, were usually the result of important causes, and were accompanied with much consideration and prayer. Nor was this case an exception to the general rule. During his ministry, the church and congregation were greatly augmented, the meeting-house was rebuilt on an enlarged scale for their accommodation, and the whole body increased in the fervor of attachment to the worthy pastor. What, then, could be the difficulty? Assuredly the people were poor, and the salary of the good man never exceeded fifteen pounds, or about seventy-five dollars a year. There was, however, an evil behind this, or poor as they were, they might have done far better. The deacons were old and decrepid men, entirely unable to discharge the active duties of their office, and the other members of the church left the whole to them. Had a proper system of giving and receiving been introduced and acted on, all had been well; but as it was, the pastor and his family had sometimes to go a whole month without the taste of animal food; nor were other matters in a better state. The church affectionately loved him, yet entirely neglected the claims of his family. Still did the good man hesitate, and wrote to his father:—"I am exceedingly divided in my own mind, and greatly need your prayers. It is well known what my situation is here, and on that account I this week received a unanimous invitation from the Baptist church at Leicester, which was joined by some of the church people, [Episcopalians,] who sit under the ministry of Mr. Robinson, of St. Mary's. If I only regarded worldly things, I should go without hesitation; but when I reflect upon the situation of things here, I know not what to do, though I think the state of things would justify my removal."

We have before us an account written by Mr. Fuller, descriptive of Mr. CAREY and his circumstances at this time. After saying "that Moulton was not a situation suited to him, either for acquiring or imparting knowledge," he goes on,—"The church at Leicester, about this time, was sunk into a melancholy state. Antinomianism, both in principle and practice, had gained the ascendency, so that the upright part of the church were unable to make any effectual resistance. An association of ministers and churches being held there in June, 1787, a solemn remonstrance was made by them against the corrupt state of the church. The consequence was, the best part of them took courage, and some of the principal offenders were separated. Both the deacons were excluded; and, Mr. Blackwell, the pastor, resigned. They were now supplied by the pastors of other churches, till they might be provided with a pastor of their own. Amongst others, Mr. CAREY sometimes went as a supply. His labors being acceptable, and it being understood that his usefulness, as well as his comfort was much confined at Moulton, it became a matter of consideration whether he should be invited to remove. At length he was invited. After carefully weighing matters on both sides, he wrote down on a sheet of paper his own thoughts and feelings, both for and against it, and gave it to some of his brethren in the ministry for advice. In this paper I well remember, there was much of the upright, disinterested man of God." The counsels of his friends and the convictions of duty led him to Leicester, but he was some considerable time before he was entirely satisfied as to the propriety of his course.

An anecdote is told by Mr. Fuller, illustrative of the manner in which Mr. CAREY was received by the Rev. Thomas Robinson, the rector of St. Mary's, and the excellent author of "*Scripture characters.*" Mr. CAREY called on him to pay his respects, and thus commenced a friendship which continued till death. Mr. Robinson, in the course of conversation, asked him if he approved of dissenting ministers getting hearers from those churches where the gospel was preached, or, as he pleasantly called it, "*Sheep-stealing?*" To this Mr. CAREY answered, "Mr. Robinson, I am a dissenter, and you are a churchman; we must each endeavor to do good according to our light. At the same time you may be assured, that I had rather be the instrument of converting a scavenger that sweeps the streets, than of merely proselyting the richest and best characters [persons] in your congregation."

On carefully examining the state of the church at Leicester, Mr. CAREY soon found that Antinomianism had taken deep root in it, and that many who stood as members were unworthy of a place in the house of God. After some attempts to purify it, which he found it difficult, if not impossible to accomplish, he, with the advice of the best members, proposed their dissolving their church-relationship, and beginning anew. This proposal was acceded to. They did not, however, refuse any one who had been a member before; but merely required the signature of a declara-

Wm. Carey. Harvey Lane Meeting House, Leicester. Page 45.

tion that they were willing and determined to keep up in future, a strict and faithful discipline, according to the New Testament, let it affect whom it might. This requisition answered the end. A considerable number of loose professors kept back, who, of course were, after a time, declared by the church to be no longer members. Thus the church was in a manner renovated. Days of fasting and prayer were appointed, in which there was much of a spirit of importunity and brotherly love; and regular prayer-meetings were constantly and well attended.

The party who refused to renew covenant, however, became Mr. CAREY'S bitter enemies. They reproached him as one who did not preach the gospel; and when he was ordained pastor, one of the boldest of them threatened, that when the members should hold up their hands as a pledge of their choice, he would make a public protest against the proceedings of the day. When he came to the trial, however, his heart failed him, and he showed no open opposition. Yet their dislike greatly distressed the new pastor, for some time, indeed, almost beyond measure. By degrees, however, they left him, for they soon found that he rose in public esteem superior to the influence of detraction.

Our readers will not here be displeased to have placed before them a view of the meeting-house in Leicester occupied by CAREY, and afterwards by the distinguished Robert Hall. Since the death of the latter excellent man, the church have erected a very large and beautiful house in another location, and the old building has been converted into school rooms for the children of the congregation.

The zealous labors of Mr. CAREY were unremitting, not only in Leicester, but in the villages near it, and wherever he could obtain access. He thus became greatly endeared to the friends of religion, while his intense thirst for learning caused him to be respected by others. Dr. Arnold, and other eminent scholars, admired his talents, and cordially threw open their libraries for his use. His great moral worth greatly contributed to raise the Baptists of Leicester, in public esteem, in which they have ever since been increasingly held.

The manner in which Mr. Carey regularly distributed his time, apportioning to every day, and almost to every hour its appropriate labor, may be learnt from a short extract of a letter to his father, which we earnestly commend to the thousands of young men among us who desire to possess his attainments:—" On Monday I confine myself to the learned languages, and oblige myself to translate something. On Tuesday, to the study of science, history, composition, etc. On Wednesday, I preach a lecture, and have been for more than twelve months on the Book of Revelation. On Thursday, I visit my friends. Friday and Saturday are spent in preparing for the Lord's day; and the Lord's day in preaching the word of God. Once a fortnight I preach three times at home; and once a fortnight, I go to a neighboring village in the evening. Once a month I go to another village on the Tuesday evening. My school begins at nine o'clock in the morning, and continues till four o'clock in winter, and five in summer. I have acted for this twelve month as Secretary to the Committee of Dissenters; and am now to be regularly appointed to that office, with a salary. Add to this occasional journeys, ministers' meetings, etc., and you will rather wonder that I have any time, than that I have so little. I am not my own, nor would I choose for myself. Let God employ me where He thinks fit, and give me patience and discretion to fill up my station to his honor and glory."

It is only important to add here, that so fully had the trials and divisions of Mr. CAREY'S church subsided, that when he was called to part from them, to enter on the work to which he devoted his life, the idea of separation was more painful than it could have been at any previous period. Still it might be said that both parties were willing to utter the final farewell; for he had taught the church to regard the general increase of the kingdom of Christ as far above their personal or social interest, and he had not taught them in vain.

CHAPTER III.

Origin of the Baptist Mission—Religious state of the Baptist denomination—Resolution of Association at Nottingham in 1784—Republication of President Edwards' Humble Attempt—Carey's Visit to Birmingham—Publication of his Pamphlet—Analysis of its reasonings—Local Meetings of the Baptists—Sermons by Sutcliff and Fuller—Association at Nottingham, 1792, and Carey's Sermon—Difficulties—Carey's Expostulation—Meeting at Kettering—Formation of the Society—The House—Remarks by Dr. Cox—Review by Dr. Godwin.

SOME of our readers will have considered it more than time that we should introduce the origin of the Baptist Missionary Society, an institution which is said by its friends of other denominations to have been "as disinterested in design, and as strenuous in exertion, as any that the Christian world ever did or ever can employ for the illumination and conversion of idolaters; and surpassing beyond comparison all former missions, and all other undertakings in the grand article of translating the Bible into the languages of the heathen." By "former missions," in this extract, must have been meant the various missions of the Roman Catholic church, the noble labors of the small body of the United Brethren, or Moravians, the efforts made in India by Danish Christians, and the foreign efforts of the Wesleyan Methodists. But up to this period, no society existed for this special object, unless indeed we must mention the old chartered "Society for the propagation of the Gospel;" but this was chiefly sustained by grants from the Government, had very little of the evangelical element in its operations, and was by its very constitution confined to the British dominions. As it is pleasant to trace the mighty oak to the acorn, let us go back to what may properly be regarded as the commencement of the society. The mustard seed—"the smallest of all seeds,"—has indeed become a great tree.

For some years before the introduction of Mr. CAREY to the Baptist church, religion had been in a very low condition throughout the denomination. We have already alluded to the False Calvinism which, to a great extent, had paralyzed Christian zeal; besides which, our ministry at that period had not generally received an adequate education; these facts, combined with the special opposition which the Baptists have always met from the established church, had brought the body into a lamentable state. At the meeting of the Northamptonshire Association, at that period one of the most respectable and vigorous of all the bodies of that kind in England, in 1784, a very deep feeling of sorrow in view of the decrease of the churches for several years past was felt, and the excellent John Sutcliff, of Olney, suggested, and the amiable John Ryland, jun., of Northampton, of both of whom we have already spoken, drew up a resolution, which we shall copy at length, with its *italics*, both because it is expressive of the simple piety of that honored fraternity, and because the reader will be glad to see the origin of all our missionary concerts, and of all our missionary institutions.

"Upon a motion being made to the ministers and messengers of the associate Baptist churches, assembled at Nottingham, respecting meetings for prayer, to bewail the low estate of religion, and earnestly implore a revival of our churches, and of the general cause of our Redeemer, and for that end to wrestle with God for the effusion of his Holy Spirit, which alone can produce the blessed effect, it was *unanimously* RESOLVED, to recommend to all our churches, and congregations, the spending of *one hour* in this important exercise, on the *first* Monday of every calendar month.

"We hereby solemnly exhort all the *churches in our connexion*, to engage heartily and perseveringly in the prosecution of this plan. And as it may be well to endeavor to keep the same hour, as a token of our unity herein, it is supposed that the following scheme may suit many congregations, viz., to meet on the first Monday evening in *May, June, and July*, from eight to nine. In *August* from *seven to eight; September and October, six to seven; November, December, January, and February*, from *five to six; March* from *six to seven*, and *April*, from *seven to eight*. Nevertheless, if this hour, or even the particular evening, should not suit in particular places, we wish our brethren to fix on one more convenient to themselves.

"We hope also, that as many of our brethren, who live at a distance from our places of worship, may not be able to attend there, that as many as are conveniently situated in a *village* or neighborhood, will unite in *small societies* at the same time. And if any *single individual* should be so situated as not to be able to attend to this duty in society with others, let him retire at the appointed hour, to unite the breath of prayer in private with those who are thus engaged in a more public manner. The grand object in prayer is to be, that the Holy Spirit may be poured down on our ministers and churches, that sinners may be converted, the saints edified, and the name of God glorified. At the same time remember, we trust you will not confine your requests to your own societies, or to our own immediate connection; let the whole interest of the Redeemer be affectionately remembered, and *the spread of the Gospel to the most distant parts of the habitable globe, be the object of your most fervent requests.* We shall rejoice if *any other Christian societies* of our own, or other denominations will unite with us, and we do now invite them most cordially to join heart and hand in the attempt.

"Who can tell what the consequence of such a united effort in prayer may be! Let us plead with God the many gracious promises of his word, which relate to the future success of his gospel. He has said, 'I will yet for this be inquired of by the house of Israel, to do it for them, I will increase them with men like a flock.' Ezek. xxxvi. 37. Surely we have love enough to Zion to set apart *one hour* at a time, twelve times in a year, to seek her welfare."

We need only add to this action of the Association, that the first printed sermon of Andrew Fuller, that on "*Walking by faith*," delivered on this same occasion, tended very deeply to strengthen this disposition to pray. The resolution was *practically regarded*, and was renewed for several years; almost immediately blessings began to descend from Heaven.

Perhaps this is the most appropriate place in which to say that in 1789, Mr. Sutcliff republished PRESIDENT EDWARDS' "*Humble Attempt to promote Explicit agreement and visible union of God's people in extraordinary prayer for the revival of Religion.*" "How much," says Mr. Fuller, "this publication contributed to that tone of feeling which in the end determined five or six individuals to venture, though with many fears and misgivings, on an undertaking of such magnitude, I cannot say; but it doubtless had a very considerable influence on it."

Little did these good men then think of the effect of their prayers; nothing was farther from their intention than to form the first society for "*the spread of the gospel to the most distant parts of the habitable globe.*" We have already seen how, three years after the resolution of 1784, such an idea was met by John Ryland, senior. Andrew Fuller says, that when it was first named to *him*, his feelings resembled those of the desponding nobleman who said, 'If the Lord should make windows in heaven, then might this thing be;'" and Dr. Ryland says, 'As to the immediate origin of a Baptist mission, I believe God himself infused into the mind of Carey that solicitude for the salvation of the heathen, which cannot fairly be traced to any other source.'

Let us now turn to see how the infinite Being led them by a way they knew not.

We have already seen that CAREY was fond of the study of geography, and we have his own testimany that his sympathy for the heathen nations was first called out by reading "*Captain Cooke's Voyages round the World.*" This zeal was not transient, and what he engaged in he did with his whole soul.

The reader is already apprized too, that soon after Mr. CAREY'S ordination at Moulton, the house of worship was rebuilt; and towards the liquidation of the debt so incurred, the pastor had to visit the different churches of the body, including the one in Birmingham, then under the pastorate of the beloved Samuel Pearce. There are others yet living, as well as the writer of this Biography, who remember one of the deacons of that church, named Thomas Potts. He was a man of plain person, and of somewhat singular habits, but greatly distinguished for simple and earnest piety. He had risen from poverty to the possession of considerable wealth by trading with the United States, chiefly, I believe, in articles of haberdashery, and was not backward in contributing to what he thought would promote the cause of Christianity. Between him and Carey there were strong points of similarity; and we are therefore quite prepared to believe the following conversation, reported in his old age by the eminent portrait painter, Mr. Medley, son of the venerable Rev. Samuel Medley of Liverpool. Mr. Medley was then [1790] a lad, and was the only person present, except Carey and Potts; we can well understand how deep an impression the scene would make on his mind:—

Mr. Potts.—Pray, friend Carey, what is it that you have got into your head about missions? I understand you introduce the subject on all occasions.

Mr. Carey.—Why, I think, sir, it is highly important that something should be done for the heathen.

Mr. Potts.—But how can it be done, and who will do it?

Mr. Carey.—Why, if you ask who, I have made up my mind, if a few friends can be found who will send me out, and support me for twelve months after my arrival, I will engage to go wherever Providence shall open a door.

Mr. Potts.—But where would you go? Have you thought of that, friend Carey?

Mr. Carey.—Yes, I certainly have. Were I to follow my inclination, and had the means at command, the islands of the South Seas would be the scene of my labors, and I would commence at Otaheite. [Tahiti.] If any society will send me out, and land me there, and allow me the means of subsistence for one year, I am ready and willing to go.

Mr. Potts.—Why, friend Carey, the thought is new, and the religious public are not prepared for such undertakings.

Mr. Carey.—No; I am aware of that; but I have written a piece on the state of the heathen world, which, if it were published, might probably awaken an interest on this subject.

Mr. Potts.—Why don't you publish it?

Mr. Carey.—For the best of all reasons, I have not the means.

Mr. Potts.—We will have it published by all means. I had rather bear the expense of printing it myself, than the public should be deprived of the opportunity of considering so important a subject.

Mr. Potts cheerfully contributed ten pounds, (about fifty dollars,) towards the publication, and in the following year the pamphlet was published. It was entitled, "*An Inquiry into the Obligation of Christians to use means for the Conversion of the Heathens.*" This pamphlet, though a new edition of it was issued some twenty-five years ago, by the late excellent Rev. Isaac Mann, of London, is very scarce; the reader, therefore, will be glad to examine a short abstract of it from the pen of Dr. F. A. Cox, who has been connected with the Society longer than any other man now living:

This tract is divided into five sections. The *first*, consists of an enquiry "Whether the commission given by our Lord to his disciples be not binding on us." It furnishes a striking evidence of the state of the public mind at that period, to find such a man as Carey, standing in the solitude of his own great missionary conceptions, constrained to plead thus: "What openings in Providence do we wait for? We can neither expect to be transported into the heathen world without ordinary means, or to be endowed with the gift of tongues, when we arrive there. These would not be providential interpositions, but miraculous ones. Where a command exists, nothing can be necessary to render it binding, but a removal of those obstacles which render obedience impossible; and these are removed already. Natural impossibility can never be pleaded, as long as facts exist to prove the contrary. Have not the popish missionaries surmounted all those difficulties which we have generally thought to be insuperable? Have not the missionaries of the *Unitas Fratrum*, or Moravian Brethren, encountered the scorching heat of Abyssinia, and the frozen climes of Greenland and Labrador, their difficult languages, and savage manners? Or, have not English traders, for the sake of gain, surmounted all these things which have generally been counted insurmountable obstacles in the way of preaching the gospel? Witness the trade to Persia, the East Indies, China, and Greenland; yea, even the accursed slave trade on the coasts of Africa." Again, "It has been said that some learned divines have proved from Scripture, that the time has not yet come that the heathen should be converted; and that first the witnesses must be slain, and many other prophecies fulfilled. But admitting this to be the case, (which I much doubt,) yet if any objection is made from this against preaching to them immediately, it must be founded on one of these things; either that the secret purpose of God is the rule of our duty, and then it must be as improper to pray for them, as to preach to them; or else that none shall be converted in the heathen world, till the universal outpouring of the Spirit in the last days. But this objection comes too late, for the success of the gospel has been very considerable in many places already."

The *second* section contains "a short review of former undertakings for the conversion of the heathen," in which is given a condensed and very excellent summary of the Acts of the Apostles, and of many of the subsequent facts of ecclesiastical history, to the eighteenth century.

The *third* section furnishes a "survey of the present state of the world;" that is, of the state of it at that period; it has, of course, been greatly altered since, by those moral and political changes which are continually occurring. It contains, however, many geographical and statistical representations worth regarding, the collection of which is demonstrative of the zeal and industry of the writer.

The *fourth* consists of "considerations on the practicability of something being done more than what is done, for the conversion of the heathen." The impediments to the carrying of the Gospel among the heathen, the author considers to be "their distance from us, their barbarous and savage manner of living, the danger of being killed by them, the difficulties of procuring the necessaries of life, or the unintelligibleness of their languages,"—all of which objections he satisfactorily refutes.

The *fifth* section embraces "an enquiry into the duty of Christians in general, and what means ought to be used, in order to promote this work." These are fervent and united prayer, and exerting ourselves in the use of means. Here he suggests the formation of a society such as was afterwards organized. "When a trading company," says he, "have obtained their charter, they usually go to its utmost limits; and their stocks, their ships, their officers, and men, are so regulated, as to be likely to answer their purpose; but they do not stop here, for, encouraged by the prospect of success, they use every effort, cast their bread upon the waters, and cultivate friendship with every one from whose information they expect the least advantage. They cross the widest and most tempestuous seas, and encounter the most unfavorable climates; they introduce themselves into the most barbarous nations, and sometimes undergo the most affecting hardships; their minds continue in a state of anxiety and suspense, and a longer delay than usual in the arrival of their vessels, agitates them with a thousand painful thoughts and foreboding apprehensions, which continue till the rich returns are safe arrived in port. But why these fears? Whence all these disquietudes and this labor? Is it not because their souls enter into the spirit of the project, and their happiness in a manner depends on its success? Christians are a body, whose truest interest lies in the exaltation of the Messiah's kingdom. Their charter is very extensive, their encouragement exceedingly great, and the returns promised infinitely superior to all the gains of the most lucrative fellowship. Let, then, every one in his station, consider himself as bound to act with all his might, and in every possible way, for God."

He concludes his pamphlet in these emphatic words:—"We are exhorted to 'lay up treasure in heaven, where neither moth nor rust doth corrupt, nor thieves break through and steal.' It is also declared, that 'whatsoever a man soweth, that shall he also reap.' These scriptures teach us, that the enjoyments of the life to come, bear a near relation to that which now is; a relation similar to that of the harvest and the seed. It is true, all the reward is of mere grace; but it is nevertheless encouraging. What a treasure, what a harvest must await such characters as Paul and Eliot, and Brainerd, and others, who have given themselves wholly to the work of the Lord! What a heaven it will be to see the many myriads of poor heathens, of Britons among the rest, who by their labors have been brought to the knowledge of God! Surely a crown of rejoicing like this is worth aspiring to! Surely it is worth while to lay ourselves out with all our might, in promoting the cause and the kingdom of Christ."

At the period of which we are writing, the Baptist churches of the midland counties of England were favored with religious meetings of intense interest. In almost every neighborhood in the spring and autumn were held what were called double-lectures;" that is, two sermons would be delivered in one service, during the forenoon; after which they would spend some hours in refreshment and social intercourse, and those who could stay, would listen to a discourse in the evening. To these meetings, members of even distant churches would flock in crowds; the preachers were usually the most acceptable who could be found, and the whole intercourse was of the best character. Unannoyed with the business trammels of "the association," every one felt at home, and in the free conversations then held, many most important plans of usefulness were suggested and matured. To these meetings, the Baptist Missionary society, during its incipient stages, and for the first twenty years of its existence, under God, owed very much. Indeed at some of these meetings its preliminaries were discussed, and at one of them it first took its actual existence. In the spring of the year 1791, one of these "Ministers' meetings," another name given to them, was held at Clipstone, a small village in Northamptonshire, where the Rev. J. W. Morris was pastor. Two sermons were preached on that occasion, both of which were afterwards printed. The first was by Mr. Sutcliff, from I Kings xix. 10, on "Jealousy for the Lord of hosts." The other was delivered by Mr. Fuller, from Haggai i. 2-, on "The pernicious influence of delay in matters of religion." Dr. Ryland, in his own simple, yet beautiful manner says, "An uncommon degree of attention seemed to me to be excited by both sermons. I know not under which I felt the most. Both were very impressive: and the mind of every one with whom I conversed seemed to feel a solemn conviction of our need of greater zeal, and of the evil of negligence and procrastination. I suppose that scarcely one idle word was spoken while I stayed, and immediately after dinner CAREY introduced the subject of beginning a mission." Mr. Morris says, "Every heart was penetrated with the subject, and the ministers retired scarcely able to speak to one another. A scene of such deep solemnity has seldom been witnessed. Mr. CAREY, perceiving the impression on all around him, could not suffer the company to separate until they had come to some resolution on forming a Missionary Society; and a society would then have been formed, but for the well-known deliberative prudence of Mr. Sutcliff." All that was really done, was to request Mr. CAREY to publish the pamphlet to which we have already referred. At the desire of the association, held at Oakham, a few weeks afterwards, these sermons were both printed.

The following sssociation was held at Nottingham, May 30, 1792, and Mr. CAREY was appointed to preach. His sermon was founded on Isaiah liv. 2, 3. Having observed that the church of God is there addressed as a desolate widow, dwelling alone in a little cottage; that the command to enlarge her tent contained an intimation that there should be an increase in her family; and that to account for so unexpected a change, she was told, that her "Maker was her husband," who should be called "the God of the whole earth," he took up what he considered to be the spirit of the passage in two exhortations; namely, EXPECT GREAT THINGS FROM GOD—ATTEMPT GREAT THINGS FOR GOD. "The effect of this discourse," says Mr. Morris, "was considerable." Dr. Ryland speaks in very much stronger terms:—"If all the people had lifted up their voice and wept as the children of Israel did at Bochim, (Judges ii.), I should not have wondered at the effect; it would have only seemed proportionate to the cause; so clearly did he prove the criminality of our supineness in the cause of God."

But even still there was ground of hesitation. Mr. Fuller says, "Some of the greatest difficulties we had to encounter were the following:—we were inexperienced in the work; we knew of no opening for a mission in any one part of the world more than another; we had no funds to meet the expense that must attend an undertaking of the kind; our situation in an inland part of the country was inconvenient for foreign correspondence; the persons who would have the management, would live at such a distance from each other as to render frequent consultation impracticable; and finally, in forming such a society, there would be danger of its falling under irreligious influence. From these and other considerations, those who were expected to engage in the work, entered upon it with much fear and trembling."

We cannot, under such circumstances, be surprised that the *ponderous* minds assembled at Nottingham moved slowly. After deliberating for a season, it is said, that they were just about to part, when CAREY, absolutely unable longer to endure disappointment, took Fuller by the arm saying, with a most imploring look, "*And are you, after all, going again to do nothing?*" This expostulation determined the matter; and a resolution was printed in the Letter [Minutes,] "That a plan be prepared against the next Ministers' Meeting at Kettering, for forming a *Baptist Society for propagating the Gospel among the Heathen.*"

The second of October, 1792, arrived, and on that day was held "The Ministers' Meeting" at

Kettering, a small country market town of less than three thousand inhabitants, commanding little wealth, and distinguished for no more intellectual power than other towns of the same general characteristics. With what anxiety must Carey have looked forward to this day. How prayerfully would he watch its movements! The brethren had their usual religious services; but the particulars of these religious services, have never, we believe, been registered. Here is the first record:—

"At the ministers' meeting at Kettering, October 2, 1792, after the public services of the day were ended, the ministers retired to consult farther on the matter, and to lay a foundation at least for a society, when the following resolutions were proposed, and unanimously agreed to.

"1. Desirous of making an effort for the propagation of the gospel among the heathen, agreeably to what is recommended in brother CAREY'S late publication on that subject, we, whose names appear to the subsequent subscription, do solemnly agree to act in society together for that purpose.

"2. As in the present divided state of Christendom, it seems that each denomination, by exerting itself separately, is most likely to accomplish the great ends of a mission, it is agreed that this society be called, *The Particular [Calvinistic] Baptist Society for Propagating the Gospel among the Heathen.*

"3. As such an undertaking must needs be attended with expense, we agree immediately to open a subscription for the above purpose, and to recommend it to others.

"4. Every person who shall subscribe ten pounds at once, or ten shillings and sixpence annually, shall be considered a member of the society.

"5. That the Rev. John Ryland, Reynold Hogg, William Carey, John Sutcliff, and Andrew Fuller, be appointed a committee, three of whom shall be empowered to act, in carrying into effect the purposes of this society.

"6. That the Rev. Reynold Hogg be appointed treasurer, and the Rev. Andrew Fuller secretary.

"7. That the subscriptions be paid in at the Northampton Ministers' meeting, October 31, 1792, at which time the subject shall be considered more particularly by the committee, and other subscribers who may be present.

"Signed, John Ryland, Reynold Hogg, John Sutcliff, Andrew Fuller, Abraham Greenwood, Ed ward Sherman, Joshua Burton, Samuel Pearce, Thomas Blundel, William Heighton, John Eayres, Joseph Timms; whose subscriptions in all amounted to £13: 2: 6."

One sentence is claimed by the house in which these proceedings took place. On that day six months preceding, had died a highly valued deacon of the church at Kettering—Mr. Beeby Wallis; in a small back parlor in the house of his widow was formed this society. Mr. Fuller, when writing of the death of Mrs. Wallis, twenty years afterwards, says, "The mention of the society being formed in *the little parlor* of her habitation, always made her eyes glisten with delight. She considered it as a high honor for so important an undertaking to have

W H VAN-INGEN.

Wm. Carey. The House at Kettering in which the Baptist Missionary Society was formed. Page 65.

been determined upon under her roof." A representation of the house, as it appeared at the jubilee of the society in 1842, is before the reader.

"The decision of this remarkable day," as Dr. Cox remarks in his excellent Jubilee "*History of the Mission*," "was not a mere extemporaneous ebullition of feeling. There were previous and preparatory movements of mind, having all the character of sacred impulses, making it evident that in the administration of providence and grace, as well as in nature, the most admirable consequences ensue from small and unpromising commencements. A thought arises in the mind of an individual. There it works secretly for a time, till it irresistibly demands expression. Then it calls into exercise the sympathies of other minds, till, attaching itself to kindred elements around, it moulds into form, and stimulates into activity a series of efforts. These issue in the salvation of innumerable souls, and by the various combinations of Christian benevolence, send down an ever-augmenting influence to distant ages. Some of the greatest events, both of secular and ecclesiastical history, have been connected with circumstances apparently the most insignificant, or with men the most obscure and unpretending, that 'the excellency of the power may be of God, and not of men.'"

"This," says Dr. Godwin, in his eloquent sermon, preached at Kettering just fifty years after, "This was precisely the way in which our mission commenced. It was neither at a time nor in such a place, nor by such means as the wisdom of this world would have selected. It was at a period when all Europe was in commotion,—when the breaking out of the French revolution affected the peace of every country, and the stability of every throne,—when the all-engrossing topic was politics, and when party spirit was high and violent. In so dark and stormy a sky who would have expected the rising of such a star? Amidst such elements of confusion and discord, who would have looked for the advent of so celestial and peaceful a visitant? Yet it was just at that time, that a few hearts, warm with the benevolence of the gospel, were found panting for the more general diffusion of its blessings, longing for the salvation of the heathen world, and devising and carrying into effect, with an enlargedness of heart which some even of their own brethren could not understand, plans for the conversion of idolaters to the knowledge and the worship of the living God. Divine Providence was about to make a new movement in the church, the set time was approaching when the vast continent of India was to receive the word of eternal life in its many languages and dialects; but who would have selected our denomination as one of its chosen instruments to take the lead in this great work?—a denomination so characteristically jealous of any thing like human authority in matters of religion, that not a few of our churches at that time looked on our single academical institution with suspicion, fearfully apprehensive lest human learning should be substituted for the teachings of the Divine Spirit. And if any one had imagined that such a movement was about to take place, where would he expect that it would commence? He might have fixed on one of our seats of learning, with its ample endowments, and its literary distinction, as most likely to originate such a project; or he might have thought of some emporium of commerce as favorable to intercourse with foreign nations; or he might have supposed that the metropolis, so rich in its resources of every kind would be a most suitable locality for the commencement of so great an enterprize; he might have said, as each of the populous and wealthy cities of the British realms occurred to his mind, as Samuel, when the sons of Jesse passed in review in his presence, "Surely the Lord's anointed is before him." But the origin of the mightiest rivers is often found in some sequestered spot. And Kettering has the honor of being the birth place of this society: and whatever political or commercial changes may pass over this town, it will descend to posterity associated with all that is great and holy in our missionary enterprize. "My thoughts are not your thoughts, neither are your ways my ways, saith the Lord of hosts."

CHAPTER IV.

An American's Visit tc Kettering—Sketches of the members of Committee—Public opinion in London—Letter from Carey respecting Thomas—Anecdote of Campbell—Thomas invited to become a Missionary—His arrival at Kettering, and affecting interview with Carey—Carey's disinterestedness and foresight—Interview with Ward—Refusal of Mrs. Carey to accompany her husband—Contributions of the churches to the Funds—Carey's visit to London—Solemn farewell services at Leicester—Embark for India—Are again set on shore—Apparent failure of the whole—Interposition of Providence—Sailing of the whole Family.

TRULY did an old man say to an American visiter to Kettering, when speaking of the origin of the Baptist missionary society, sixty years afterwards, "It was a wonderful thing, my young friend, but they did not know it; and they were wonderful men. I shall never forget them, boy as I was. They are all gone." "There was no need," says the visiter, "of asking questions—he told the whole story. I don't wonder at his not forgetting the event. Had he been but six, instead of sixteen, he would have remembered it, for his memory has been refreshed every month since. At length we took our leave, receiving the blessing of the pleasant old deacon."

In going back to the very early history of the society, it may be gratifying to look upon CAREY and his associates some two months after the organization of the body, as they are assembled at a committee meeting. There is RYLAND, often the chairman; he is of middle size, near-sighted, and has a singularly squeaking voice; he is profound in Hebrew learning, and scriptural theology; is eminently serious, and intensely anxious that deep piety should pervade every action;—there is CAREY, small in stature, lowly in spirit, and of cool and steady enthusiasm; he has infused much of the missionary spirit into the hearts of his brethren, and now only wishes they should understand that he is willing to go wherever they may send him, quite content that all the details should be settled by them;—there is HOGG, a respectable gentlemanly man, once a Congregational minister; he seems to wish it felt that he is *rich;* he never was very active nor very liberal, and soon withdrew from regular attendance on the committee, very properly resigning the office of treasurer into the hands of a layman. He survived all his brethren, attended, in second childhood, the JUBILEE meeting at Kettering, and died soon after at ninety, leaving a legacy to the society of the paltry sum of one hundred pounds;—there is PEARCE, somewhat small and thin in person, with his long hair hanging down over his shoulders; his intensity of character was now, as always, apparent, his temper all sweetness and love, and his devotion, like a vestal flame—pure, consecrated, inextinguishable. His character is described in one of his own sentences,—"O to be a Mercury, for ever rolling round and *near* the sun;"—there is SUTCLIFF, of rather large size, and the very personification of fatherly kindness; every look is benignity; he can counsel, but not control, and will carry caution and prudence to the utmost; in a word, he has exactly the qualities, in a very large degree, that Fuller needs;—yes, there, too, is FULLER, a sturdy unbending oak of the forest, who is rather dominant than attractive; no man would do any thing without asking his counsel, and assuredly he has both courage and perseverance enough to carry out any plan on which his brethren may determine, while kindness will often melt him down, and make him gentle as a lamb. Such was this first missionary cabinet, wise and humble. Never did the providence of God bring together men more suitable to harmonize in the work they had to do.

But what said other ministers and other churches of these brethren and their designs? The truth must be told; the great majority thought of the scheme as utopian, and of the men as disposed to take God's own work into their hands. A meeting was held in London to consider the propriety of forming an auxiliary society; thirty-ono persons were present, eight of whom were ministers. In a letter to Mr. Fuller, Dr. Rippon, the chairman, stated that some who were invited did not attend; and that two of the principal men in a leading church spoke decidedly against the formation of such a society. The objection was sustained by an hour's appeal from Dr. Stennett, the most distinguished of the ministers. "I asked," says he, "what must be said, in case any one wants to know the opinion of the meeting." It was universal, so far as I observed, that they were willing to assist the society as individuals; but if they were formally to take up the society, they should *commit the whole denomination.*"

And, suppose they had done so, what then? But it is important it should be well understood that it is not possible, however large a meeting, or respectable the persons of which it is composed, to *commit the whole denomination* to any thing. This is a fact which may sometimes be profitably remembered, both by large organizations, and by "city pastors." Any meeting, however called, can represent itself only; every Baptist church must perform its own duties, and has no power to transfer any duty whatever to delegates. They can appoint no representatives. All the duties of a church are those of each of its individual members.

Turn we now again to CAREY. On November 13th, a meeting of the committee was held at which CAREY was not present; but a letter was read from him, saying that a Mr. Thomas, a surgeon from Bengal, was then in London, raising a fund for a mission to that country, and was also endeavoring to obtain a companion to assist him in the work. He expressed a doubt lest this should interfere with their more enlarged plan, and a wish, if it could be done, to amalgamate their funds. Mr. Fuller was commissioned to make inquiries respecting Mr. Thomas,—his character and proceedings.

Here is the suitable place to introduce a singular circumstance related by the late Rev. John Campbell, of Kingsland, London, afterwards the distinguished missionary traveller in Africa. Mr. Campbell then resided in Edinburgh, and had heard of Mr.

Thomas, by letters from Malda, sent to one of the Scotch Bishops who had "an enthusiastic friend, that was always *pestering* him about the success of the gospel in Bengal, and with questions about religion at home." "The bishop," says Mr. Campbell, "knew little of the religion which the Bible contains. I answered his friend's questions as well as I could. I then heard nothing more of the affair until 1792, when in London." While there, he called on the Rev. Abraham Booth, and found with him a gentleman in the garb of a minister. It appears that Mr. Booth had felt some doubt about the claims of this gentleman, and did not know what weight to attach to his testimonials. Mr. Campbell regarded it as providential that he went in "just at the nick of time" to authenticate them; for upon the conversation turning upon Malda, he asked, "Did you ever hear of a Mr. Thomas, a surgeon, who began to preach in India?" After allowing him to proceed with some remarks, he said, "I am the man." All parties were much struck with the coincidence of facts. Mr. Campbell, who much resembled Carey in size, spirit of Christian simplicity, and persevering zeal, used to remark, in his own quaint manner, when speaking of the Baptist mission, "Thus I had a finger in that pie too."

Enquiry about Mr. Thomas ascertained that he was the son of a Baptist deacon at Fairford, in Gloucestershire, and that he went out in early life as a surgeon to India. About 1784 he returned from his first voyage as a medical officer, deeply affected with what he had heard and seen in that region of idolatry, and in 1785 was baptized by the late Rev. Dr. S. Stennett, was admitted into the church in Little Wild Street, London, and was licensed to preach. At the time of which we have already spoken, he had returned a second time from India to make efforts for a country, where he had some years before advertized for a Christian without finding one. It may be easily supposed that Mr. Booth immediately corresponded with the brethren in Northamptonshire on the subject.

At a committee meeting, held in Mr. Fuller's study, January 10th, 1793, the report given by the secretary, respecting Mr. Thomas, was highly satisfactory; and "the committee being fully of opinion that a door was now open in the East Indies, for preaching the gospel to the heathen, agreed to invite Mr. Thomas to go out under the patronage of the society; engaging to furnish him with a companion, if a suitable one can be obtained. Brother CAREY was then asked, whether, in case Mr. Thomas should accede to our proposal, he was inclined to accompany him. To this he readily answered in the affirmative." Late that same evening, while they were in full deliberation, to their great surprise, the arrival of Mr. Thomas was announced. Impatient to see his colleague, he entered the room in haste, and Mr. CAREY rising from his seat, they fell on each other's necks and wept. "From Mr. Thomas's account, we saw," said Mr. Fuller, "there was a gold mine in India, but it seemed almost as deep as the centre of the earth. Who will venture to explore it? 'I will go down,' said Mr. CAREY to his brethren, 'but remember that you must hold the ropes.' We solemnly engaged to do so; nor while we live shall we desert him."

The heart of CAREY was now exclusively fixed on his mission. Writing to his father soon after, he thus speaks:—"The importance of spending our time for God alone is the principal theme of the Gospel. 'I beseech you, brethren,' says Paul, 'by the mercies of God, that ye present your bodies a living sacrifice; holy and acceptable, which is your reasonable service.' To be devoted like a sacrifice to holy uses, is the great business of a Christian, pursuant to these requisitions. I consider myself as devoted to the service of God alone, and now I am to realize my professions . . . . I hope, dear father, you may be enabled to surrender me up to the Lord for the most arduous, honorable, and important work that any of the sons of men were ever called to engage in. I have many sacrifices to make."

The Rev. Eustace Carey, the nephew of Mr. C., and his first biographer, very truly remarks, that "he seemed in this undertaking to have 'his work before him,' and to possess almost a foresight of the issues of things. In his '*Inquiry*,' he wrote as if all denominations of Christians were to be stirred up to the same efforts, and expresses his judgment of what should be their conduct." And so, shortly after this time, when he went into Yorkshire, to take his farewell of a brother, he visited the town of Hull, and while walking with the Baptist pastor in the streets, he was introduced to a very young man, a printer, who had recently united with the church there. "We shall want you," said Carey, "in a few years, to print the Bible: you must come after us." Such was the first idea of missionary service conveyed to William Ward, so many years his eminent colleague at Serampore. These few words, Mr. Ward used to say, so remained on his mind, that he could never forget them; and who does not bless God for the result? Who does not resolve henceforth to have "a single eye" to the glory of his Lord?

CAREY spoke correctly when he said to his father, "I have many sacrifices to make." We have already remarked that the church at Leicester, though they ardently loved him, felt it to be their duty to say, as did the brethren at Cesarea to Paul, "The will of the Lord be done." But he had trials nearer home. Mrs. Carey was a woman of piety, but was not blessed with a very comprehensive mind; she loved her husband, but had very little sympathy with his missionary feelings; in a word she was decidedly averse to going to India, and insisted that, come what might, she and her children would remain in England. This was, both to him and the Committee, a very severe trial. They could distinctly foresee, that though men are allowed to leave their wives, and families for a time, to engage in mercantile and military expeditions, yet in religion, there would not only be a great outcry against such conduct from worldly men, but even many Christians, who had thought but little on the subject, would join in the general censure. At length, however,

CAREY resolved at all events to go; and if his wife could not be persuaded to accompany him, he would take Felix, his eldest son, with him, and leave the rest of his family under the care of the Society. She might, he thought, be afterwards persuaded to follow him; or, if not, he could but return, after having made the trial, and ascertained in some measure the practicability of the undertaking. So things for a while remained.

In the meantime, money was needed to meet great approaching expenses. Fuller toiled through London to solicit contributions from reluctant givers, and often retired from the more public streets into the back lanes, that he might not be seen by other passengers to weep for his having so little success. But while some who were presumed to possess a leading influence in the metropolis, were afraid of "committing the denomination" by its public acts, very many in the rural districts evinced a fine noble spirit of sympathy with the movement. Mr. Thomas, Mr. Pearce, and others, visited several parts of the kingdom, and met with warm responses to their appeals. Even where some hesitation was at first manifested, both ministers and people in the end assisted. Private letters contained some curious details, of which the following may be regarded as a specimen:—At Worcester, Mr. Thomas writes, that on his arrival, he had poor encouragement; but there was speedily a change. After a collection, "one poor woman, who had put five shillings into the plate in the evening, came next morning, with tears in her eyes, and blessings in her mouth, and willingly gave sixteen shillings and sixpence more. I asked her name, but she would not have it used; 'but *set me down as worthless dust and ashes;*' which I did." Mr. Thomas manifested considerable tact, as well as zeal in his missionary excursions. After being wet through in a storm, between Horsley and Bath, he arrived in the latter city at a very late hour. He preached at the Baptist church the next morning; but as they had a rule not to have more than one or two [distinct benevolent] cases in a year, and no collections, "I thought," said he, "that I should have nothing there; but some woman, after hearing the case, sent in a penny. I thanked them, and said I should set down—'*Bath, one penny!*' On farther thinking of it, and on the emergency of the case, they agreed to a collection, and at my brother's table, there was a plate handed round, and seven guineas collected; which, together with what was collected at the doors, amounted to twenty-two pounds, six shillings, and eight pence farthing."

Once, and I think only once, till after his first embarkation, CAREY visited London, and that about this time. Though so much coldness had been shown towards the mission, he described the cordial reception with which he was met by Dr. Stennett, and by Mr. Booth. During his visit, too, he made the acquaintance of the venerable John Newton. This excellent man advised him with the fidelity and tenderness of a father; and encouraged him to persevere in his missionary purpose, despite of all opposition. "What," asked CAREY, "if the company should send us home upon our arrival at Bengal?" "Then conclude," was the answer of Newton, "that your Lord has nothing there for you to accomplish. But if he has, no power on earth can hinder you."

In prospect of the missionaries taking their final departure, it was resolved, to hold at Leicester, on March the 26th, a holy convocation—a season of farewell services. The day was anticipated with solemn feeling. "I am willing," says Samuel Pearce, writing to Andrew Fuller, "to go any where, and do any thing in my power; but I hope no plan will be suffered to interfere with the affecting—hoped for—dreaded day. Oh, how the anticipation of it at once rejoices and afflicts me! Our hearts need steeling to part with our much loved brethren, who are about to venture their all for the name of the Lord Jesus." The former part of the day was wholly devoted to prayer. In the afternoon, Mr. Thomas preached from Psa. xvi. 4. "Their sorrows shall be multiplied that hasten after another god;" and a public collection was made for the mission. In the evening Mr. Hogg, of Thrapstone, delivered a suitable discourse on the solemn occasion, from Acts xxi. 14. "And when he would not be persuaded, we ceased, saying, The will of the Lord be done." Mr. Fuller addressed the missionaries from John xx. 21. "Peace be unto you; as my Father hath sent me, even so send I you." "Every part of the solemnities of this day," said he, "must be affecting; but if there be one part which is more so than the rest, it is that which is allotted to me, delivering to you a solemn parting address. But the hope of your undertaking being crowned with success, swallows up all my sorrow. I could myself go without a tear, (so at least I think,) and leave all my friends and connexions, in such a glorious cause." In closing, he says, "Go then, my dear brethren, stimulated by these prospects. We shall meet again! Crowns of glory await you and us. Each, I trust, will be addressed in the last day—'Come, ye blessed of my Father, enter ye into the joy of your Lord.' In CAREY'S Diary, Jan. 29, 1794, he says, "This evening, after a day of dejection, I had much relief in reading over Mr. Fuller's charge to us at Leicester; the affection there manifested almost overcame my spirits."

But, alas, pleasantly as things now seemed to move, CAREY and Thomas have yet no small trials to pass through; and CAREY and Fuller have to experience almost broken-heartedness. At that period, the East India Company, in whom was vested by the English government, vast political powers, was controlled almost entirely by a spirit of Infidelity, some of their Directors being placed in the British House of Commons, purposely to prevent any steps being taken for the introduction of Christianity into India, lest the government there should meet with difficulties. Hence, the greatest caution had to be observed, as to the measures to be taken in obtaining a passage for CAREY. Thomas, on this matter, had no difficulty, because he had already been in the service of the Company; and he ventured to take CAREY on board, without giving any particulars of the design of the voyage. But Thomas himself had his peculiar trials, and was in danger of imprisonment for debts which had involved him in bankruptcy; and on the very eve of embarkation he was arrested for comparatively a small sum; he fully stated his circumstances, and was set free. CAREY and he now joyfully went on board the Earl of Oxford, expecting in a day or two to sail for the far distant East. But CAREY'S own letter to Fuller shall tell a sad tale:—

Ryde, May 21, 1793.

"MY VERY DEAR FRIEND,

I have just time to inform you that all our plans are entirely frustrated for the present. On account of the irregular manner of our going out, an information is laid against the captain, (I suppose by one of Mr. T's. creditors,) for taking *a person* on board without an order from the company. The person not being specified, both he and myself, and another passenger are ordered to quit the ship, and I am just going to take all my things out.

"Our venture must go, or it will be seized by the custom-house officers. Mrs. Thomas and daughter go. I know not how to act, but will write you more particularly as soon as I can get to some settled place. I leave the island [Isle of Wight,] to-day or to-morrow, and on Thursday the ship sails without us. All I can say in this affair is, that however mysterious the leadings of Providence are, I have no doubt but they are superintended by an infinitely wise God.

"I have no time to say more. Mr. T. is gone to London again on the business. Adieu.

"Your's affectionately,

W. CAREY."

Alas, poor Fuller! Sturdy oak as he was, he transmitted this letter to Dr. Ryland, writing on it as follows:—

Kettering, May 24th.

"MY DEAR BROTHER,

Perhaps CAREY has written to you.—We are all undone.—I am grieved—yet, perhaps 'tis best.—Thomas' debts and embranglements damped my pleasure before.—Perhaps 'tis best he should not go.—I am afraid leave will never be obtained now for CAREY, or any other,—and the adventure seems to be lost.—He says nothing of the £250 for voyage. 'Tis well if that be not lost.—Yours, ever,

A. F."

No arrangement could be made by Mr. Thomas with the company in London, and the captain peremptorily refused to take them; but returned £150 of the money they had paid for the voyage; and CAREY with his companions were in London, depressed and almost overwhelmed with disappointment. In the course of a few days, however, the scene began to brighten, and their spirits to improve. The elasticity of Thomas' mind, his alacrity, and enterprize, together with the spirit of self-denial which he now manifested were truly surprising, and justly entitle him to the grateful remembrance of all who feel an interest in this Mission. And so speedily and evidently propitious were the interpositions of Providence, that before the larger number of their friends could be informed of this apparent frustration of their hopes, all was resolved into one of the most beneficial dispensations that could have possibly been imagined. Let us look at the facts.

CAREY sat down to write to his wife, to tell her that he was coming to see her, and Thomas went to a coffee-house to examine the papers, whether any Swedish or Danish vessel was expected to sail from Europe to Bengal, or any part of the East Indies that season; "when to the great joy of a bruised heart," said Thomas, "the waiter put into my hand a card, whereupon were written these life-giving words: '*A Danish East Indiaman, No.* 10 *Cannon Street.*' No more tears that night." They "fled to the office," the ship was supposed to have sailed from Copenhagen, was hourly expected in Dover Roads, and would make no stay there. "We went away wishing for money," of which they could not muster half enough. No time could be lost; that night they set off, and breakfasted with Mrs. Carey the next morning; she was suffering from weakness, having but three weeks before given birth to an infant; still she refused to go; and they reasoned with her to no purpose. They set off to Dr. Ryland at Northampton to obtain money, and on the way Thomas saw that all CAREY'S hope of his wife going with them had expired. "I proposed," says Thomas, "I will go back." 'Well, do as you think proper,' said he; 'but I think we are losing time.' I went back, and told Mrs. Carey her going out with us was a matter of such importance that I could not leave her so;—her family would be dispersed and divided for ever—*she would repent of it as long as she lived.*" She now felt afraid to stay at home, and in a few minutes, trusting in the Lord, determined to go, on the condition that her sister, now staying in the family, would go with her. This was agreed to. And, says Thomas, "We now set off for Northampton, like two different men; our steps so much quicker, our hearts so much lighter."

But even yet, there were vast difficulties to be surmounted. The seven hundred pounds needed for the voyage could not by any means be obtained. "What Dr. Ryland had," says Thomas, "he was heart-willing should go, and faith gave credit for the rest. So within the space of twenty-four hours, the whole family packed up, and left all, and were in two post-chaises on their way to London, where we were authorized to take up money if we could." The Rev. Messrs. Booth, Thomas, and Rippon, two of them new converts to the Mission, did what they could; and Thomas went to the agent, and was delighted to find that the ship had not arrived. He told the agent the facts of the case, who was so struck with the despatch which had been manifested in the business, that he accepted Thomas' offer of three hundred guineas for the whole. "I was moved with wonder," says Thomas, "to see the hand of God on this occasion, in his accepting these terms, the lowest, I suppose, that were ever heard of." For this sum the captain treated them all with the greatest kindness, admitted all to his table, and furnished them all with handsome cabins. Thus on June 13, 1793, this missionary band put to sea on board the *Kron Princessa Maria.* Of this voyage and subsequent proceedings we shall have something to say hereafter.

One remark we deem it important to make before we close this chapter:—How very different are the plans of God from those of man! We have already seen more than one illustration of this in our narrative; and who can look at the remarkable fact, that CAREY now goes to India instead of the South Sea Islands, without admiring the movement of the Divine hand? Had his original purpose been fulfilled, whatever might have been the result, it would have been not only a far different sphere from that which he did occupy, but of far less importance and appropriateness to his peculiar talents. The providence of God had otherwise designed; wisely frustrating those views which must have greatly restricted his usefulness, and directing him, by an invisible but mighty control, to a country, where, in a wonderful degree, he enlarged the bounds of literature, and extended the influence of Religion. Dr. Cox well remarks, "He *intended* to go to Otaheite; God *sent* him to India;" and we may add, raised up JOHN WILLIAMS for the South Seas, who never could have done much in the East.

CHAPTER V.

Effects produced in England by the Mission—Not generally sustained—Opinion of Mr. Beddome—Voyage—Carey's difficulties and poverty in India—Voyage up the Jubona—Meeting with Captain Short—Kindnesses received—Attachment to American Theology—Brainerd—Carey's feelings under trials—Missionary labors—Commences to build—Invited by Mr. Udney to Mudnabatty—Receives a handsome income, and relinquishes his salary—Love to the Society—A church organized—Letter of dismission from Leicester—Trials—Sickness—Domestic bereavement—Piety—Active labors—Character of the Bengalese—Worship of the Sun—Ridicule of Missions in England—Speech of Charles Marsh, Esq.

HAVING now dispatched CAREY and his family on their voyage, it may not be improper to look to the effects which followed the movement he had originated at home. In reviewing the recent proceedings, Mr. Fuller says, speaking of the benefits which had already resulted to the churches from the undertaking:—"A new bond of union was furnished between distant ministers and churches. Some who had backslidden from God were restored; and others who had long been poring over their unfruitfulness, and questioning the reality of their personal religion, having their attention directed to Christ and his kingdom, lost their fears, and found that peace, which, in other pursuits, they had sought in vain. Christians of different denominations discovered a common bond of affection; and instead of always dwelling on things wherein they differed, found their account in uniting in those wherein they were agreed. In short, our hearts were enlarged; and, if no other good had arisen from the undertaking, than the effect produced upon our own minds, and the minds of Christians in our own country, it was more than equal to the expense."

Nor is it possible for a Christian, even at this distance of time, to read the facts we have related, without admiring the wisdom and kindness of God in opening a way for an elevated devotion to display itself at a crisis, and under circumstances of such remarkable discouragement. From such interpositions, too, we must be inspired with confidence in attempting the most arduous Christian service, and offering the most costly sacrifice to which an enlightened conscience can urge us.

It must not be supposed, however, that even after all this, the missionary project met with very general support, or that those who withheld their sanction were all men either of narrow minds, or of hyper-Calvinistic tendencies. The subject, as applied to the case of modern Christianity, was new to them. The sentiments expressed by the learned and venerable Benjamin Beddome, whom Robert Hall considered the most distinguished Baptist minister in his day, in a letter to Mr. Fuller, may be taken as representing the views of many very excellent men:—"I think your scheme, considering the paucity of well-qualified ministers, hath a very unfavorable aspect with respect to destitute churches at home, where charity ought to begin. I had the pleasure once to see and hear Mr. CAREY; it struck me he was the most suitable person in the kingdom, at least whom I knew, to supply my place, and make up my great deficiencies when either disabled or removed. A different plan is formed and pursued, and I fear that the great and good man, though influenced by the most excellent motives, will meet with a disappointment. However, God hath his ends, and whoever is disappointed, he cannot be so. My unbelieving heart is ready to suggest that the time is not come, the time that the Lord's house should be built."

To detail all the particulars of the voyage, would be entirely unnecessary. Five months were thus occupied, and on the whole pleasantly, as one storm only, of importance, excited their fears. The kind treatment of the captain, the good health and cheerful spirits of Mrs. Carey and the whole family, opportunities for daily worship and Sabbath preaching, and especially the great work of the translation of the Scriptures, all animated and delighted CAREY. Thomas says, "We have finished a translation of the book of Genesis on the passage; and brother CAREY helped me out in passages which I could have made nothing of without him. So let the goldsmith help the carpenter, and the carpenter the goldsmith, that the work of God be done."

Poor CAREY! We are called to see him in trouble again. He arrived in India, a stranger in a strange land, and soon began, with his family, to feel the bitter effects of poverty. Thomas was, as may have been already perceived, of very different habits from CAREY. He directed the expenditure till there was nothing left to spend, and then turned his attention to medicine as the source of his own maintenance, while CAREY was left to do as he best might. In addition to this, Mrs. Carey soon began to show that her mental powers were unequal to her task, and indeed already furnished some symptoms of the monomania which marked her last years, and at length entirely deprived her of reason.

We may here furnish, partly from a narrative given by Mr. Fuller, but chiefly from Dr. Cox's interesting "*History of the English Baptist Mission*," a most remarkable illustration of the kindness of God to his servant, connecting with the narrative a lively display of the simplicity and Christian devotedness of CAREY.

When CAREY took his family to India, they carried with them a small investment, elsewhere called "a venture," which was designed as a means of their support and establishment; but these goods proved of little value. One authority says, that the boat which contained them was sunk in the Hoogly river, and another, that Mr. Thomas disposed of them for their immediate supply. Certainly, CAREY and his family were in great want.

In a strange land, with a wife's sister, a wife and four children, without money, without friends, and without employment, the good man must needs have felt himself in a sad condition. It occurred to him, that he might by possibility secure a little rough land, and by bringing it under cultivation, obtain food for his family. Having, too, the offer of a Bungalow, belonging to the East India Company, at Dehartar, about forty miles east of Calcutta, in which he and his family might reside, till he could provide a more permanent residence, he was induced about the beginning of February, 1794, to make preparations for his departure. He engaged as the guide of himself and his budgerow, or boat, a sensible native, called Ram Booshoo, and sailed with his family up the country, all but totally destitute of the means of subsistence, uncheered by the sweet associations of friendship, uncountenanced by the ruling authorities, and carrying with him a reluctant family, who thought it hard to be forced away from Calcutta, and carried through salt rivers, lakes, and a river of the Sunderbunds, the habitation of fierce animals prowling for prey. The humble missionary was intent, not on the acquisition of wealth or of fame, but solely on a voluntary expatriation to the distance of fifteen thousand miles from his native land, to rescue the wretched children of men from idolatry and vice; and more than willing to labor, to suffer, or to die for their salvation! What is the glory of ambition to this sublimity of benevolence!

As the family party proceeded up the Jubona, they found themselves not only desolate, but in utter destitution. Their strength was exhausted, and their provisions had failed. At this critical juncture, a gentleman was seen walking along the banks of the river, with a gun in his hand seeking for amusement. The guide said that a house which they saw, built after the English fashion, was occupied by an English gentleman. This led Mr. CAREY to think of calling there. At this moment, the gentleman with the gun, who was the very English resident described by the guide, perceiving the boat, which he saw was occupied by Europeans, approached, and invited them all to his mansion. This gentleman,—Charles Short, Esq., was a military officer, and nobly did he sustain his character. Mr. CAREY, with all his accustomed frankness, told him that his design in leaving England was to convert the Hindoos, and explained the difficulties in which he was now placed. The Captain was unhappily destitute of all true religion, and very naturally ridiculed the idea of converting the natives of India to Christianity. Cordially adding, however, that he was at perfect liberty to make his house a home for himself and his family, for six or twelve months, till he should see what he could do. Kindness like this must have powerfully affected them. Especially as it was continued in the most handsome manner for some months. CAREY saw in this unbeliever a subject on whom he did not cease to urge the evidences and the importance of the religion of the Bible, till he conducted him to the cross of Christ. He soon afterwards married Mrs. Carey's sister, and became a warm friend to the mission, till he was removed by death.

It seems proper to remark here, that some years before Mr. CAREY left England, his mind had been imbued with what was in that country called "*The American Theology.*" President Edwards, its great master, was his most admired author. The strong and absorbing view in which that great man exhibited some leading principles in the system of revealed truth, seemed so clearly to explode the errors of Armi nianism on the one hand, and of false Calvinism on the other, and to throw such a flood of irresistible light on the mediatorial dispensation, as perfectly captivated, and almost entranced the ministerial circle with which CAREY was connected. David Brainerd was supposed by President Edwards, to exemplify and irradiate the main features of his own system. This, indeed, was a principal reason why he compiled the history of his religious experience and labors; and hence it became the constant manual of the devoted admirers of that great man's theological system; while its intrinsic worth, as offering a sublime and experimental display of religious affections, through a scene of arduous labor and patient suffering, rendered it the devotional guide of multitudes who remained strangers to that grand theory of evangelical sentiment which it was supposed to illustrate. Dr. Ryland, the intimate friend of CAREY, was often heard to say that Brainerd's life ranked with him next to the Bible. In his esteem of this eminent saint and prince of Missionaries, Mr. CAREY was not behind him. His trials, during the early period of his residence in India, were not less than those of Brainerd; they were even more severe, complicated, and perplexing, and the religious devotion he manifested under them was equally pure, if not equally intense. Of this the reader will soon have proof. The missionary spirit was so incorporated with all he thought, and felt, and did, that to commemorate the missionary is to describe the Christian. "Why," asks the good man, as he writes to the society, at the very darkest moment of his history, when he had justly to complain of the conduct of Mr. Thomas, and had reason to say, "I have a place, but cannot remove my family to it, for want of money." "Why is my soul disquieted within me? Things may turn out better than I expect: every thing is known to God, and God cares for the Mission. O for contentment, delight in God, and much of his fear before my eyes! Bless God, I feel peace within, and rejoice in having undertaken the work, and shall, I feel I *shall*, if I not only labor alone, but even if I should lose my life in the undertaking."

Even before CAREY and his family were found in the house of Captain Short, he had begun missionary labor. He must have made astonishing progress in the language, and must have strongly felt that weeping must not hinder sowing. On the 19th of January, 1794, he writes in his Diary:—"This day, as every Sabbath since we have been in the country, we went among the natives. For these three last Lord's days we have discoursed to a pretty large congregation at Manicktullo bazaar or market; for we have just the same business done here on that day as any other. Our congregation has consisted principally of Mahommedans, and has increased every Lord's day. They are very inquisitive, and we have addressed them upon the subject of the gospel with the greatest freedom, and in the following manner: —A burial place, with a consecrated tomb, where offerings are daily made to the spirit of the departed person, was near; some enquiries about the reason of their offerings were made, which led on to questions on their part; and then the Gospel and the Koran insensibly became the subject of conversation. They alleged the divine original of the Koran; we enquired, 'Have you ever seen or read it?' The universal answer was 'No!' But to-day a man came who pretended to have seen it. We asked him if he knew the beginning of every chapter, for the chapters all begin with these words: 'In the name of God, gracious and merciful:' but he said, no, for it was written in Arabic, and no one could understand it. The question now was, 'Then how can you obey it?' and 'Wherefore are you Mahommedans?' To this they could not reply. They said, and so says the Koran, that the Koran was sent to confirm the words of Scripture. We insisted that the Bible said, 'Whosoever shall add to or diminish from the word of God, shall be under the curse of God;' but the Koran was written after the Bible, and pretends to Divine authority; therefore, if the Gospel be true, the Koran cannot be so, for that, you say, was to confirm it. They answered, that the Jews and Christians had corrupted the Bible, which was the reason why God made the revelation by Mahommed. We answered, 'Then how could the Koran come to confirm it? If it was corrupted, it needed correction not confirmation.' Being driven to the last shift, they said, 'Mahommed was the friend of God, but Esu, (by whom they mean Jesus,) was the spirit of God;' to which Mounshi, [the Interpreter,] shrewdly replied, 'Then which would you think highest, your friend, or your soul or spirit?' All this they bore with great good temper; but what effect it may have, time must determine. Many more things were said to recommend the Gospel, and the way of life by Christ; and as night came on we left them."

Almost immediately after CAREY and his family accepted the kindness of Captain Short, he obtained some land, and began to erect a tent, or rather very humble house, for the residence of his family; and was soon very much encouraged to find that he was rapidly gaining the confidence of the natives, four or five hundred families of whom had determined to take up their abode in his vicinity. He now thought, that as soon as he had fully acquired the language, he would have an abundant opportunity for useful exertions, both among the Hindoos and the Mussulmen. But again was he called to remove, though in this instance the change was more than pleasant. His temporal privations were about to be relieved, and troubles of this character to cease for ever.

At Malda, about three hundred miles from Calcutta, resided a gentleman of high rank in the service of the East India Company, named Udney. He was a Christian man, who in former years had been intimately acquainted with Mr. Thomas, but some unhappy differences had separated them. This gentleman was now in great distress, occasioned by the dangerous illness of his mother. Mr. Thomas hastened, far as it was, with characteristic ardor, to pay him a visit of sympathy. They met each other with tears, and far more than a renewal of their former friendship took place. This gentleman was about to erect two indigo factories in addition to those he already possessed, and knowing the destitution of the two missionaries, he invited them to superintend the new establishments, offering them such a sum of money as would afford competent support to their respective families and leave a surplus which might be applied to the furtherance of their missionary labors. In addition to all this, it was supposed that these factories, which were some seventy miles apart, would furnish a shelter for any of the heathen who might lose caste by the reception of the gospel; and that in every way the great object of the Mission might be thus advanced. On the 15th of June, 1794, CAREY arrived, after a sail of more than three weeks, at the factory, "and had once more the happiness of joining in prayer with those who love God."

Mr. CAREY was now placed in a state of comparative affluence, and although his wife's health was so feeble that she was utterly unfit to attend to his domestic concerns, and he was constantly exposed to the peculation of native servants, yet he was able to spare from one-third to one-fourth of his income for missionary purposes. With a disinterestedness which we might well expect from him, he wrote to the society in England to stop the salary he had been accustomed to receive from them. His labors, however, in the holy cause were by no means relaxed. On the contrary, he felt himself bound, now that he had become, in a pecuniary way, independent, to devote his energies, as far as possible, to the great objects which had brought him to India. Besides fulfilling the duties of his civil employment with the utmost diligence and assiduity, he attempted native education, acquired the dialect of the province in which he lived, daily addressed the idolatrous natives, often travelled considerable distances to preach in English, maintained an extensive correspondence, and conquered the elements of one of the most difficult and classic languages of the world. At the same time, his letters describe his feelings of deep regret that he could not do more, for want of an enlarged acquaintance with the native languages; and complained, too, that many infidel Europeans whom he found in India, endeavored to discourage his attempts to convert the natives by urging the utter impracticability, as they imagined, of such an enterprize. It was pleasant to him to know that his views of duty were sustained by the Committee at home, who, however, united caution with their consent, in the following resolution:—that, "though, upon the whole, we cannot disapprove of the conduct of our brethren, in their late engagement, yet, considering the frailty of human nature in the best of men, a letter of serious and affectionate caution be addressed to them."

We must stay here a moment to admire CAREY, now that we can see him again entirely *at home*. In the letter in which he resigns his salary, he adds, "At the same time it will be my glory and joy to stand in the same near relation to the Society as if I needed supplies from them, and to maintain the same correspondence with them. The only favor that I beg is, that I may have the pleasure of seeing the new publications that come out in our connexion, and the books that I wrote for before, namely, a "*Polyglott Bible*," "*Arabic Testament*," "*Malay Gospel*," and "*Botanical Magazine*." I wish you also to send me a few instruments of husbandry, namely, scythes, sickles, plough-wheels, and such things; and a yearly assortment of all garden and flowering seeds, and seeds of fruit trees, that you can possibly procure; and let them be packed in papers, or bottles well stopped, which is the best method: all these things, at whatever price you can procure them, and the seeds of all sorts of field and forest trees, etc., I will regularly remit you the money for every year; and I hope that I may depend upon the exertions of my numerous friends to procure them. Apply to London seedsmen and others, as it will be a lasting advantage to this country; and I shall have it in my power to do this for what I now call my own country. Only take care that they are new and dry."

In this letter he also gives an encouraging account of several Christian people; and expresses hopes of some natives, who, however, afterwards disappointed his expectations. *Caste* was already found to be a great obstacle in the way of Christian profession. But with five or six Baptists only, they were about to organize a church.

The reader has long since been struck with the Christian simplicity which eminently distinguished the early proceedings of the Missionary Society and its friends. This admiration will not be lessened as he reads the following extract from the church book of Harvey Lane, Leicester, written, probably, by the Rev. B. Cave, the successor of Carey:

"By a letter from Mr. W. Carey (our former pastor, and whom we resigned to the Mission in Hindostan in Asia,) we were informed that a small church was formed at Mudnabatty; and he wished a dismission from us to it, that he might become a member, and have also an opportunity of becoming its pastor. We therefore agreed, not only to send his dismission, but also to insert it at large in our Church-Book, to preserve to posterity, the memory of an event, so pleasing and important—the planting of a Gospel Church in Asia."

"The church of Christ, meeting in Harvey Lane, Leicester, England, in Europe; to the church of Christ, of the same faith and order, meeting in Mudnabatty, Hindostan, in Asia, sendeth greeting:

"DEAR BRETHREN,

"As our brother William Carey, formerly our beloved pastor, requests a dismission from us to you as a member, we comply. We earnestly desire that he may be very useful among you, both as a member and as a minister. Though few in number, may you be as a handful of genuine corn in Hindostan, which may fill all Asia with Evangelical fruit! The Lord has already done great things for you, whereof you have cause to be glad; we hope you will make it your great concern to prize and conform to the glorious gospel and its holy institutions. That ye may be filled with spiritual light, and joy; and abound in the practice of all the fruits of righteousness, is the ardent prayer of

"Your affectionate brethren in Jesus Christ."

[*Signed by Pastor and Deacons.*]

An extract from the Diary of Mr. Carey, under date of Sept. 1794, will go very far to show the trials of Missionaries, especially in the early history of the enterprize:—

"During this time [month] I have had a heavy and long affliction, having been taken with a violent fever. One of the paroxysms continued for twenty-six hours without intermission, when, providentially, Mr. Udney came to visit us, not knowing that I was ill, and brought a bottle of bark with him. This was a great providence, as I was growing worse every day; but the use of this medicine, by the blessing of God, recovered me. In about two days I relapsed, and the fever was attended with a violent vomiting and a dysentery; and even now I am very ill, Mr. Thomas says, with some of the very worst symptoms. On the last of these days it pleased God, to remove, by death, my youngest child but one; a fine engaging boy of rather more than five years of age. He had been seized with a fever, and was recovering; but relapsed, and a violent dysentery carried him off. On the same day we were obliged to bury him, which was an exceedingly difficult thing. I could induce no person to make a coffin, though two carpenters are constantly employed by us at the works. Four Mussulmans, to keep each other in countenance, dug a grave; but though we had between two and three hundred laborers employed, no man would carry him to the grave. We sent seven or eight miles to get a person to do that office; and I concluded that I and my wife would do it ourselves, when at last a servant, kept for the purpose of cleaning, and a boy who had lost caste, were prevailed upon to carry the corpse, and secure the grave from the jackals. This was not owing to any disrespect in the natives towards us, but only to the cursed caste. The Hindoos burn their dead, or throw them into the rivers to be devoured by birds and fishes. The Mussulmans inhume their dead; but this is only done by their nearest relations; and so much do they abhor every thing belonging to a corpse, that the bamboos on which they carry their dead to the water or the grave, are never touched or burnt, but stand in the place and rot; and if they only tread upon a grave, they are polluted, and never fail to wash after it.

"The points of coincidence between the Jewish people and the Hindoos are so very numerous, that alike in their religious, and ceremonial, and throughout their domestic economy, you are continually reminded of some scriptural term, incident, or usage. When engaged in preparing a Harmony of the four Gospels in the Bengali language, my pundit would often interpose the remark, 'Sir, there can be no doubt but the Jews were originally Hindoos.'

"During this affliction my frame of mind was various: sometimes I enjoyed sweet seasons of self-examination and prayer, as I lay upon my bed. Many hours together I sweetly spent in contemplating subjects for preaching, and in musing over discourses in Bengali; and when my animal spirits were somewhat raised by the fever, I found myself able to reason and discourse in Bengali for some hours together, and words and phrases occurred much more readily than when I was in health. When my dear child was ill, I was enabled to attend upon him night and day, though very dangerously ill myself, without much fatigue; and now, I bless God that I feel a sweet resignation to his will. I know that he has wise ends to answer in all that he does, and that what he does is best; and if his great and wise designs are accomplished, what does it signify if a poor worm feels a little inconvenience and pain, who deserves hell for his sins?"

The passage we have just given furnishes a fair specimen of CAREY's Diary at this important period. It is very evident that he lived too near the throne of God for the secular engagements which occupied his attention to injure his soul; nor can it excite any degree of surprize that such a Christian should be successful in the cause of his Great Master. He had now acquired enough of the language to preach more or less in about two hundred villages, within a circle of twenty miles. "My manner of travelling," he says, "is with two small boats; one serves me to live in, and the other for cooking my food. I carry all my furniture and food with me from place to place; namely, a chair, a table, a bed, and a lamp. I walk from village to village, but repair to my boat for lodging and eating."

It may not be improper here to occupy a page or

two in describing the Hindoos, to whose spiritual welfare this eminent man had now devoted his life. They are usually regarded as the aborigines of the country; from the period, however, of the conquest of India by Tamerlane, in the year 1398, a great part of Hindostan has been under the Mahommedan power; but the Hindoo subjects of the Mogul empire are incomparably more numerous than their conquerors. Their character has been recently described by an eloquent pen as follows:—"The physical organization of the Bengalee is feeble even to effeminacy. He lives in a constant vapor bath. His pursuits are sedentary, his limbs are delicate, his movements languid. During many ages, he has been trampled upon by men of bolder and more hardy breeds. Courage, independence, and vivacity, are qualities to which his constitution and his situation are equally unfavorable. His mind bears a singular analogy to his body. It is weak, even to helplessness, for purposes of manly resistance; but its suppleness and its tact move the children of sterner climates to admiration, not unmingled with contempt. All those arts which are the natural defence of the weak, are more familiar to this subtle race than they were to the Ionians of the time of Juvenal, or to the Jew of the dark ages. What the horns are to the buffalo, what the paw is to the tiger, what the sting is to the bee, what beauty, according to the old Greek song, is to woman,—deceit is to the Bengalee. Large promises, smooth excuses, elaborate tissues of circumstantial falsehood, chicanery, perjury, forgery, are the weapons, offensive and defensive, of the people of the lower Ganges. All these millions do not furnish one sepoy to the armies of the company. But as usurers, as money-changers, as sharp legal practitioners, no class of human beings can bear a comparison with them, With all his softness, the Bengalee is by no means placable in his enmities, or prone to pity. The pertinacity with which he adheres to his purposes, yields only to the immediate pressure of fear. Nor does he lack a certain kind of courage, which is often wanting in his masters. To inevitable evils, he is sometimes found to oppose a passive fortitude, such as the stoics attributed to their ideal sage. A European warrior, who rushes on a battery of cannon, with a loud hurrah, will shriek under the surgeon's knife, and fall into an agony of despair at the sentence of death. But the Bengalee, who would see his country overrun, his house laid in ashes, his children murdered or dishonored, without having the spirit to strike one blow, has yet been known to endure torture with the firmness of Mucius, and to mount the scaffold with the steady step and even pulse of Algernon Sydney."

We might here occupy many pages by presenting the sad moral, or rather, *idolatrous* condition of India, and show the harrowing cruelties connected with the worship of Juggernaut, and a thousand other things, fully illustrative of the fact that "the dark places of the earth are full of the habitations of cruelty." But it may suffice to give from one of CAREY'S own letters a description of *the worship of the Sun*, as practised in some parts of Bengal:—

"The Sun, called Soorjya, or Deelahar, is supposed to be the governor of all bodily diseases, and is therefore worshipped, to avert his anger, and to prevent diseases. Some valetudinarians worship him every Sunday, by fasting and offerings; but he is annually worshipped the first Sunday in the month of May. The name of this worship is Dhomma Bhau, or Soorjya Bhau. In these parts, (for the manner is different in different places,) women appear to be the principal actors in the worship, though none are excluded, and even Mussulmans have so far Hinduized as to join in the idolatry. It was thus conducted:—At the dawn of the morning a great number of offerings were carried into the open field, and placed in a row. The offerings which I saw consisted of fruits, sweet-meats, pigeons, and kids; and I suppose other things, as deer and buffaloes, might be offered. By each person's offering is placed a small pitcher-like pot, containing about a pint and half of water. A device, made of a water-plant, a species of phylanthus, made to represent the sun, is placed on the edge of the pot, as people in England place flowers. The pot, with all its appendages, represents the sun, perhaps as the vivifier of nature. By each offering also is placed a ——, what shall I call it?—an incense altar, or censer. It resembles a chafing-dish, is made of copper, and stands on a pedestal about a foot long. It is called a dhoonachee. It contains coals of fire, and has a kind of incense from time to time thrown into it, principally the pitch of the saul tree, called here dhoona. By each offering also stands a lamp, which is kept burning all day; and the women who offer take their stations by their offerings. At sunrise, they walk four times round the whole row of offerings, with the smoking dhoonachee placed on their heads, and then resume their stations again, where they continue in an erect posture, fasting the whole day, occasionally throwing a little dhoona into the dhoonachee. Towards evening, the Brahmin who attends the ceremony, throws pigeons up into the air, which, being young, cannot fly far, and are scrambled for and carried away by any one who gets them, for the purpose of eating. The Brahmin also perforates the ears of the kids with a pack-needle; after which, the first who touches them gets them. About sunset, the officers again take up the smoking dhoonachees, and make three more circuits round the row of offerings, making the whole number seven times in the day. I have not learned the reason of this number. After this, each one takes his or her offering home, and eats it, the worship being ended. Then the lamps are extinguished. I had some of these things presented to me; but in order to bear a testimony against the idolatry, I not only refused them, but others also brought on purpose for me by one present, telling them that it was a very wicked thing to eat things sacrificed to idols, which are God's enemies. I preached to them from Rev. i. 16, 'His countenance was as the sun shining in his strength,' and told them of the glories of the Lord of the sun, as Creator, Governor, and Saviour. I had a rich Fakir Mussulman come in the morning to hear me; he came from a distance. I had much talk with him afterwards, in the hearing of the people, who were so credulous as to believe that he had actually that morning turned a pot of water into milk. I asked him to dine with me, (this no native would do on any account,) and observed to the people, that if he could change water into milk, he could change pork into mutton; pork being never eaten by Mussulmans."

In a word, the immense difficulties that stood in the way of a successful mission were so formidable, that nothing but a steady faith in him who has "all power in heaven and in earth," could have induced CAREY and his companions to encounter them. Languages of very difficult acquirement met them at the very threshold of their labors; the intellectual and moral habits of the Hindoos were in the highest degree unfavorable to the reception of Christianity; the Brahmins, who had every thing that was dear to the pride and power of the priesthood to lose by the prevalence of the gospel, had an ascendency over the Hindoo mind scarcely equalled by that of the papal ecclesiastics in the darkest ages, or the Druids of the ancient Britons; and the institution of caste by which, to use the eloquent language of an enemy to missions in the British parliament, "the soul and all its powers were bound to Brahminism, as by an indissoluble and adamantine chain," was pronounced to be "an invincible barrier to the proselytism of the Hindoos;" so that some new power hitherto undiscovered in the moral world, and equivalent to that which the old philosopher required in the physical, would be requisite to pull down this consolidated fabric of pride and superstition, which has stood, unmoved and undecaying, the sudden shock of so many revolutions, and the silent lapse of so many ages." Added to this was the extreme jealousy of the English Indian government, and its determined hostility to missionary movements, together with the irreligion and profaneness of European residents, and the suspicions created in the minds of the government in England, by those who having returned from India, and professing a perfect knowledge of the condition and character of the natives, declared that "every European throat would be cut, if the missionaries were encouraged, and the attempt at conversion persisted in;" and proclaimed in the British Senate the utter hopelessness of an enterprize which none but mad and ignorant fanatics could be induced to undertake. "Will these people," asked the gentleman already quoted,—Charles Marsh, Esq.,—"crawling from the homes and caverns of their original destination, apostates from the loom and anvil, and renegades from the lowest handicraft employments, be a match for the cool and sedate controversies they will have to encounter, should the Brahmins condescend to enter into the arena against the maimed and crippled gladiators that presume to grapple with their faith? What can be apprehended but the disgrace and discomfiture of whole hosts of tub preachers in the conflict?" We shall see.

CHAPTER VI.

CAREY'S acquaintance with the Missionary field—Difficulties—His manner of preaching—Hymn by Ram Ram Boshoo, and metrical version—Unexpected arrival from England—Carey's visit to Bootan, Thibet, etc.—Importance of a Bengali Bible—Printing Press—Fountain's account of Carey—Carey's account of the Mission—Conversation with a Brahmin—New Missionaries in England—Ward—Brunsdon—Grant—Marshman—Failure of factory at Mudnabatty—Conduct of the British government in connection with Missions—Reply of Carey to the Governor-General—Arrival of the new Missionaries at Serampore—Death of Mr. Grant—Reflections of Marshman—Visit of Ward and Fountain to Carey—Removal to Serampore—Language of Mr. Denham.

IT will have been perceived that by this time the Missionaries, especially Mr. CAREY, had become well acquainted with the field to be occupied, the difficulties in the way of duty, and the prospect of ultimate, though, probably, distant success. CAREY had pleased himself with the thought that Ram Ram Boshoo, his Pundit, Parbotee, and other natives, were under the influence of the gospel, but one of them after another entirely disappointed his hopes, and returned to their idols. Other difficulties, too, existed, of which he thus speaks in a letter to his valued friend, Mr. Pearce of Birmingham:—"I cannot send you any account of sinners flocking to Christ, or of any thing encouraging in that respect; but I can send you an account of some things which may be viewed as forerunners to that work which God will certainly perform. The name of Jesus Christ is no longer strange in this neighborhood. And the hymn of Mounshi is well known, especially the chorus :—

"O who can save sinners except the Lord Jesus Christ!"

"We have Divine worship constantly every Lord's day, and conduct it in the manner of the English churches; and on the week days I take opportunities of conversing with the natives about eternal things.

"The Bible has, that part which has been translated, been read to several hundreds of natives, and I trust will gain ground.

"But now I must mention some of the difficulties under which we labor, particularly myself. The language spoken by the natives of this part, though Bengali, is yet so different from the language itself, that, though I can preach one hour with tolerable freedom, so that all who speak the language well, or can write or read, perfectly understand me, yet the poor laboring people can understand but little; and though the language is rich, beautiful, and expressive, yet the poor people, whose whole concern has been to satisfy their wants, or to cheat their oppressive merchants and Zemindars, have scarcely a word in use about religion. They have no word for love, for repent, and a thousand other things; and every idea is expressed, either by quaint phrases, or tedious circumlocutions; a native who speaks the language well, finds it a year's work to obtain their idiom. This sometimes discourages me much; but blessed be God, I feel a growing desire to be always abounding in the work of the Lord, and I know that my labor shall not be in vain in the Lord. I am much encouraged by our Lord's expression, 'He who reapeth,' in the harvest, 'receiveth wages, and gathereth fruit unto eternal life.' If I, like David, only am an instrument of gathering materials, and another build the house, I trust my joy will not be less."

In a letter to the society, very soon after, he says: —"I wish to say something about the manner of my preaching, but scarcely know how. As a specimen, however, I will just describe one season at a large village, about four miles from Mudnabatty, called Chinsurah. I went one Lord's day afternoon to this place, attended by a few persons from Mudnabatty. When I got into the town, I saw an idolatrous temple, built very finely with bricks. In order to excite attention, I asked what place that was; they said that it was Thakoorannee, that is, a debta. I asked if it was alive; they said yes; well, said I, I will see her, and accordingly went towards the place, when they all called out, 'No, Sir, no; it's only a stone.' I, however, mounted the steps, and began to talk about the folly and wickedness of idolatry. A bazaar, or market, near, was very noisy; I therefore removed to a little distance under a tamarind tree, where we began by singing the hymn, in Bengali, composed by Ram Ram Boshoo:

CHORUS.—O who besides can recover us,
O who besides can recover us,
From the everlasting darkness of sin,
Except the Lord Jesus Christ.

1. Lo! that Lord is the Son of God,
The intermediate of a sinner's salvation:
Whosoever adores him,
Will get over his eternal ruin.
O who besides can recover us, etc.

2. In all this world there is none free from sin,
Except the Saviour of the world,
And his name is Jesus.
O who besides can recover us, etc.

3. That Lord was born into the world
To redeem sinful men:
Whosoever has faith to adore him,
That's the man that will get free.
O who besides can recover us, etc.

4. With and without form, an holy incarnation,
That's the Lord of the world:
Without faith in him, the road to heaven
Is inaccessible.
O who besides can recover us, etc.

5. These words of his mouth, hear, O men,
For his sayings are very true;
"Whoso is thirsty, let him come,
I will give him the living water."
O who besides can recover us, etc.

6. Therefore adore, O my soul,
Having known him substantial;
And besides himself
There is no other Saviour.

O who besides can recover us,
O who besides can recover us,
From the everlasting darkness of sin,
Except the Lord Jesus Christ!

The following metrical version of this hymn, by the late Rev. Dr. FAWCETT, will be acceptable to our readers, and might be useful in the Conference room:

1. Jesus descended from above,
   To save our souls from guilt and shame;
O may we then admire his love
   And render praises to his name.
Jesus alone whom we adore,
The ruined sinner can restore.

2. He came to bear our sins and die,
   That he might save our wretched race;
Yet he's the Son of God most High,
   Adorned with purity and grace.
Jesus alone whom we adore,
The ruined sinner can restore.

3. Angelic hosts the tidings bring,
   And hail the long expected morn,
'Go, shepherds, visit Christ your king,
   The promised Saviour now is born.'
Jesus alone whom we adore,
The ruined sinner can restore.

4. Sinners he ransoms by his blood,
   He that believes the tidings lives;
Sinners he reconciles to God:
   Pardon and peace he freely gives.
Jesus alone whom we adore,
The ruined sinner can restore.

5. By humble faith to him apply;
   His words are kind and ever true;
'Ye thirsty souls to me draw nigh,
   Water of life I give to you.'

Jesus alone whom we adore,
The ruined sinner can restore.

6. O may we still adore his name,
We who have known his saving power;
Ascribe salvation to the Lamb,
And love and praise him evermore.
Jesus alone whom we adore,
The ruined sinner can restore.

"By this time a pretty large concourse of people was assembled, and I began to discourse with them upon the things of God. It is obvious that giving out a text, and regularly dividing it, could not be of any use to those who never heard a word of the Bible in their lives; I therefore dwelt upon the worth of the soul and its fallen state, the guilt of all men who had broken God's righteous law, and the impossibility of obtaining pardon without a full satisfaction to Divine Justice. I then enquired what way of life, consistent with the justice of God, was proposed in any of their shastras. They, said I, speak of nine incarnations of Vishnu, past, and one to come, yet not one of them for the salvation of a sinner. They were only to preserve a family, to kill a giant, to make war against tyrants, etc.; all which God could have accomplished as well without those incarnations. An incarnation of the Deity, said I, is a matter of too great importance to take place in so ludicrous a manner, and for such mean ends and purposes. The Mutchee Obeetar, or fish incarnation, said I, was to become the rudder of a boat, and preserve a family in a great flood; and the wild hog incarnation was to kill a giant, and draw up the earth out of the sea when it was sinking; but this, God, who created it, could have accomplished without any such interposition. I then observed how miserable they were, whose religion only respected the body, and whose shastras point out no salvation for the sinner. I then spoke of the way of life by Christ, his substitution in our place, suffering in the sinner's stead, and the like.

"At another place, I preached from Christ being a blessing, sent to bless men in turning every one from his iniquities. I observed the superiority of the gospel to all other writings, and Christ to all pretended saviours in that point; that believing on Christ was universally accompanied with turning from iniquity; and that their worship must be false, for they made images and offerings to them, and were abundant in their worship; but, said I, there is not a man of you yet turned from his iniquity. There are among you liars, thieves, whoremongers, and men filled with deceit. And as you were last year, so you are this, not any more holy; nor can you ever be so, till you throw off your wicked worship and wicked practices, and embrace the gospel of our Lord Jesus Christ.

"This is the method of preaching that I use among them; nothing of this kind affronts them; many wish to hear; many, however, abhor the thought of the gospel. The Brahmins fear to lose their gain; the higher castes their honor; and the poor tremble at the vengeance of their debtas. Thus we have been unsuccessful."

In September 1796, CAREY was both surprised

and delighted by receiving help from England. The Society had felt the importance of strengthening the missionary force, and sent Mr. John Fountain, with his wife, who was afterwards Mrs. Ward. The senior missionary writes, "Mr. Fountain arrived quite unexpectedly, and except a hint or two in a letter from England, some months before his arrival, we had not heard a word of his coming out. He therefore arrived at Mudnabatty before I knew of his arrival in India, and took me quite by surprize." Mr. Fountain says, "Brother Carey most kindly received me. When I entered, his pundit stood by him, teaching him Sanscrit. He labors in the translation of the Scriptures, and has nearly finished the new Testament."

About this time CAREY visited Bootan, Thibet, and Dinagepore, by which his zeal for Missions was greatly increased, and fervent were his prayers for the advancement of the kingdom of Christ. His own labors were fixed especially on the translation of the Scriptures, in which also Thomas felt a great interest. The latter says in a letter to England, "I would give a million pounds sterling, if I had it, to see a Bengali Bible. O most merciful God, what an inestimable blessing would it be to these millions! The angels of heaven will look down upon it to fill their mouths with new praises and adorations. Methinks all heaven and hell will be moved at a Bible's entering such a country as this. O Lord, send forth thy light and thy truth." CAREY lived to see the sacred volume, or parts of it, translated and circulated, not only in Bengali, but in more than *forty* other languages of the east. At this time, on the whole, the missionaries considered their prospects more pleasing than at any former period. Shortly after this, the Committee at home determined to send paper from England on which to print the New Testament; in the mean time a printing press was purchased at Calcutta, and preparatory measures were adopted for procuring types. CAREY made the following curious record—"September 18, 1798. This day we set up the printing press at Mudnabatty. Some of the natives, who came in to look at it, went away and said it was a *balatle dhourga;* that is, an English idol!"

The reader will certainly feel interested in the account given of the subject of our Memoir by Mr. Fountain in the autumn of 1796—"As to brother Carey, his very soul is absorbed in the work of the Mission. His dear friends in England had no grounds for their fears, that riches might alienate his heart from that work. He does not possess them. I am persuaded there is not a man who has not learned to deny himself, but would prefer his situation when at Leicester to that in this country. But he, like a Christian minister, as described in his own publication, considers himself as having 'solemnly undertaken to be always engaged as much as possible in the Lord's work, and not to choose his own pleasure and employment, or to pursue the ministry as a thing which is to serve his own ends or interests, or as a kind of by-work.' He has told me, that, whatever his future circumstances may be, he durst not lay by a shilling for his children, for his all is devoted to God. The utmost harmony and love subsist between him and brother Thomas. They are fellow laborers in the Gospel of the grace of God." Shortly after he says:—"I think the society, and all who feel for the wretched millions in India, perishing for lack of knowledge, can never be sufficiently thankful to God that brother CAREY so cheerfully embarked in the Mission. His amazing knowledge of the languages and customs of countries; his assiduity in translating the scriptures; his diligence in preaching; his patience under trials; and his perseverance, though without apparent success, are admirable. He seems every way fitted to lay the foundation of future good in this country." CAREY, himself, says to his sisters in this year:—"I know not what to say about the Mission. I feel as a farmer does about his crop; sometimes I think the seed is springing, and thus I hope; a little time blasts all, and my hopes are gone like a cloud. They were only weeds which appeared; or if a little corn sprung up, it quickly died, being either choked with weeds, or parched up by the sun of persecution. Yet I still hope in God, and will go forth in his strength, and 'make mention of his righteousness, and of his only.' I preach every day to the natives, and twice on the Lord's day constantly, besides other itinerant labors; and I try to speak of Jesus Christ and him crucified, and of him alone: but my soul is often much dejected to see no fruit."

A conversation between Mr. CAREY and a Brahmin, will tend to convey to the reader a correct idea of the Hindoo mind, and to show the kind of men who ought to be employed as missionaries to that land. "I was," says CAREY, "pressing upon him the necessity of believing in Christ for salvation, when he asked how it was that the worship of idols had been followed from the beginning, and how it was that, according to the scripture itself, the worship of the Debtas was professed through the whole world, except one small nation, from the beginning. And, said he, 'if the gospel be the way of life, how is it that we never heard of it before?' I answered, 'God formerly suffered all nations to walk in their own way, but now commandeth all men every where to repent.' 'Indeed,' said he, 'I think God ought to repent for not sending the Gospel sooner to us.' I then tried to convince him that God had never done injustice to men, and that it was his settled purpose finally to overcome all the power and craft of the devil. To this I added, 'suppose a kingdom had been overrun by the enemies of its true king, and he, though possessed of sufficient power to conquer them, should yet suffer them to prevail, and establish themselves as much as they could desire, would not the valor and wisdom of that king be far more conspicuous in exterminating them, than it would have been if he had opposed them at first, and prevented their entering the country? Thus, by the diffusion of gospel light, the wisdom, power, and grace of God will be much more conspicuous in overcoming such deep-rooted idolatries, and in destroying all that darkness and vice which have so universally prevailed in this country, than they would have been if all had not been suffered to walk in their own ways for so many ages past."

The year 1798 brought great changes in connection with the Mission, both in England and in India, which indeed soon altered its whole character. We have already referred to an interview which CAREY had before he left England, with Mr. Ward, a printer at Hull. This young man had since that period been encouraged to enter the ministry, and had pursued his preparatory studies for that office under the Rev. Dr. Fawcett, at Ewood Hall. He now offered his services as a Missionary, and was accepted. Mr. Daniel Brunsdon was also accepted as a companion. A third candidate was found in Mr. William Grant, a member of Dr. Ryland's church in Broadmead, Bristol. The history of this young man was remarkable. At the age of sixteen, he had associated himself with a young deist, with whom he read "*Voltaire's Philosophical Dictionary*," and united in ridiculing Christians as fanatics. Two years afterwards, he was partially reclaimed by "*Priestley's History of the Corruptions of Christianity;*" but soon relapsed into his former principles, and plunged into profanity and vice. He was conscious, however, of the inconsistency of atheistical opinions, became convinced at length, of their falsehood, and by an attention to natural philosophy and anatomy, perceived such demonstrations of the intelligent First Cause, that he believed in the Being of a God. Soon afterwards, he met with Mr. Joshua Marshman, a member also of Broadmead church, in a book-seller's shop. Observing him looking at a

Latin dictionary, he enquired of Mr. Marshman if he understood that language; and finding that he did, requested some instruction. This new friend and teacher soon heard him sneer at the absurdities of Calvinism, particularly at the doctrine of the Atonement. This, with its associate doctrines, became the subject of frequent conversation; thus, and by other means of grace, he was brought to a saving knowledge of Christ, and made a public profession of his name. Hearing of the Mission to India, and reading the accounts received from that country, a strong desire was excited personally to engage in that work, and with the full approbation of his pastor, he gave himself up to it. Simultaneously with Mr. Grant's wish, arose a similar feeling in the heart of his friend Mr. Marshman, who was a schoolmaster, and was now attending daily lectures in Bristol college, who gave himself to the service at the age of thirty-two, with cheerful disinterestedness and fervent zeal. These four young men, with their wives, sailed in the *Criterion*, Captain Wickes, who was an elder in the Presbyterian church, Philadelphia, in May, 1798.

Turning now to Mudnabatty, we become acquainted with some important facts. It had always been felt that the district had nothing to recommend it as the permanent seat of an important mission. It was no place of public resort; and had no celebrity attached to it, either religious, literary, or commercial. Nothing could be more entirely providential than were the circumstances which led Mr. CAREY there. His residence in it had also answered some very important ends. His object had become known, and his character appreciated, throughout a respectable circle of European observers, whose esteem he had conciliated, whose liberality in the cause of Christianity now began to evince itself, and whose respect and fervent attachment he continued to enjoy, unimpaired, to the close of his life. Here, too, he had, by the most untiring industry, prepared himself for future and far more eminent service. Here the Mission to India was well cradled; but to mature its strength and to put forth its energies, it must be translated to another and more favorable region.

The indigo works which Mr. Udney had erected at Moypauldiggy and Mudnabatty, the superintendence of which had furnished support to CAREY and his colleague in the time of their extremity had entirely failed; and the successive and severe losses which this benevolent friend had experienced, led him to determine to break them up. Mr. CAREY had commenced in the same business on his own account, at Kidderpore, about ten miles distant, at considerable outlay, and without any advantage, but rather to his loss. His way was hedged in, and his temporal resources, there is reason to fear, were fast drying up.

We may here, as it is very closely connected with our main topic, write a few sentences on the strange and anomalous conduct of the British authorities in India in reference to the subject of religion. This arose partly from ignorance of the true genius of Christianity, and the legitimate means of diffusing it, and partly from a profane indifference to the spiritual welfare of the millions they governed, and hostility to whatever might seem to interfere with their own interests. It is a matter equally undeniable and to be deplored, that no class of persons are to be found less acquainted with the nature and design of Christianity than are professedly Christian legislators and rulers. And how can it be otherwise, when so few among them ever give its consideration an hour of their serious attention? Is it to be supposed that their spirits should be found in affinity with principles they never study, and to the majesty of which they never bow? And yet they hesitate not to make laws, and to interpose their authority to regulate the faith, and to control the religious profession and conduct of mankind. What then it may be asked, have professedly Christian legislators nothing to do,—no function to discharge with respect to religion? Yes, they are called to two duties, but both in common with other men, the one is cordially to embrace the religion of Christ for themselves, and the other to afford equal protection to all men, that they may safely profess and freely promulgate what they believe. They ought never to view religion and its maintenance in the world as a matter of mere expediency; if they do so, as they read the page of history, it can be no matter of surprise if their fears should sometimes be alarmed.

When, many years ago, an interference on the part of government was sought to be averted, it was asked by his Excellency the Governor-General of India, "Do you not think, Dr. CAREY, it would be wrong to force the Hindoos to become Christians?"

"My Lord," it was replied, "the thing is impossible; we may indeed compel men to be hypocrites; but no power on earth can force men to become Christians."

The young missionaries of whom we have spoken, arrived in India, October 12; and as the government would not allow them, *as missionaries*, to remain under British protection,* on the following day they proceeded to Serampore, a village on the banks of the river Hoogly, fifteen miles from Calcutta, described by Mr. Grant as "a beautiful little town, and esteemed the most healthy spot in all India." It was then a Danish settlement, and very much resorted to by decayed tradesmen and gentlemen

* The Rev. Dr. Boaz, a Congregational Missionary from Calcutta, in his speech before the annual meeting of the Baptist Missionary Society in London, in the year 1849, stated, that on the subject of the missionaries' staying in Calcutta being discussed in the Council, one of the members of that Council said, "If these men had belonged to the English church, and had been missionaries, one might have borne with them. If they had belonged to any of the more respectable sects of the Dissenters, they might have been tolerated; but to think of tolerating *Baptists*, the smallest of the sects, and the straitest; that is not to be borne!" Dr. Boaz stated it as remarkable, that the son of that very member of Council was brought to a knowledge of the truth in one of the Hill Stations in India, by having a newspaper, edited by a Dissenter, and printed at the Baptist Missionary press, put into his hands, containing an extract from the writings of Baxter or Doddridge. He came down from his solitary hill station to seek Christian instruction; and was baptized and added to one of our churches. One cannot help seeing how different are the ways of God to ours. Humanly speaking, could that father have had his will, his son had never been brought to the knowledge of Jesus Christ.

who had been unsuccessful in business at Calcutta. It contained about fifty houses, and was inhabited by Danes, English, Scots, Germans, Greeks, Armenians, Irish, Bengalese, and Portuguese. They remained there at a hotel a few days, awaiting the arrival of Mr. CAREY. But a dark cloud overshadowed them. On the 27th, Mr. Grant was prevented from attending the public worship which they conducted by a cold accompanied with stupor. No serious apprehensions respecting him were entertained, till the morning of the 31st, when he died in peace. He was interred in the Danish burying ground, and a funeral discourse was delivered by Mr. Ward; on which occasion the governor, with two other gentlemen, mingled with the little band of mourners. "The Lord's dealings," observes Mr. Marshman, "strike me with amazement; that he who was so earnest in the missionary cause, should thus be taken off, before he had the least opportunity of doing any thing for that cause, appears mysterious. That the Lord should make use of him to stir me up, and loosen me from those many connections in which I seemed so firmly fixed; and that I should, after seeking to God with many tears, be determined to go immediately, not waiting, as I had at first resolved, till he had gone to India first, and sent me an account how matters stood, in which case, my coming at all might have been prevented;—I say, that he should be raised up for this purpose, and then be taken to glory, is to me quite astonishing."

All this seemed as though God were training his servants by disappointments and trials of almost every kind, for an extraordinary career; and as though he were giving a practical lesson to the whole church, on the importance of pursuing missionary undertakings, not only with entire devotedness, but in the spirit of humble dependence on him alone; and how easily, as John Howe has beautifully remarked, he can polish an instrument and make it fit to accomplish much work, and then lay it aside, to show how readily he can do without it.

About the middle of November, Messrs. Ward and Fountain went to Mudnabatty, to consult with Mr. CAREY respecting the removal of the whole Missionary family to Serampore. He had found it impracticable, for the reasons we have already assigned, to remain at Kidderpore, and with all the interest he could employ, he was unsuccessful in obtainining permission of the government for the Missionaries to settle in the British territory. Besides this necessity, other considerations urged them with great force, to unite in one place. The chief purposes of the mission would thus be best carried on; the printing of the Scriptures most advantageously effected, as Mr. Ward would then have the inspection of the press; other Missionaries might be allowed to join them at Serampore; and the population was far more numerous in that district than around Mudnabatty. While on his journey to Serampore, CAREY thus communicates his feelings to his friend Mr. Yates of Leicester, under date, *Gobra, January* 6, 1800:—"You will inquire, what is become of those natives concerning whom some hopes have been entertained? What is become of the rising interest at Dinagepore? And is all preaching given up at Malda? Is the school dissolved, and all the fruits of five years' labor relinquished at once? I answer,—none but myself can tell the conflict, and the exercises of my mind, on this trying event. But necessity has no law; our resources are too small to permit us to live separately, and the work of printing the Bible requires my inspection. I hope well of Sookmun and Hurry Charron. The very last conversation I had with them gave me much encouragement. Our labors at Dinagepore have not been in vain. The Christians, also, in the neighborhood of Malda, please me much. We hope to visit those places once or twice in the year, besides corresponding with our friends by letter. The school at Mudnabatty is necessarily relinquished; though not till we have the pleasure of knowing that about fifty lads have been taught to read and write, who could otherwise have known nothing. The name and doctrines of Christ are known by many; so that a foundation is laid for our future efforts to become effectual."

Mr. CAREY arrived at Serampore on the 10th of January, 1800, and the next day, on being presented to the Governor, was very kindly received. "We have," says Mr. Ward, "purchased of the Governor's nephew a large house in the middle of the town, for six thousand rupees, or about eight hundred pounds [$4,000]; the rent, in four years, would have amounted to the purchase. It consists of a spacious veranda and hall, with two rooms on each side. Rather more to the front, are two other rooms separate: and on one side, is a storehouse, separate

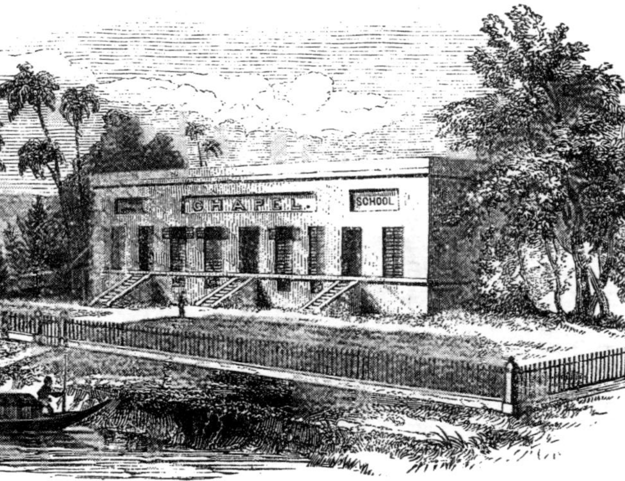

Baptist Missionary Premises at Serampore, Bengal.

Page 126.

also, which will make a printing office. It stands by the river side, upon a pretty large piece of ground, walled round, with a garden at the bottom, and in the middle a fine tank or pool of water. The price alarmed us, but we had no alternative; and we hope this will form a considerable missionary settlement. Being near to Calcutta, it is of the utmost importance to our school, our press, and our connection with England."

In a few days they prepared a set of rules for the government of the family. They were to preach and pray in turn; one was to superintend the affairs of the family for a month, and then another; CAREY was treasurer, and had the regulation of the medicine chest; Fountain was appointed librarian. One of their resolutions was, that "no one should engage in private trade; but that all be done for the benefit of the Mission."

We will close this chapter with the beautiful language of the Rev. W. H. Denham, the present excellent pastor of the church at Serampore, who, in 1845, wrote:—"Of Serampore itself it would be a work of supererogation to pen a sentence. Who can recall its name without veneration? On its sages rested a second pentecostal fire, and from their hands India and its hundreds of millions have received the regenerating word of life. Honored names! honored instrumentality! their works shall praise them so long as the waters that lave the banks of Serampore shall roll. The press is the friend of India: still to its interests may it long be devoted, a fountain of moral influence, a potent instrument of social and eternal good!"

CHAPTER VII.

Anxieties of Carey at Serampore—Encouragements of the Mission—Baptism of Krishna Pal—His subsequent usefulness—Montgomery's View of the Subject—Conduct of the Governor General on the Bengali Bible—Hymn by Dr. Marshman—Interest felt in the Translations in England—Zealous Efforts of Mr. Ralston and others in the United States—Letters from Captain Wickes—Carey, and Fuller—British and Foreign Bible Society—Carey elected Professor in the College of Fort William—Marquis of Wellesley's testimony to him—Dr. Marshman and Lord Ellenborough—Prohibition of Missionary labors by the Government—Conduct of Carey in the matter—Proceedings in England—Attack in the Edinburgh Review—Defence of the Missionaries in the London Quarterly Review.

It must not be supposed that Carey could enter on his duties at Serampore without anxiety, nor could that anxiety be easily allayed. Writing to Mr. Fuller, Feb. 5, 1800, he says:—"The last year has been a remarkable one for changes in our circumstances; some afflicting, but the greatest part encouraging; and I trust the whole will eventually turn out for the benefit of the Mission. Our removal from Mudnabatty to this place is among the most remarkable of these providences which have occurred, and was at first so afflicting to my mind that I scarcely ever remember to have felt more on any occasion whatever: it was, however, so clearly the leading of Divine Providence, that no one of us can entertain the shadow of a doubt respecting it. I was, and am still, much distressed on account of the heavy expenses and losses incurred by this providence. But we could not oppose the resolutions of the Government; nor would it have been advisable to have been separated; the setting up of the press would have been useless at Mudnabatty, without brother Ward, and perhaps might have been ruined, if it had been attempted. At this place, we are settled out of the Company's dominions, and under the government of a power very friendly to us and our designs. Here is a more populous neighborhood; we can work our press without fear, and pursue our work with security. People also hear us with considerable attention, and in considerable numbers; so that we are not discouraged, but trust that our Lord will appear, at length, and set up himself over this part of the earth."

After having detailed their necessities, spoken of the sum of money they wanted, and expressed his fear that Mr. Pearce had been removed by death, he goes on somewhat gloomily to remark to his correspondent, "You, brother Ryland, and a few of the most active to provide funds for the Mission, may also soon die; and the work may fall through for want of active persons who will feel interested in it as you do." On this part of the letter, good Dr. Ryland, when it passed under his eye, wrote very truly, "This hardly corresponds with CAREY's usual faith."

The year 1800, the first of the settlement of the Mission, was every way a remarkable one. Mr. Fountain was somewhat suddenly called from his brethren and his family by death, and the event caused no small grief; but on the other hand, two of Carey's sons, though only fifteen and thirteen years of age, began to give decided evidences of piety. In addition to these things, the Mission field began to afford fruits. Writing, Nov. 22, to Mr. Fuller, Carey says, "Last Lord's day we had perhaps the most mixed congregation that you ever heard of. It consisted of English, Danes, Norwegians, Germans, Americans, Armenians, a Greek, and a Malabar, whom I addressed from Isa. lv. 1, 2. We preach in the evening of the Lord's day in our own house. This was originally designed for the instruction of the servants; several others, however, attend, and among them a good number of Portuguese have lately come to hear. Yesterday Ram Boshoo was here, to revise his piece against the Brahmins, in order to its being printed. It is very severe; but it must be so to make them feel. Notwithstanding all his caution, he is obliged to dispute for the Gospel sometimes, and meets with more severity from the Brahmins than he would in all probability meet with if he were wholly on the side of Christ. I hope he may not be able to hold it out much longer."

But happiness far greater than this was at hand. On the 29th December, he writes to Mr. Sutcliff:—"Yesterday was a day of great joy. I had the happiness to desecrate the Ganges, by baptizing the first Hindoo, namely Krishnu, and my son Felix; some circumstances turned up to delay the baptism of Gokul, and the two women. Gokul's wife came on Saturday to make a trial what could be done

Wm. Carey. Krishna Pal. Page 131.

towards getting him back; and the women, who stood persecution very stoutly, were brought to a state of hesitation, by the tears and entreaties of their relations. We went to them again and again, but though they all declared themselves steadfast on the side of Christ, they wished to defer their baptism a week or two. Krishnu's coming forward alone, however, gave us very great pleasure, and his joy at both ordinances was very great. The river runs just before our gate, in front of the house, and, I think, is as wide as the Thames at Gravesend. We intended to have baptized at nine in the morning; but, on account of the tide, were obliged to defer it to nearly one o'clock, and it was administered just after the English preaching. The governor and a good number of Europeans were present. Brother Ward preached a sermon in English, from John v. 39, 'Search the Scriptures.' We then went to the water side, where I addressed the people in Bengali, after having sung a Bengali translation of the hymn,

'Jesus, and shall it ever be,' etc.,

and engaging in prayer. After the address, I administered the ordinance, first to my son, then to Krishnu. At half past four, I administered the Lord's supper; and a time of real refreshing it was."

It would be an act of injustice to the beloved Krishnoo, or rather *Krishna Pal*, if we did not say here, that for a period exceeding twenty years, with great ability, diligence, and success he preached the gospel of salvation, exemplifying a character in entire harmony with the religion of Jesus. And it is cheering to know, that in the solemn hour of his dissolution, he evinced the composure and tranquil reliance upon a crucified Saviour, which are the genuine products of evangelical principles. "I myself," says the present excellent Dr. Sutton, "witnessed the last moments of Krishnoo, and heard his aged and quivering lips speak of the preciousness of Christ. In this we cannot but admire the Divine goodness, and consider the strong consolation and heavenly maturity which this first Hindoo disciple attained, as an earnest of what God will do for India."*

Yes, all these things were of God; and by them we are reminded of the remark of the venerable and excellent James Montgomery, some years since at a public meeting. One of the speakers alluded to the *first thought* which set all these things going; the poet started from his seat, as though inspired, and exclaimed, "It was a spark dropped from heaven, and has set the world in a blaze." Here indeed was a combination of truth and poetry!

About this time we meet, in a letter from CAREY to Mr. Fuller, with the following passage:—"Yesterday, at the house, or rather as I was leaving the house of a friend, in Calcutta, I met with the Rev. [Claudius] Buchanan, [afterwards D. D.] It is three years since I saw him, but he remembered me and we had a very pleasant conversation in the yard.

* An interesting Memoir of this excellent man, under the title of "*The First Hindoo Convert*," has been published by THE AMERICAN BAPTIST PUBLICATION SOCIETY.

He was very friendly and invited me to his house. We had much talk about the Governor General's dispositions towards the Mission. He informed me that he was sure that we should have been perfectly secure in Calcutta, and might have preached any where in the town, if we had not assembled a congregation before the Government house, which would have been improper. He said that the Marquis Wellesley, when he first heard of a printing press at Serampore, supposed that some wild democrat might have run from Calcutta, and got protection under the Danish governor; but that now he was perfectly satisfied, and perfectly well understood the design of our Mission." In this somewhat indistinct manner, has this subject of his lordship's views of the circulation of the Scriptures in India rested till the present time; but as all parties are now beyond human applause or censure, the whole tale may be told; especially as it strikingly illustrates the Providence of God in connexion with his word. For the facts I am about to relate I am indebted to the late Rev. John Dyer, for twenty-five years the indefatigable and excellent successor of Andrew Fuller, as Secretary of the English Baptist Missionary Society.

My readers all know that the Marquis Wellesley was brother to the late Duke of Wellington, and was at this period the Governor General of India. At the same time, the Rev. David Brown was a chaplain of the East India Company, and minister of the church where his lordship attended. He was a faithful and devoted servant of Jesus Christ, cordially attached to Dr. CAREY and his colleagues, and ever ready to favor them with his counsel. When the Bengali Scriptures were ready for printing, the question became a very serious one, as to the manner in which they should be published. It is true that the press was at Serampore, and that the Missionaries were under the protection of the Danish governor; but it was also true, that they were British subjects, and that the government at Copenhagen would be very unwilling to refuse any demands which the Governor General of India might make upon them. How then would the Governor General look on the publication of a Bengali Bible, was a question of no small moment. The missionaries conferred with Mr. Brown, who took an intense interest in the matter, but saw little clearer than they did. It was true, they might have printed and published without any regard to consequences; and then also they might be sent to England by the first ship that went, and so the whole mission might be ruined; or they might ask permission of the Governor General; but then, if he refused, of course they could not do it; here then was a difficulty which claimed much consideration, and much prayer. At length Mr. Brown suggested, that on a certain day the Missionaries should advertise the Scriptures as about to be issued from the Mission press, and that when the advertisement was printed, immediately before the hour of publication, he engaged to see the Governor General, and endeavor to arrange the matter. Such was the plan adopted.

But it was not exactly carried out. By some means the visit of Mr. Brown to "Government

House" was delayed, and the first intimation his Lordship received of the affair was from the newspaper itself. His excitement was great. "Why, sir," he asked of his secretary, "do you know who these fellows are, and what this Mission press is? Write immediately to the Danish Governor, and request him to put that press down." The secretary at once prepared to obey, and half the despatch was written, when his Lordship said, "Leave that letter, sir, at present, and send immediately for Mr. Brown, as I should like to know whether he has heard any thing concerning it." A messenger was instantly sent off, but long before he could have reached the residence of that gentleman, Mr. Brown was announced as in waiting, wishing to see his Excellency. The conversation was, substantially, as follows:—

Governor General.—Mr. Brown, I am glad to see you; here is a most extraordinary advertisement in the paper this evening. It seems there are some fellows at Serampore who are going to publish a Bengali translation of the Bible; have you heard any thing about it, sir?

Mr. Brown.—Yes, my Lord, and that very business has brought me here; I intended to have communicated the fact to your Lordship two hours ago, but was prevented from coming here till now.

Governor General.—Well, Mr. Brown, it will not do to allow it; and I have directed Mr. ——— to write to the Governor to get that press put down.

Mr. Brown.—Of course your Lordship knows

best; but I submit, my Lord, that such a decision requires very grave consideration.

Governor General.—But you know, sir, that the Bible tells us that all men are on a level; now it will never do to circulate that in this country. If the natives get the idea that they are equal to us, farewell to the British government in India.

Mr. Brown.—I submit, my Lord, with all due respect, that that opinion is incorrect. Let the Hindoos embrace Christianity, and I will guarantee their loyalty to our government.

Governor General.—It cannot be, sir; the consequences of reading the Bible among the natives of this country would be tremendous. Indeed, sir, it must not be allowed.

Mr. Brown.—I submit, my Lord, whether any interposition to stop the publication, now it is announced, would not produce a great excitement among the religious people of England; and would they not be likely to appeal to Christianity as being the religious establishment of the whole empire? Of course, of this your Lordship is the best judge.

Governor General.—Do you know these translators? Are they competent men; and, especially, are they loyal to the British government?

Mr. Brown.—My Lord, I know them well. They are gentlemen, and men of high learning, and most devotedly attached to the British constitution and government.

Governor General.—Well, sir, this is a most perplexing business. What do *you*, Mr. Brown, consider the best course to adopt in the case?

Mr. Brown.—Whatever I venture to say, my Lord, on this subject, is with the utmost deference to your Lordship's better judgment; but I should venture to suggest, that as no *official* information has been laid before you, by any party, on this subject, whether it would not be better to suspend action of any kind till you see that evil does really arise out of it.

Governor General.—I am afraid, sir, that I cannot act on your counsel; however, I will think it over again.

Here the matter rested. The conduct of his Excellency to Dr. CAREY shortly after, will soon be before the reader, and will clearly show how all hearts are in the hand of God.

I shall be more than forgiven if I insert in this place, a hymn, written by Dr. Marshman, and sung in the Mission family, with thrilling effect, on the completion of the Bengali Bible. Who can describe the results of the work they thus celebrated!

Hail, precious book divine!
Illumined by thy rays,
We rise from death and sin,
And sing a Saviour's praise;
The shades of error dark as night
Vanish before thy radiant light.

We bless the God of grace
Who hath his word revealed,
To this bewildered race,
So long in darkness held;
His love designs, his people pray!
His Providence prepares the way.

Now shall the Hindoos learn
The glories of our King;
Nor to blind gooroos turn,
Nor idol praises sing;
Diffusing heavenly light around,
This Book their Shasters shall confound.

Deign, gracious Saviour, deign
To smile upon thy word;
Let millions now obtain,
Salvation from the Lord;
Nor let its growing conquests stay,
Till earth exult to own its sway.

It will be no matter of surprise, that this subject of the translation of the scriptures into the languages of the East, soon began to excite no small interest among Christians of all denominations, both at home and abroad. An eminent physician in one of the principal towns in Yorkshire, determined to collect *one thousand pounds* in that neighborhood, as an expression of deep sympathy with the great object; the committee of the then newly formed British and Foreign Bible Society, hearing of this arrangement, proposed that the money thus raised should pass into their treasury, and that they would cheerfully assist the Bengali and future translations by their money and their influence. It will be remembered, that for a series of years the Missionaries at Serampore were the most prominent of their translators, while, on the part of the society, abundant Christian liberality was shewn to each successive edition of the holy volume, till the occurrence of events to which we shall hereafter refer.

And, happy am I to record, that the flame of holy

zeal was not confined to the British isles, but extended itself across the Atlantic, and lit up a fire in these United States. Our readers are aware that no small difficulty existed in sending money to the missionaries, and they have been already introduced to Captain Wickes, a worthy presbyterian elder of Philadelphia. From "*The Assembly's Missionary Magazine; or Evangelical Intelligencer,*" for April 1806, I copy the following paper:—

"*Philadelphia, Feb.* 4, 1806.

"PROPAGATION OF THE GOSPEL.

"*To all who love the prosperity of Zion, and are disposed to aid in propagating the Gospel among the Heathen.*

"The subscriber lately returned from a voyage to the East-Indies, touched in Europe, and was in London in August last, where he received from the Baptist Missionary society in England, for propagating the gospel among the heathen, one thousand guineas, to be sent in the Spring to the missionaries in Bengal, for the purpose of printing the sacred scriptures in one of the languages of that country. There are seven languages that the missionaries there aim to translate and publish the scriptures in. They have made such progress in three of them that it is expected that the above sum will enable them to complete the work. The money is now in the hands of ROBERT RALSTON, Esquire, of Philadelphia, who will forward it in due time. Should any individual, society, or congregation of people in the United States of America, be disposed to contribute to this good work, Mr. Ralston will gladly receive whatever may be sent to him for that purpose, and add to it the above sum, to be forwarded to the missionaries at Serampore, near Calcutta.

"(Signed)

BENJAMIN WICKES, Sen."

Accompanying this paper was an address from a large committee of clergymen of different denominations, strongly urging the importance of aiding the great cause, and requesting the newspapers of the United States, who were friendly to the object, to aid them in the grand undertaking. In October following, we learn that "the amount collected, principally in Philadelphia, and remitted by Mr. Ralston, was *nearly five thousand dollars*," and that after this remittance was made, very liberal encouragement had been given to the object in Boston. *Two thousand dollars* had been already received, and two thousand more were expected. I believe that the five thousand dollars here referred to, was *the first money ever subscribed in this country for* FOREIGN *missions*.

I shall make no apology for introducing two letters in this place, which will, at all events, when this volume shall cross the Atlantic, be new in England; and in this connection, they must of necessity be interesting in this country. The first is from the pen of CAREY, addressed to Mr. Ralston, and though without a date, bears internal evidence of its being written the early part of 1806:—

"I shall now give you a brief sketch of the state of the mission in India. Last year our four brethren, who came by way of America, arrived, all safe, and soon after six missionaries from the London Missionary Society arrived at Madras. Three of these are settled in Ceylon, two at Vizagapatam, and one at Tranquebar. Since that [time] two more from the same society arrived in India, designed for Surat, one of whom (Dr. Taylor) is now with me, having come to see us, and spend a little time with us before he goes to the place of his destination. We are on very friendly terms with all these our brethren. Thus you see the enemy's kingdom in this country is invested on all sides. One of these, last mentioned, is about to marry an American lady from New-York, who, with Mr. Smith and family of that city, attended our worship this evening.

"Since my arrival in this country eighty-four persons have, by baptism or letter, been joined to the church. Eight out of this number have been removed by death, all of them in the Lord: six have been excluded, and of those who remain, I reckon ten doubtful characters. There are now about fifteen persons under hopeful impressions, all natives, several of whom I hope to baptize next ordinance [communion] day. We have already baptized sixteen this year. On account of the widely separated state of our members, it is in contemplation to divide the church into four churches, and to appoint native pastors of at least three of them. I trust this scheme, which I doubt not will be for the furtherance of the gospel, will very soon be put in execution.

"The third volume of the Bible from Job to Canticles inclusive, is published. The second edition of the New-Testament will be out in about a month; the prophets are begun, and we intend to begin printing the historical books from Joshua forwards in a few weeks. The gospel by Matthew is printed (nearly) in the Mahratta language; nearly the whole New and some parts of the Old are translated into that language, that of Orissa, the Hindostannee, and Persian. The gospels in Hindostannee, and Matthew in Persian are printed for the college at another press. We have some more extensive plans for translations in contemplation, if God prosper us.

"W. CAREY."

The other letter was from Andrew Fuller, the excellent secretary of the Baptist Missionary Society in England. Justice demands that it should be said, the missionaries and their wives, referred to in this letter, with all their goods, were taken to India without the expense of a single penny to the Society. I willl add, too, that it was seldom the worthy secretary wrote a letter in such an animated strain as this, indeed it was by no means often that he had such a correspondent:—

"*Kettering*, 3*d of June*, 1806.

"DEAR SIR,

"I this day received your kind favor of April 26. What can I say, my dear sir, respecting the very liberal and brotherly exertions of yourself and friends on your side the Atlantic? To express our grateful acknowledgements seems too little; yet what more can I add, save that like David and the elders of Israel, I rejoice with you and bless the Lord that you have offered willingly, and with a perfect heart. I trust what has been so offered is acceptable to God as well as to your brethren in Europe and Asia, and will turn to your account, and that of all those dear Christian ministers and people who have helped forward the good work.

"What happiness does Christianity produce; and what a tendency is there in every Christian duty to unite the friends of Jesus! We should not have known or loved one another as we do, but for these exertions for his name.

"Our last intelligence from India comes down as late as October 20, 1805, and you will find it in print, in No. xv. [of the Periodical Accounts of the Society.] The Lord is more and more opening the hearts of his people in Britain to contribute. We make an annual collection in London. I have several times made it, but never till this Spring collected above four hundred pounds. This time the collection amounted to upwards of eight hundred pounds.

"Of all the nations upon earth, I think it is the duty of Britain and North America to disseminate the gospel. We have more commerce with mankind, more gospel knowledge, more liberty, and more wealth, than perhaps any other nations; and while we are thus employed, or rather while there is amongst us a body of Christians thus employed, I have little or no apprehension of our falling a prey to the destroyer.

"In the tract which good Mr. Carey published prior to his engaging in the mission, I remember he introduces Isaiah lx. 9, in proof that navigation and commerce should become subservient to religion. Truly we have seen the accomplishment of this already in a measure.

"I know not in what way to express the gratitude of the Baptist missionary society, to the numerous friends who have assisted it in America. The Lord reward them, and think upon them for good!

"Capt. Wickes was well and very happy in seeing his old friends in London, as we were in seeing him. We have got a good portrait of him. He took out besides our four young people, a young woman from the London missionary society, who is gone to be a companion to a Mr. Loveless,* one of their missionaries in the east.

"Grace and peace be with you my dear sir, and with your obliged and affectionate friend.

"ANDREW FULLER."

One short paragraph from a letter of Captain Wickes, written in London, April 2, 1806, to his friends in Philadelphia, shall be quoted to show the

* This worthy missionary of the cross was many years a devoted and successful laborer at Madras, where he lost this excellent wife. He returned to England in shattered health, labored in the ministry a very few years, and died with a mind destroyed by the climate of India.

deep interest he still continued to take in the Mission:—

"Yesterday morning I had on board the ship to breakfast, the missionaries and their wives, several ministers of different denominations, and others to the number of about thirty. Here we had an exercise of prayer and praise, until near twelve o'clock, committing the missionaries, the ship, and the crew, to the care of the blessed God, and praying for the spread of the gospel among the heathen. In the evening there was a meeting held at one of the Baptist meeting houses, for the purpose of dismissing the missionaries from their country and kindred, to go among the heathen in Bengal. This was a crowded and solemn assembly."

Thus began a work which went on till from that press, thus established at Serampore, there issued before the death of CAREY *two hundred and twelve thousand* copies of the sacred Scriptures in *forty* different languages—the vernacular tongues of *three hundred and thirty millions* of immortal beings, of whom more than *one hundred millions* were British subjects; and he lived till he had seen expended upon that noble object, on behalf of which the first small offering at Kettering was presented, a sum little less than *half a million of dollars.*

To detail the various events connected with the Mission, is no part of our design, or we might write with pleasure that Mr. and Mrs. Marshman originated, and carried on for a long succession of years a ladies' boarding school, the whole large profits of which were devoted to the general fund; and that

Mr. Ward superintended a public printing press, from which the fund annually derived a very large sum; indeed these sources of income, together with CAREY'S salary as Professor, for many years furnished an annual amount of not less than *twenty-five thousand dollars.* The spirit in which this was given, may be seen from a solemn Instrument which was drawn up and signed by the whole body of the Missionaries in 1805:—"Let us give ourselves up unreservedly to this glorious cause. Let us never think that our time, our gifts, our strength, our families, or even the clothes we wear, are our own. Let us sanctify them all to God and his cause. Oh! that he may sanctify us for his work! Let us for ever shut out the idea of laying up a dowry for ourselves or our children. If we give up the resolution which was formed on the subject of private trade when we first united at Serampore, the Mission is from that hour a lost cause. A worldly spirit, quarrels, and every evil work will succeed, the moment it is admitted that each brother may do something on his own account. Wo to that man, who shall ever make the smallest movement towards such a measure! Let us continually watch against a worldly spirit, and cultivate a Christian indifference towards every indulgence. Rather let us bear hardness as good soldiers of Jesus Christ; and endeavor to learn in every state to be content." It cannot be supposed, that the increasing missionary families could always continue to reside in one house, or that, as the number of their children increased, a sum of about six dollars per month would be sufficient for their personal expenses, but assuredly the *spirit* of this agreement was admirably preserved, and every one of its contracting parties died very poor.

Were we presenting a History of the Mission, we might also tell of the liberality of *the British and Foreign Bible Society*, who selected a committee in India, and most freely contributed to the cause of Biblical translations at Serampore, till it was found that the words in reference to Baptism were translated in accordance with the idea of immersion; when, as on the one hand, the translation was "inconvenient" to Pedobaptists, and on the other, the consciences of the translators would not admit of a change, all farther aid was withheld; which led to the formation of the American and Foreign Bible Society in this country, and to the Bible Translation Society in England. We now return especially to CAREY.

In the spring of 1801, Serampore, chiefly by diplomatic arrangement, quietly passed into the hands of the English; and happily CAREY and his brethren still found themselves as much unmolested as under the Danish government. The missionaries were summoned to the Government House, and informed by Governor Bie, that they were allowed to proceed with their labors as under his protection, while the English commissioner apologized for the inconvenience to which they had been put in leaving their occupations. The influence of all this on CAREY and the Mission will soon be seen.

Just at this time, his success in the study of the vernacular languages of India, recommended

CAREY for an honorable and lucrative appointment under the Government. It appears that the general ignorance of the East India Company's servants with the languages in which they were required to communicate with the natives of India, had been the occasion of frequent complaint on the part of both the local authorities and those in Europe; and not unfrequently it had been productive of serious inconvenience in the administration of affairs. Means of inducing a more diligent attention to the study of the languages had not been neglected, but all had failed. At length the Governor General, the Marquis Wellesley, took upon himself the responsibility of founding a college, in which CAREY soon became a professor, and remained so till it was closed by the authorities in England, about the time that the College at Serampore was founded.

Even at the risk of being thought tedious, I cannot withhold from the reader an extract of a letter from the pen of CAREY to his friend Dr. Ryland, on this subject. Its date is June 15, 1801: "A college was founded, last year, in Fort William, for the instruction of the junior civil servants of the Company, who are obliged to study in it three years after their arrival. I always highly approved of the institution, but never entertained a thought that I should be called to fill a station in it. The Rev. David Brown is provost, and the Rev. Claudius Buchanan, vice-provost; and, to my great surprise, I was asked to undertake the Bengali professorship. One morning, a letter from Mr. Brown came, inviting me to cross the water, to have some conversation with him upon this subject. I had but just time to call our brethren together, who were of opinion that, for several reasons, I ought to accept it, provided it did not interfere with the work of the Mission. I also knew myself to be incapable of filling such a station with reputation and propriety. I, however, went over, and honestly proposed all my fears and objections. Both Mr. Brown and Mr. Buchanan were of opinion, that the cause of the Mission would be furthered by it; and I was not able to reply to their arguments. I was convinced that it might. As to my ability, they could not satisfy me; but they insisted upon it that they must be the judges of that. I therefore consented, with fear and trembling. They proposed me that day, or the next, to the Governor General, who is Patron and Visiter of the college. They told him that I had been a missionary in the country for seven years or more; and as a missionary, I was appointed to the office. A clause had been inserted in the statutes, to accommodate those who are not of the Church of England, (for all professors are to take certain oaths and make declarations;) but for the accommodation of such, two other names were inserted, namely, lecturers and teachers, who are not included under that obligation. When I was proposed, his Lordship asked if I was well affected to the state, and capable of fulfilling the duties of the station, to which Mr. Buchanan replied, that he should never have proposed me, if he had had the smallest doubt on those heads. I wonder how people can have such favorable ideas of me. I certainly am not disaffected to the state; but the other is not clear to me. When the appointment was made, I saw that I had a very important charge committed to me, and no books or helps of any kind to assist me. I therefore set about compiling a grammar, which is now half printed. I got Ram Boshoo to compose a history of one of their kings, the first prose book ever written in the Bengali language; which we are also printing.* Our pundit has, also, nearly translated the Sanscrit fables, one or two of which brother Thomas sent you, which we are also going to publish. These, with Mr. Foster's Vocabulary, will prepare the way to reading their poetical books; so that I hope this difficulty will be gotten through. But my ignorance of the way of conducting collegiate exercises is a great weight upon my mind. I have thirteen students in my class; I lecture twice a week; and have nearly got through one term, not quite two months. Most of the students have gotten through the accidence, and some have begun to translate Bengali into English. The examination begins this week. I am also

* Since the completion of the manuscript of this volume, the following interesting statement has appeared in that invaluable little paper, "*The American Messenger.*" It is a very fine illustration of great results from small beginnings:—"At Calcutta are not less than forty native presses established for the purpose of publishing Bengali books, which send out 30,000 volumes annually. It is fifty-one years since the Serampore missionaries published the first book in the Bengali language. Within this period, every ancient Bengali book but one, all of which were full of idolatry and obscenity, has ceased to be published, while nearly four hundred works of a better character have taken their place."

appointed teacher of the Sanscrit language; and though no students have yet entered that class, yet I must prepare for it. I am, therefore, writing a grammar of that language, which I must also print, if I should be able to get through with it, and perhaps a dictionary, which I began some years ago. I say all this, my dear brother, to induce you to give me your advice about the best manner of conducting myself in this station, and to induce you to pray much for me, that God may, in all things, be glorified by me. We presented a copy of the Bengali New Testament to Lord Wellesley, after the appointment, through the medium of the Rev. D. Brown, which was graciously received. We also presented Governor Bie with one."

We shall only add in connexion with this appointment of the humble, but well-qualified CAREY, that it most essentially advanced the prosperity of the Mission; for though it occasioned him much employment and anxiety, it presented a favorable opportunity for the extension of his useful influence; while he availed himself with indefatigable zeal of every interval of his public duties to converse with any natives to whom he could obtain access; and at the same time it furnished him with large pecuniary means, all of which were sacredly devoted to the great object to which he had consecrated his life.

In February, 1805, CAREY wrote to his old friend and pastor, Mr. Sutcliff, and from his letter we shall give an extract, showing a strong contrast with the opinion of the Governor General formed of him when he first met with his name as a translator of the

Scriptures :—" In September last I was, as moderator at the public disputation, called to deliver a public speech in the Bengali language, and another in Sanscrit, before the Governor General and all the chief officers of government. The Sanscrit speech, being the first one delivered in that language by a European, was ordered to be translated, and, with its translation, printed among the college essays and theses.* I took that opportunity to address part of the speech to his Excellency, Lord Wellesley; and after it was translated, I sent it to Mr. Buchanan, desiring him to suggest any alterations or additions.

He considerably enlarged the address to Lord Wellesley, and inserted some expressions of flattery, which I totally disapprove. Without saying any thing to me, he sent the speech thus enlarged and amended to his lordship, for his approbation, previously to its publication. As it involved some things

* Dr. Claudius Buchanan in the Introduction to his valuable "*Christian Researches in Asia*," refers to this truly important address, which it seems was, particularly directed to the student who had pronounced an oration in Sanscrit. In the American edition of this book, is given an extract from it, which is so beautiful in itself, yet so unlike CAREY'S usual style, that I make no apology for its transcription :—

" Sanscrit learning, say the Brahmins, is like an extensive forest, abounding with a great variety of beautiful foliage, splendid blossoms, and delicious fruits; but surrounded by a strong and thorny fence, which prevents those who are desirous of plucking its fruits and flowers, from entering in. The learned Jones, Wilkins, and others succeeded in breaking down the fence in several places, but by the college of Fort William a high-way has been made in the midst of the enclosure, and you, sir, by means of it have entered."

respecting the Mission, particularly an open avowal of my having been in the habit of preaching constantly to the natives, and superintending schools for the instruction of Hindoo children in the principles of Christianity, he was very anxious about the result, but said nothing to me till it was returned, with a letter written by his lordship's hand, of which, as nearly as I can recollect, this is a copy:—

"I am much pleased with Mr. Carey's truly original and excellent speech; I would not wish to have a word altered. I esteem such a testimony from such a man, a greater honor than the applause of courts and parliaments. W."

"Both Mr. Brown and Mr. Buchanan were astonished; and yet more so, when on the 6th of February last, Mr. Brown and I, before dinner at Government House, were talking together, Lord Wellesley came up, and expressed nearly the same sentiments to me, in nearly the same words, adding, 'I then desired Mr. Buchanan to tell you this, and have the pleasure now to tell it you yourself.'* He then asked several questions about our family, told me

* It may create a smile to tell here a little anecdote of Dr. Marshman, the well known colleague of CAREY, and who for a short period survived him. He had a remarkably handsome foot and ancle; and Lord Ellenborough, then Governor General of India, being about to have a full length portrait of himself taken, Dr. M. was applied to for the favor of his leg and foot in the painting. "Ah," said the old gentleman, "when we first came to this country they thought us a poor mean set, and drove us from place to place, trying to get us out of it; now they are very glad to make use of a poor Missionary's *understanding*."

that he had been informed about our establishment by Dr. Buchanan, [a physician,] and expressed the highest satisfaction with the whole, He had, a week before, sent me a great number of copies of inscriptions, and other curious documents, in the Kurnata and Tamul languages, collected by Dr. Buchanan in Mysore, for me to translate. I have given in an estimate of the expense, and it will probably fall on me to superintend the translation, if it be done, which, as it is ordered by the Court of Directors, will, I suppose, be the case.

"Within the last year, the Mahratta language has been taught in the college; this was placed under me. On the 6th of February last, a gentleman who had studied it, delivered a public declamation therein at the public disputations at the Government House, with very great reputation. In consequence of this, it was proposed to make me a Professor, and to double my income. Mr. Buchanan informed me that it was approved by his lordship, and would, in all probability take place."

But trials still mingled with the happiness and success of the missionary. During this period of labor and honor, his wife, while in a state of mental derangement, was called to her eternal home. Mr. Thomas, in a similar state, also died; and John Chamberlain, an excellent and devoted fellow-laborer, likewise exchanged his toils for everlasting rest. Other, and different scenes now open before us.

In 1805 CAREY, who had, very unexpectedly to himself, received the degree of D. D., published his grammar of the Mahratta language, opened a Mission church in the Loll bazar in Calcutta, and received intimation of the sailing of two additional Missionaries and their wives from Europe. So far all promised well; but in the early part of the following year the Marquis of Wellesley left for Europe, and Sir George Barlow had the temporary charge of the Government. When Messrs. Chater and Robinson, the new Missionaries, arrived, August 23, 1806, in an American ship, the Benjamin Franklin, commanded by Captain Wickes, our American friend, on presenting themselves at the police office, some demur arose as to their being allowed to go on to Serampore. The Vellore mutiny had just occurred, and it was convenient to some parties to consider it as the result of attempts forcibly to proselyte the natives; so that when Dr. CAREY applied at the office of the magistrates on the subject of the new Missionaries going to Serampore, one of the magistrates intimated that a message had come to him, from the Governor General, " that as Government did not interfere with the prejudices of the natives, it was his request that Mr. Carey and his colleagues would not." As explained by the magistrates, the message amounted to this,—They were not to preach to the natives, nor suffer the native converts to preach; they were not to distribute religious tracts, nor suffer the people to distribute them; they were not to send forth converted natives, nor to take any step, by conversation or otherwise, towards persuading the natives to embrace Christianity." Dr. CAREY enquired if they had any *written* communication; and being answered in the negative, he retired, saying, that neither he nor his brethren, wished to do any thing disagreeable to the Government from which they could conscientiously abstain. In the discussions which immediately followed this communication, CAREY maintained with great ability, but with expressions of due deference to the orders of the Government, the inexpediency and even inconsistency with the dictates of Christianity, of such an utter abandonment of its claims, and virtual denial of its divine authority, as the order in question appeared to imply. The order, therefore, was very much modified; and although preaching in the Lol Bazar in Calcutta was for a time discontinued, the Missionaries were assured that the Government was "well satisfied with their character and deportment, and that no complaint had ever been lodged against them."

The proceedings in India consequent on the Vellore mutiny led, of course, to agitation and discussion in England, in the Court of Directors, in the Court of Proprietors, and in the British Parliament, and from the Press; in which Messrs. Twining and Scott Waring stepped forward as the opponents of Missions, and, among others, the late Lord Teignmouth and Mr. Charles Grant, afterwards Lord Glenelg, as the advocates and apologists of the Missionaries. It became evident in the course of the discussions, that the Vellore mutiny did not originate in any apprehension on the part of the natives of India of attempts at forcible proselytism, but that it was occasioned by the inconsiderate enforcement of military costume, in matters not necessarily connected with religion. The ultimate result was favorable to the Missionaries and their cause. They had in the mean time commenced the Burmese Mission, which was afterwards given up to the beloved Judson.

By this time the subject of Missions had become a very popular topic of discussion in England. We have already seen the ridicule poured on the great enterprize by Mr. Marsh, in the British Senate, and it may not be improper here to show how a large portion of the Press acted. I have before me "*The Edinburgh Review for April* 1808," which contains an article extending to more than thirty pages, professing to be a critique on eight recently published works on the controverted subject of diffusing Christianity in India, in which all the Missionaries, especially Dr. CAREY, are the objects of ridicule. The writer was the late facetious, talented, and, alas that I must add—*impious*—REVEREND Sydney Smith, Prebendary of St. Paul's, London. It might have been hoped that this effusion of impiety and of spleen was the thoughtless production of a young man, and charity might have suggested its burial in oblivion, had not Mr. Prebendary Smith, in 1839, when an old man, included it in a collected edition of his works, edited by himself, at a time when the world had become well acquainted with the doings of CAREY and others in British India. We transcribe two or three paragraphs.

"The duties of conversion appear to be of less importance, when it is impossible to procure proper persons to undertake them, and when such religious embassies, in consequence, devolve on the lowest of the people. Who wishes to see scrofula and atheism cured by a single sermon in Bengal? who wishes to see the religious hoy riding at anchor in the Hoogly river? or shoals of jumpers exhibiting their nimble piety before the learned Brahmins of Benares? This madness is disgusting and dangerous enough at home. Why are we to send out little detachments of maniacs to spread over the fine regions of the world the most unjust and contemptible opinion of the Gospel? The wise and rational part of the Christian ministry find they have enough to do at home to combat with passions unfavorable to human happiness, and to make men act up to their professions. But if a tinker is a devout man, he infallibly sets off for the East. Let any man read the anabaptist mission;—can he do so, without deeming such men pernicious and extravagant in their own country; and without feeling that they are benefitting us much more by their absence, than the Hindoos by their advice?

"It is somewhat strange, that in a duty which is stated by one party to be so clear and so indispensable, that no man of moderation and good sense can be found to perform it. And if no other instruments remain but visionary enthusiasts, some doubt may be honestly raised whether it is not better to drop the scheme entirely.

"Shortly stated, then, our argument is this. We see not the slightest prospect of success;—we see much danger in making the attempt; and we doubt if the conversion of the Hindoos would ever be more than nominal. It is a duty of general benevolence to convert the heathen, it is less duty to convert the Hindoos than any other people, because they are already highly civilized, and because you must infallibly subject them to infamy and present degradation. The instruments employed for these purposes, are calculated to bring ridicule and disgrace upon the Gospel; and in the discretion of those at home, whom we consider as their patrons, we have not the smallest reliance; but on the contrary, we are convinced they would behold the loss of our Indian empire, not with the humility of men convinced of erroneous views and projects, but with the pride, the exultation, and the alacrity of martyrs."

There was something remarkable in the fact, that while "*The Edinburgh Review*," a professedly liberal journal, thus censured the Serampore Missionaries, "*The Quarterly Review*," a high Tory Church and King publication, came to their rescue. Speaking of the anti-missionary men, who called them fools, madmen, tinkers, Calvinists, and schismatics, keeping out of sight their love of man and zeal for God, their self-devotement, their indefatigable industry, and unequalled learning, the Quarterly Review adds —"These low-born and low-bred mechanics have [Feb. 1809] translated the whole Bible into Bengali, and have by this time printed it. They are printing the New Testament in the Sanscrit, the Orissa, Mahratta, Hindostani and Guzarat, and translating it into Persic, Felinga, Karnata, Chinese, the languages of the Seiks and of the Burmans; and in four of these languages they are going on with the

Bible. Extraordinary as this is, it will appear more so, when it is remembered that of these men one was originally a shoemaker, another a printer at Hull, and the third the master of a charity school at Bristol. Only fourteen years have elapsed since Thomas and CAREY set foot in India, and in that time have these missionaries acquired this gift of tongues; in fourteen years these low-born and low-bred mechanics have done more towards spreading the knowledge of the Scriptures among the heathen, than has been accomplished by all the world besides."

CHAPTER VIII.

CESSATION of the Difficulties with the Government—Second Marriage of Dr. CAREY—His illness—Grateful Review—Letter to his Nephew—Fire at Serampore—Description of the Printing Office—Mr. Thomason and Dr. Carey at the Fire—His fine spirit after the calamity—British Liberality—Visit of Mr. and Mrs. Judson to Calcutta and Serampore—And of Mr. and Mrs. Newell—Baptism of Mr. and Mrs. Judson and Mr. Rice—Carey's Letter to Dr. Staughton—Conversion of Jabez Carey—His Ordination—Character of Carey, Marshman and Ward—Piety of Carey as seen in his Letters—His recreations—Montgomery's Poem on the Daisy—Carey the Founder of the Agricultural and Horticultural Society of India.

HAPPILY the difficulties between the government of India and the Missionaries were soon ended. Dr. CAREY wrote to Mr. Fuller, from Calcutta, under date of October 14, 1807:—"I rejoice to inform you that the storm is gone over. On Tuesday last, the Governor of Serampore, received a letter from the government, revoking their order for the removal of the Press to Calcutta, and only requiring to be apprized of what we print, as the productions of our press are designed for distribution within the British territories. We shall send copies of what we intend to print to the Governor of Serampore, who will transmit them to the British government. The same day, a letter to the same purport was sent to me. We had little expectation of a formal revocation of the former orders, but had hopes that they might not be enforced. We intend to keep a day of thanksgiving for this deliverance as soon as I return to Serampore. Our public work will not be greatly interrupted by this occurrence, and I have reason to hope that the obstacles which yet remain will be gradually taken away. Perhaps our situation is, even now, better than it was before. There are, however, many here who would rejoice to see Christianity wholly expelled the country, and, particularly, to see any embarrassment thrown in our way. We, therefore, have no security but in God. I this evening preached from Isaiah li. 1—3. I think I feel a trust in God, as it respects the concerns of his church. The example of his preserving and increasing Abraham, who was alone when called, and the circumstance of this being held up to encourage the hope that God will comfort, repair, beautify, and fill with gladness his church, as promised in the third verse, is a support to me. I have, for many months past, had my mind much drawn to Isaiah xl., 27, 28, particularly the 28th verse, 'God is the Lord, the everlasting God, the Creator of the ends of the earth.' Thus he can do all that is necessary for the extension and benefit of his church. Thus God fainteth not, neither is weary, notwithstanding the wickedness of the world, and the ingratitude of his own people. He knows how to accomplish all that he has promised, for there is no searching of his understanding."

In another letter shortly after, addressed to Mr. Sutcliff, referring to the kindness of God to his church in India, he says, "I have lately made a comparison between the state of India when I first landed here, and its present state, as it respects the progress of the Gospel; which I shall send you. When I arrived, I knew of no person in Bengal who cared about the Gospel, except Mr. Brown, Mr. Udney, Mr. Creighton, and Mr. Brown, an indigo planter, besides brother Thomas and myself. There might be more, and probably were, though unknown to me. There are now in India thirty-two ministers of the gospel." About this time his son Felix was enrolled among the missionary band, being the second of his sons called to this work.

Dr. CAREY was now in his forty-seventh year, and was most devotedly engaged in his work; perhaps at no period of his life was he more active or more useful. We have already mentioned the death of his wife, after twelve years of melancholy derangement, uncheered by a single ray of pleasure during that long period. May 9, 1808, he entered a second time into the marriage union; the object of his choice being Lady Charlotte E. Rumohr, a person about his own age, ardent in her piety, and warm in her attachment to the Mission. She was of a noble family. With this excellent lady he lived in the enjoyment of great happiness for thirteen years.

In the following year, Dr. CAREY was visited with an alarming attack of fever, which for several weeks threatened to be fatal. He gives the following account of it, after his recovery, to his friend and former pastor, Mr. Sutcliff:—"I have been lately brought to the gates of death by a severe fever. I was first seized with it the last Sabbath in June, as

I was returning from Calcutta with brother Marshman. For the first two or three days I took medicine according to my own judgment; but getting worse, medical aid was called in from Barrackpore, a military station on the opposite side the river from Serampore. For several days I took medicine, which appeared to answer the designed end; but a delirium, attended with considerable fever, supervened, and for a few weeks together my life was in doubt. One or two days I was supposed to be dying. I believe Dr. Darling, who attended me, well understood my case, and treated me with the utmost skill; but I believe my life was given back in answer to prayer. From all that I can find, there was a remarkable spirit of prayer poured down upon the church and congregation at Calcutta, on my account; and I have reason to believe that it was not confined to our congregation, but was pretty general among the serious people in Calcutta and its environs. On the Monday, the day after I was taken ill, I put the finishing stroke to the translation of the Scriptures into the Bengali language, which some of my friends considered as the termination of my labors. Now I am raised up, I beg that I may be enabled to go on with more simplicity of heart, and more real despatch and utility, in the work of the Lord." It seems remarkable, that on his recovery, his letters to Europe took a more decidedly spiritual view of the Mission and its successes than at any previous time; God evidently intended this affliction to do him great good.

In the present state of the churches and the ministry in this country, it cannot be improper here to give a short extract of a letter addressed by Dr. CAREY to his nephew, Mr. Eustace Carey, who afterwards joined his venerable uncle as a Missionary in India. Under date of March 12, 1812, he says:—"Whether you come to India or not, be assured that the work of publishing the gospel is the most important work you could have chosen. Engage in it with humble dependence on God, and with a single eye to his glory, and I doubt not but he will give a blessing to your undertaking. I am fully of opinion that every person to whom God has given abilities for the work, is bound to devote himself to the work of the ministry. It is not at the option of such a person, whether he will engage in it or not, nor is it at the option of a church whether it will send one to the work of the ministry upon whom God has bestowed spiritual gifts. If the church neglect to send a member into the ministry, the guilt lies on them. The number of persons now required to spread the gospel through the earth is unspeakably great. If fifty thousand ministers, besides those actually employed, were now to go forth, they would be so thinly spread about, as scarcely to be perceived. The harvest is indeed great, but the laborers are very few."

Little did CAREY suppose while writing this letter, that within a few hours, even before he could close it, he would hear of the most affecting calamity which had ever befallen the Mission,—nothing less than the destruction of the Missionary printing office at Serampore. Introductory, however, to the details of this sad catastrophe, we will give the reader a graphic view of it as sent by Mr. Ward to a clerical relative in England, but little more than three months before the painful occurrence:—"I am in the very work, beyond which I have nothing to wish for, except more success in it. No place on earth presents itself in which I should be likely to be doing more good. Could you see your cousin in his printing-office, surrounded by forty or fifty servants, all employed in preparing the Holy Scriptures for the nations of India, you would, I am sure, be highly pleased. One man is preparing the Book of God for the learned Hindoos, in the Sanscrit language; another for the people of Bengal; another for those of Hindostan; another for the inhabitants of Orissa; another for the Mahrattas; another for the Sikhs; another for the people of Assam; and for the Mussulman in all parts of the East, in the Persian and Hindostannee languages; others for the Chinese; others for the Talingas; and others are soon to begin the Cingalese, Tamul, and Malay languages.

"As you enter the office, you see your cousin, in a small room, dressed in a white jacket, reading or writing, and at the same time looking over the whole office, which is one hundred and seventy-four feet long. The next persons you see, are learned natives translating the Scriptures into the different languages, or correcting the proof-sheets. You walk through the office and see, laid out in cases, *types* in Arabic, Persian, Nagaree, Talinga, Sikh, Bengali, Mahratta, Chinese, Orissa, Burman, Carnata, Keshomena, Greek, Hebrew, and English. Hindoos, Mussulmans, and converted natives are all busy. Some composing, others distributing, others correcting. You next come to the presses, and see four persons throwing off the sheets of the Bible in different languages; and on the left are half a dozen Mussulmans employed in binding the Scriptures for distribution; while others are folding the sheets, and delivering them to be placed in the store-room till they can be made up into volumes. This store-room, which is one hundred and forty-two feet long, is filled with shelves from side to side, upon which are laid, wrapt up, the sheets of the Bible before they are bound. You go forward, and in a room adjoining to the office, are the *type-casters*, busy in preparing the types in the different languages. In one corner, you see another party busy in grinding the printing ink; and in a spacious open place, walled round, you see a paper mill, and a number of persons employed in making paper for printing the Scriptures in all these languages. I think you will acknowledge that I am at my post, and where I ought to be."

Alas, that on the evening of the 11th of March, 1812, this vast establishment with 2000 reams of paper, and the types of nine languages, were all destroyed by fire,—it was believed by an incendiary. I have lying before me a long letter written by Dr. Marshman to Dr. Ryland, detailing the sad events of the calamity, the extent of which was estimated at twelve thousand pounds, or about sixty thousand dollars. The late Rev. T. T. Thomason, the worthy chaplain of the India Company at Calcutta, first assistant, and afterwards successor to the Rev. David Brown, thus writes of the sad occurrence:—"I could scarcely believe the report; it was like a blow on the head, which stupifies. I flew to Serampore to witness the desolation. The scene was indeed affecting. The immense printing office, two hundred feet long and fifty broad, reduced to a mere shell. The yard covered with burnt quires of paper, the loss in which article was immense. CAREY walked with me over the smoking ruins. The tears stood in his eyes. 'In one short evening,' said he, 'the labors of many years were consumed. How unsearchable are the ways of God! The Lord has laid me low that I may look more simply to him!' Who could stand in such a place—at such a time—with such a man, without feelings of sharp regret, and solemn exercise of mind? I saw the ground strewed with half-consumed paper, on which, in the course of a very few months, the words of life would have been printed. The metal under our feet amidst the ruins was melted into misshapen lumps—the sad remains of beautiful types consecrated to the service of the sanctuary. All was smiling and promising a few hours before—now all is vanished into smoke, or converted into rubbish."

But let us listen to CAREY only fourteen days after this sad event, and pitiable indeed is the man who cannot admire his sorrowful, but still more hopeful and grateful spirit. Writing to Mr. Fuller, he says:—"The loss cannot be estimated at less than seventy thousand rupees. By this providence several important manuscripts were lost. I believe, in my own case, it will require twelve months' hard labor to replace what has been consumed. This affliction is severely felt, as it will occasion a considerable delay in the publications of the different versions of the Bible, in which we are engaged, and the loss of English paper cannot, if our funds were ever so large, be soon replaced in this country. Many very merciful circumstances, however, attended this providence, and I rather wish to record them, than to dwell upon the gloomy side of the event. 1. No life was lost, and no one's health was injured, though brother Ward was in very great danger of being suffocated with the smoke, through running into the place, as soon as the fire broke out. Another man, who ran in after the oxygen of the air had been nearly consumed with the fire, fell down senseless before he could get out, and was rescued from death by the people who were near. 2. We had a strong proof of the kindness of our neighbors of every description, both European and native, and of the lively sympathy of all who knew us, from the highest to the lowest. 3. The matrices of the oriental types, and the punches are all recovered, and the presses saved, so that with the metal of the types which was melted down in the fire, we are able immediately to commence casting, and shall, in another fortnight, if nothing unforeseen intervene, be able to begin printing again in one language. Another month will enable us to begin in another, and I trust that in six months our loss in oriental types will be repaired. 4. The printing offices in Calcutta have sold or lent us a few English types, so that we can hobble on till you can send the articles ordered by our overland letter of yesterday. 5. Our paper manufactory is not injured, so that we shall not be stopped for want of country paper, on which to print our own editions of the Scriptures. 6. Our premises are not injured, except the printing office; and, providentially, a large building, larger than the one consumed, which we had let to a merchant of Calcutta, as a warehouse, was vacated only four days before the fire, so that we are not under the necessity of building before we can begin work. 7. None of our sources of income are dried up, and, besides our regular income from the school and the college, we have pretty large funds which we can use. Mr. Brown wished us to draw immediately upon the Bible Society, for the three thousand pounds voted us for the ensuing three years; but I trust we shall get through without that. The loss of manuscripts of the Telinga, Kurnata, Shikh, Sanscrit and Assam languages, is a very heavy loss; but as the travelling a road the second time, however painful it may be, is usually done with greater ease and certainty than when we travel it for the first time, so I trust the work will lose nothing in real value, nor will it be much retarded by this distressing event, for we shall begin printing in all these languages the moment types are prepared. The ground must be labored over again, but we are not discouraged. Indeed, the work is already begun again in every language; we are cast down, but not in despair. 8. We have all of us been supported under the affliction, and preserved from discouragement. To me, the consideration of the Divine sovereignty and wisdom has been very supporting; and, indeed, I have usually been supported under afflictions by feeling that I and mine are in the hands of an infinitely wise God. I endeavored to improve this our affliction, last Lord's day, from Psalm xlvi. 10. 'Be still, and know that I am God.' I principally dwelt upon two ideas:—1. God has a sovereign right to dispose of us as he pleases. 2. We ought to acquiesce in all that God does with us and to us. To enable us to do which, I recommended realizing meditation upon the perfections of God,—upon his providence, and upon his promises, including the prophecies of the extension of his kingdom."

Greatly must it have delighted the heart of CAREY and his colleagues to know, that no sooner did the mournful intelligence arrive in England, than the Christian public, of all denominations, hastened to repair the loss by an unexampled liberality. The British and Foreign Bible Society immediately sent out two thousand reams of paper; the London Missionary Society, as a mark of esteem to their Baptist brethren, voted one hundred pounds from their funds, and pulpits every where were opened to the leading ministers of the denomination, that they might solicit contributions; so that in *fifty days* afterwards, Fuller entered the room in which the committee had been convened, exclaiming, with eyes sparkling with joy and gratitude, "Well, brethren, the money is all raised, the loss by the Serampore fire is all repaired; and so constantly are the contributions pouring in, from all parties, in and out of the denomination, that I think we must in honesty publish an intimation that the whole deficiency for which we appealed to them, is removed. They are of so ready a mind that we must even stop the contributions."

Assuredly this fire was eminently useful in making the Mission known throughout India, and in extending a spirit of regard to the society in England, the happy effect of which continues even till now. Nor ought we to omit saying that it gave to the work of translation a mighty impetus, which soon began to show itself by a variety of new versions of the sacred volume. On all these accounts, what was so great a calamity at the time, became, in the kind providence of God, a very distinguished blessing.

Scarcely had the pressure of business arising from the fire subsided, when a series of events occurred in which our readers cannot but feel a special interest. On the eighteenth of June, 1812, the first Christian Missionaries connected with the *American Board of Commissioners for Foreign Missions*, arrived from the United States in Calcutta, where they were met and cordially welcomed, and invited to make their home in the Missionary family at Serampore, till another band of brethren and sisters then on their way from the same land should arrive. Mrs. Judson, in her own interesting way, shall introduce us to the scenes we have to narrate:—"Mr. Judson came on board with an invitation from Dr. CAREY to spend the night with him. I got into a palankeen—Mr. Judson walked to the house. It was with considerable fear I rode, as the streets were full of natives and English carriages. Those who carried me went so much faster than Mr. Judson, that I soon lost sight of him, and did not know where they would carry me. They, however, stopped before a large stone building, which I soon found to be Dr. CAREY'S house. We were directed up a pair of stairs, through one or two large rooms, into his study. He arose, shook hands with us, and gave us a cordial welcome to this country. His house is curiously constructed, as the other European houses are here. There are no chimneys or fire-places in them, the roofs are flat, the rooms are twenty feet in height, and proportionably large. Large windows without glass, open from one room to another, that the air may freely circulate through the house. They are very convenient for this hot climate, and bear every mark of antiquity. In the evening we attended meeting in the English Episcopal church. It was the first time of our attending meeting for above four months, and as we entered the church, our ears were delighted with hearing the organ play our old favorite tune, Bangor. The church was very handsome, and a number of punkahs, something like a fan several yards in length, hung around, with ropes fastened to the outside, which were pulled by some of the natives, to keep the church cool. We spent the night at Dr. CAREY'S, and were rejoiced to find ourselves once more in a house on land. Very near the house is a charity-school, supported by this mission, in which are instructed two hundred boys and nearly as many girls. They are chiefly children of Portuguese parents, and natives of no caste. We could see them all kneel in prayer, and hear them sing at the opening of the school. It was really affecting to see these poor children, picked up in the streets, learning to sing the praise and read the word of God."

Let us give here another picture, for those early days of Missions, so far as Americans are concerned, were of deep interest; and the lovely Harriet Newell, that first American martyr to the cause, ought to be heard, even though her description be of the same scenes as those presented to us by Mrs. Judson, and very similar as to the colors in which they are painted:—

She writes, June 18, 1812, "Yesterday afternoon we left the vessel, and were conveyed in a palanquin through crowds of Hindoos to Dr. CAREY'S. No English lady is here seen walking in the streets. This I do not now wonder at. The natives are so numerous and noisy, that a walk would be extremely unpleasant. Calcutta houses are built almost entirely of stone. They are very large and airy. Dr. C.'s house appeared like a palace to us, after residing so long in our little room. He keeps a large number of Hindoo servants. Mrs. Carey is very ill at Serampore. The Doctor is a small man and very pleasant. He received us very cordially. This morning we saw some of the native Christians. Ram-mo-Hund was one. They cannot talk English. A son of Dr. C.'s is studying law at Calcutta. He is an amiable young man. An invitation to go to Serampore to-morrow."

Two days afterwards, she writes, "At Serampore.

We came here last evening by water. The dear missionaries received us with the same cordiality as they would, if we had been their own brothers and sisters. This is the most delightful place I ever saw. Here the missionaries enjoy *all* the comforts of life, and are actively engaged in the Redeemer's service. After a tedious voyage of four months at sea, think, my dear mother, how grateful to us is this retired and delightful spot. The mission-house consists of four large commodious stone buildings—Dr. Carey's, Dr. Marshman's, Mr. Ward's, and the common house. In the last we were accommodated with two large spacious rooms, with every convenience we could wish. It has eight rooms on the floor, no chambers; namely, the two rooms above mentioned, with the two other lodging rooms, the dining hall, where an hundred or more eat, a large elegant chapel, and two large libraries. The buildings stand close to the river. The view of the other side is delightful. The garden is larger, and much more elegant than any I ever saw in America. A few months since, the printing office was destroyed by fire. This was a heavy stroke; but the printing is now carried on very extensively. There is a large number of out-buildings also; the cook-house, one for making paper, etc., etc."

On the day following she writes, "Mr. N. [Newell,] preached this morning in the Mission chapel. Mr. W. [Ward] in the afternoon, in the Bengali language, to about fifty Hindoos and Mussulmen. This afternoon I shall ever recollect with peculiar sensations. The appearance of the Christian Hindoo, when listening to the word of life, would have reproved many an American Christian. Had you been present, I am sure you could not have refrained from weeping. Had an opposer of missions been present, his objections must have vanished. He would have exclaimed, 'What hath God wrought!' To hear the praises of Jesus sung by a people of a strange language; to see them kneel before the throne of grace; to behold them eagerly catching every word which proceeded from the mouth of their minister was a joyful affecting scene. Rejoice, my mother; the standard of the blessed Immanuel is erected in this distant pagan land; and here the gospel will undoubtedly continue, till the commencement of the bright millenial day. In the evening brother J. [Judson] preached. How precious the privileges I now enjoy."

One short passage, written the next day, shall close our extracts:—"I have every thing here which heart could wish, but American friends. We are treated with the *greatest possible kindness*. Every thing tends to make us happy and excite our gratitude. You would love these dear missionaries, could you see them."

The two missionaries, Messrs. Judson and Newell, with their wives, stayed at Serampore several weeks, to the high gratification of all parties, so far as Christian intercourse was concerned; but here, also, they learned that the jealousy of the government would not allow them to settle within the British dominions. A letter from CAREY to Dr. Staughton, under date of October 12, 1812, gives, in his own simple way, information of a fact which every

American Baptist now well understands :—" Since their arrival in Bengal, brother and sister Judson have been baptized. Judson has since that preached the best sermon upon Baptism, that I have ever heard on the subject, which we intend to print. I yesterday heard that brother Rice had also fully made up his mind upon baptism.

" As none of us had conversed with brother Judson before he showed strong symptoms of a tendency towards believers' baptism, I enquired of him what had occasioned the change. He told me, that on the voyage he had thought much about the circumstances, that he was coming to Serampore, where all were Baptists; that he should, in all probability have occasion to defend infant sprinkling among us; and that in consequence, he set himself to examine into the grounds of Pedobaptism. This ended in a conviction, that it has no foundation in the word of God, and occasioned a revolution in his sentiments, which was nearly complete before he arrived in India. He mentioned his doubts and convictions to Mrs. J., which operated to her conviction also, and they were both of them publicly baptized at Calcutta. I expect, however, that he will give the account of this change in an appendix to his sermon, which will, of course, be more correct than my statement.

" Brother Rice was on the voyage thought by our brethren to be the most obstinate friend of Pedobaptism, of any of the Missionaries. I cannot tell what has led to his change of sentiment, nor had I any suspicion of it, till one morning, when he came before I was up, to examine my Greek Testament. From some questions which he asked that morning, I began to suspect that he was enquiring; but I yesterday heard that he was decidedly on the side of believers' baptism. I expect, therefore, that he will soon be baptized." The results of this movement are well known to our readers, and need not here be detailed.

This seems a very proper place to state a few facts relating to Jabez, the third son of Dr. CAREY. His two eldest, we have already seen, had professed Christianity, and were now employed in Missionary labors; but Jabez had hitherto shown nothing but aversion to religion, and was at a proper age articled to an attorney. About this time, the year 1812, was held the first annual public meeting of the society in London, when Dr. Ryland and Mr. Fuller preached. During Mr. Fuller's sermon, which was on the *Power of the Gospel*, the venerable preacher adverted to the happiness of the beloved CAREY in seeing two of his sons devoted to the Mission, but added he, "there is a third who gives him pain; he is not yet turned to the Lord;"—then making a long and solemn pause, during which tears flowed abundantly from his eyes, he exclaimed in a loud and shrill voice, which seemed to spring from a soul full of feeling, "Brethren, let us send up a united, universal, and fervent prayer to God, in solemn silence for the conversion of Jabez Carey." The appeal was like a sudden clap of thunder, and the pause afterwards as intensely solemn as silence and prayer could make it. Two minutes, at least, of the most profound devotional feeling pervaded an assembly of perhaps two thousand persons. The result was striking. Among the first letters afterwards received, was the announcement of that conversion which had been so earnestly sought; and which occurred nearly, if not just at the season of fervent supplication.

During the following year, the president of the island of Amboyna wrote to Dr. CAREY, requesting him to send some missionaries there, stating that there were twenty-thousand professing Christians in the Island, with places of worship and schools, but without a minister. The government also applied to them for aid in the schools. At this time, when help seemed far off, Jabez Carey proposed himself, and most cheerfully relinquished secular prospects the most promising to give himself to the self-denying work of the Mission. His offer was accepted, and his ordination took place. On this occasion a very pleasing coincidence occurred. Felix Carey arrived from Burmah, just previously to the commencement of the exercise. Thus Dr. CAREY, with two of his sons, Felix and William, united in laying hands on the third. "I trust," said the good father, "this will be a matter of everlasting praise. O praise the Lord with me, and let us exalt his name together! To me the Lord has been very, *very* gracious. I trust all my children love the Lord, and three out of four are actually engaged in the important work of publishing his Gospel among the heathen; two of them in new countries."

It would be ungrateful to the memory of the holy dead, if we did not dedicate a page to the manifestations of the Divine kindness in connexion with

CAREY'S associates at Serampore. As Dr. Godwin has well remarked, in his *Jubilee* sermon, "For between twenty and thirty years were associated together in that hallowed spot, CAREY, MARSHMAN, and WARD; names honorable to the denomination to which they belonged, dear to the whole Christian church, and destined to live in the fragrant recollections of distant ages as long as devoted piety and missionary zeal are revered amongst men. Here were three men, of dispositions, and characters, and talents very diverse, and not without their respective imperfections, but all glowing with intense ardor for the glory of God and the salvation of men, full of faith and zeal, making efforts which astonished both the church and the world, and devoting, with a sublime generosity seldom equalled, and perhaps never surpassed, thousands, yes, tens of thousands, the produce of their own labors and talents, to the Missionary cause. These were men adapted to each other, and perhaps we may say, necessary to each other, who continued in an unbroken friendship till, one after another, they entered into their rest; and who, by the blessing of God on their joint labors, accomplished a work which will remain a monument of their devoted piety and zeal more lasting than our empire in India, or than the great globe itself. These men stood in front of the battle of India missions, and during the arduous struggle which terminated with the charter of 1813, in granting missionaries free access to India, they never for a moment deserted their post, or despaired of success. When, at a subsequent period, Lord Hastings, who honored them with his kind support, had occasion to refer in conversation to the severe conflict they had passed through, he assured them that, in his opinion, the freedom of resort to India which missionaries then enjoyed was owing, under God, to the prudence, the zeal, and the wisdom which they had manifested, when the whole weight of government in England and in India was directed to the extinction of the missionary enterprise. Must we not acknowledge the hand of God in this remarkable adaptation of men to their work?"

It has been well remaked, by the late excellent Dr. Jeremiah Chaplin, that "Dr. CAREY furnishes a most satisfactory proof of the possibility of uniting deep and ardent piety with an assiduous and successful cultivation of science and literature. That he was eminently pious, no man who has read his life can dispute; and there is as little difficulty in believing him to have made rapid and great progress in natural history and in many languages." We would labor to encourage our rising ministry to aim at both these features of character, by giving them a few specimens of the piety which regulated his mind, and guided every study. We shall introduce but a few extracts from his letters diffused over a series of years, but they will be sufficient to show the influence under which he lived, and constrain us to glorify God in him; they will tend also to illustrate a passage in his early diary for 1794, when he says, "O what is there in all this world worth living for, but the presence and service of God! I feel a burning desire that all the world may know this God and serve him."

Writing to Mr. Sutcliff, in 1803, he says:—"I see that I have inadvertently written some things to England which savor strongly of vanity, and which, when they have been printed, have made me wish that they had never been written. I am not conscious of having felt the workings of vanity while writing them, and believe that the sentiments were what lay uppermost at the moment of writing; but I wish they had not been published, at least in their present form.

"My time is so much occupied with the second edition of the New Testament, and the remaining part of the Old, that, together with my other necessary avocations, the whole is completely engrossed, and my mind has acquired so much bias towards seeking out words, places, and idioms of speech, that it is unprepared for any other undertaking, and I feel that there is a possibility of having the mind secularized whilst employed in Biblical criticisms. This, however, is an absolutely necessary work, and cannot be done without much repeated and close attention, and frequent revision. I therefore comfort myself with the thought, that I am in the work of the Lord."

To his sister, he says in the following year:—"I have this evening been preaching in English, from 2 Peter iii. 18. I endeavored to define the grace of God, as consisting in sorrow for, and forsaking of sin; in holy jealousy over ourselves, and care not to transgress; and in participation of that mind which was also in Christ Jesus. 'The knowledge of our Lord Jesus Christ,' I considered as a hearty trusting in him for salvation, and receiving him as exhibited in the gospel. I defined growing in grace as consisting in frequently looking into ourselves; always seeking for more than we have already; and a continual desire to lay out for God's glory what we do obtain from him."

To his friend, Dr. Ryland, he says in 1810:—"It is now nearly seventeen years since I left England for this country. Since that time I have been witness to an astonishing train of circumstances, which have produced a new appearance of all things relating to the cause of God in these parts. The whole work, however, has been carried on by God in so mysterious a manner, that it would be difficult for any one person to fix on any particular circumstance, and say, 'I am the instrument by which this work has been accomplished.' At the same time, all has been done by the instrumentality of one or another, or, more properly speaking, by the instrumentality of all so combined, compounded and recompounded, that direct instrumentality can scarcely be perceived. We see the effect; each one rejoices in it; and yet no one can say how it has been wrought. I have often thought that the work must be obstructed by me, and that the God who aboundeth in all wisdom and prudence in the dispensations of his grace, could not give a blessing to the labors of such a one as I am, without deviating from that wisdom and prudence which he always observes.—Yet I do desire, to give myself such as I am, wholly to the cause of my God, and to be wholly employed in his service. I do indeed plod on in my work, but without the life and spirit necessary to excite me to do it as a spiritual service to God."

In 1815, he says to Mr. Fuller:—"Through Divine goodness, I still live, and am in as good a state of health as perhaps I ever was; well would it be, if my soul were in as good a state as my body. I think I trust in the Lord Jesus, and I cannot say that I ever get further than to cast my perishing soul from day to day on the Saviour of sinners. What I have always lamented as the great crime of which I am constantly guilty, is want of love to Christ. That fervency of spirit which many feel, that constant activity in the ways of God, and that hunger and thirst after righteousness which constitute the life and soul of religion, I scarcely feel at all, or if I do perceive a small degree of it, its continuance is so short, and its operations so feeble, that I can scarcely consider it as forming a part of my character. I live a kind of mechanical life, going through the labors of each day as I should go through any other work, but in a great measure destitute of that energy which makes every duty a pleasure."

At the close of 1816, he says to Dr. Ryland:—"How important is it to live in that state of continual communion with God, and lively faith in Christ, as to have the great point of our acceptance with God quite clear while we are in health. In my illness, great weakness and great stupor so prevailed, that I found it impossible to do more than cast my sinful soul on the Redeemer, and hope in the mercy of God for eternal life."

To Mr. Burls, an eminent Christian merchant of London, he wrote about two months after the letter from which we have just quoted:—"I trust in Christ alone for pardon and acceptance with God. I deserve everlasting destruction from his presence, and the glory of his power; yet I hope in his mercy, and believe his faithful word, 'Him that cometh unto me, I will in no wise cast out.'"

And in 1831, he thus writes to his son Jabez:—"I am this day seventy years old,—a monument of Divine mercy and goodness; though, on a review of my life, I find much, very much, for which I ought to be humbled in the dust. My direct and positive sins are innumerable; my negligence in the Lord's work has been great; I have not promoted his cause, nor sought his glory and honor as I ought. Notwithstanding all this, I am spared till now, and am still retained in his work. I trust for acceptance with him to the blood of Christ alone; and I hope I am received into the Divine favor through him. I wish to be more entirely devoted to his service, more completely sanctified, and more habitually exercising all the Christian graces, and bringing forth the fruits of righteousness to the praise and honor of that Saviour who gave his life a sacrifice for sin. . . . . I trust I am ready to die, through the grace of my Lord Jesus, and I look forward to the full enjoyment of the society of holy men and angels, and the full vision of God for evermore."

This appears to be an appropriate place to state a few facts as to what may be described the recreations or amusements of Dr. Carey. Every one must be aware, that to a man engaged every day at least ten hours, in lecturing and translating, some relaxation is indispensable. CAREY had his; but it was connected with the welfare of the great country which he regarded as his own. We have already seen him, even at Moulton, devoting his spare hours in examining the plants and the animals of his neighborhood, and carefully studying their history. These studies were resumed in India. He wrote to England from time to time for books on Botany and kindred subjects; he formed, when at Mudnabatty, an intimate friendship with Dr. Roxburg, the superintendent of the Company's Botanical Garden, who called a newly discovered tree by CAREY'S name; writing to Mr. Fuller, September 7, 1803, he says:—"I may mention a thing which I have long designed, but for want of funds, have never been able to accomplish. I suppose that the expense of doing it might be thirty rupees a month. I have always had a strong turn for natural history, and know nothing more fit to relax the mind after close application to other things. I have long wished to employ a person to paint the natural history of India, the vegetable productions excepted, which Dr. Roxburg has been about for several years. The birds, insects, lizards, fishes, and serpents, (many of the last have been drawn by Dr. Buchanan and Dr. Russel with descriptions,) would be amusing, would take little time, and might be of use. I could do it for that sum, and indeed intend to employ my own little property for that purpose, as soon as it can be spared from the family." Six years afterwards, he wrote to Mr. Sutcliff:—"I have written for some works of science, which I hope you will send. I think your best way is to send my list of roots, seeds, etc., to some nurseryman of note in London, with orders to ship them on the Providence, directed to me. Were you to give a penny a day to a boy to gather seeds of cowslips, violets, crowfoots, etc., and to dig up the roots of bluebells, etc., after they had done flowering, you might fill me a box every quarter of a year; and surely some neighbors would send a few snow-drops, crocuses, and other trifles. All your weeds, even your nettles and thistles, are taken the greatest care of by me here. The American friends are twenty times more communicative than the English in this respect; indeed, though we can not buy a little cabbage seed here under about two guineas, yet I have never been able to extort an ounce, or a quart of kidney-beans, from all the friends in England. Do try to mend a little."

A beautiful little poem, which made its appearance in England in 1821, records an instance strikingly illustrative of the feelings of such a mind as CAREY'S when unexpectedly led back in the prosecution of his studies to the scenes of his infancy, in a country from which he had, at an early age, expatriated himself for the remainder of his life. After having carefully unpacked a bag of seeds, which he had received from a friend in England, in order to make experiments on them in his garden at Serampore, he shook out the bag in one corner of the garden, and shortly afterwards discovered something spring up on the spot, which, when it reached maturity, proved to be nothing less nor more than one of those *daisies* with which the meadows of England abound. The delight with which this

"Wee, modest, crimson-tipped flower,"

one of the humblest, but most pleasing ornaments of the English Flora, inspired him, he described to some of his European correspondents in very strong and glowing language, and the incident suggested to the amiable James Montgomery the following lines, which we need make no apology for transcribing:—

"ADDRESSED TO DR. CAREY.

"Thrice welcome, little English flower
My mother-country's white and red,
In rose or lily, till this hour
Never to me such beauty spread;
Transplanted from thine island-bed,
A treasure in a grain of earth,
Strange as a spirit from the dead
Thine embryo sprang to birth.

"Thrice welcome, little English flower!
Whose tribes beneath our natal skies
Shut close their leaves while vapors lower;
But when the sun's gay beams arise,
With unabashed, but modest eyes,
Follow his motion to the west;
Nor seek to gaze till day-light dies,
Then fold themselves to rest.

"Thrice welcome, little English flower!
To this resplendent hemisphere,
Where Flora's giant offspring tower
In gorgeous liveries all the year;

Thou, only thou, art *little* here,
Like worth unfriended or unknown,
Yet to my British heart more dear
Then all the torrid Zone.

Thrice welcome, little English flower!
Of early scenes beloved by me,
While happy in my father's bower,
Thou shalt the blithe memorial be
The fairy sports of infancy,
Youth's golden age, and manhood's prime,
Home, country, kindred, friends, with thee
Are mine in this fair clime.

Thrice welcome, little English flower!
I'll rear thee with a trembling hand:
Oh, for the April sun and shower,
The sweet May dews of that fair land,
Where DAISIES, thick as star-light stand
In every walk!—that here might shoot
Thy scions, and thy buds expand,
A hundred from one root!

"Thrice welcome, little English flower!
To me the pledge of hope unseen:
When sorrow would my soul o'erpower
For joys that *were or might have been*,
I'll call to mind how fresh and green,
I saw thee waking from the dust,
Then turn to heaven with brow serene,
And place in God my trust."

The important services rendered to India, by Dr. Carey, as the founder of the Agricultural and Horticultural Society of that country will be detailed in their proper place towards the close of this volume. Suffice it to say here that in 1817, after conversation with some of the leading persons of influence in India, the society was formed, under the patronage of Lord Hastings, then Governor General, and that many of the most opulent natives joined it; it has, unquestionably, proved of great benefit to the country.

CHAPTER IX.

Dr. Carey's Resumption of labor after the fire—Letter to Fuller—Carey's extraordinary labors and diligence—Renewal in England of the East India Company's Charter—Religious Freedom secured—Misunderstanding of Carey and his brethren with the Society in England—Church at Serampore—Letter to the American Triennial Convention—Carey's Views of the Duty of American Baptists—Progress of the Cause in India—Death of the second Mrs. Carey—Visit of Messrs. Tyerman and Bennett—Mr. Leslie's View of Dr. Carey—Visit of Mr. and Mrs. Jones—Serious Accident to Dr. Carey—His daily Engagements—Extraordinary Results of his Labors—Honors conferred on the Doctor—His third Marriage—Description of Dr. Carey and his doings, by Mr. Leechman.

If any one should be disposed to draw an inference from the close of the preceding chapter, that Dr. Carey had begun to lessen his labors in the Missionary cause, he will be under a great mistake. Let us look in on him at Serampore, a very few months after the fire, and see him at work. Let us remember, to use the language of Haldane, in his recently published Memoir of his father and uncle, "He who was sneered at as '*the consecrated cobbler*,' who stole into a Danish settlement at Serampore and began those translations of the Bible which have already shaken the superstition of India to its foundations." We will here furnish an extract of a letter to Mr. Fuller, under date of March 20, 1813: "I was never so closely employed as at present. I have just finished for the press my Telinga Grammar; the last sheet of the Punjaba Grammar is in press. I am getting forward with my Kurnata Grammar; indeed it is nearly ready for the press. I am also preparing materials for Grammars of the Kashmeer, Pushto, and Billochi languages, and have begun digesting those for the Orissa. The care of publishing and correcting Felix's Burman Grammar lies on me, besides learning all these languages, correcting the translations in them, writing a Bengali Dictionary, and all my pastoral and collegiate duties. I therefore can scarcely call an hour my own in a week. I, however, rejoice in my work, and delight in it. It is clearing the way, and providing materials for those who succeed us to work upon. I have much for which to bless the Lord. I trust all my children know the Lord in truth. I have every family and domestic blessing I can wish; and more than I could have expected. The work of the Lord prospers. The church at Calcutta is now become very large, and still increases. The Mission, notwithstanding its heavy losses, has been supported, and we have been enabled, within one year from a very desolating calamity, to carry on our printing to a greater extent than before it took place. I wish we could have communicated to you our real situation on the day you received the news of the fire. It would have greatly raised your drooping spirits could you have looked forward, or could you have known how we had been supported till then."

The following year, Dr. CAREY states, in a letter to the same correspondent, that the number of languages into which the Scriptures were either wholly or in part translated by himself and his brethren at Serampore, was twenty-six. And when we consider, that the labor of correcting and revising all these translations devolved upon CAREY himself, we may readily conceive that his exertions must have been truly astonishing. Diligent application and unwearied industry, could alone have carried him through his unparalleled labor. For be it remembered, that so essentially different in their entire structure and idiom are the languages of the East from those of the western parts of the world, that the Rev. W. Buyers, of Benares, a highly accomplished missionary, and a competent authority, has recorded it as his opinion, that any six of the principal languages of Europe, might be learnt with as little labor as one of those of India. It must ever therefore, stand as an instance of extraordinary skill and prodigious learning, that, in less than four years from his arrival, CAREY had translated the New Testament into Bengali, and that this first translation was so rapidly followed by others into the venerable Sanscrit, and the various dialects and languages of British India. Well, might the Marquis Wellesley, once so much afraid of CAREY, pronounce on a public occasion, a high encomium, designating him, "as the venerable Protestant Missionary," acknowledging his literary attainments, and recording the benefits which he had conferred upon the College of Fort William.

Important events in the mean time had occurred in England. As the charter of the East India company would expire in the year 1815, two years before that period, a very powerful and extensive agitation commenced among Christians of all classes in Great Britain. The pens of Claudius Buchanan, Robert Hall, Andrew Fuller, and others, and the eloquence of Wilberforce and other Christian legislators, were employed in the House of Commons, to obtain a clause in the New Charter securing to Missionaries of all denominations entire freedom in the pursuit of their great work. The object was secured, and no further annoyance has since been felt by them, except that which a religious hierarchy will always in some way or other create. For this kind interposition of Divine Providence, and manifestation of the deep interest in their work on the part of European Christians, CAREY, and Christian missionaries in India, of all the sections of the one church were devoutly grateful.

It may not, however, be uninteresting or useless to place on record the character of the opposition to this measure which was shown in the British Parliament. CAREY writes to Mr. Fuller from Calcutta, Feb. 24, 1814 :—" I have received a letter from Mr. B. informing me of the debates, and containing an extract from the *Times* paper, in which Mr. Pendegrast stated his having seen me on a hogshead, haranguing the natives ; that a mob was raised, and I was saved by the police. Not a syllable of that statement is true. I never mounted hogshead, pipe, or tun in my life. I never preached in Calcutta streets in my life. I need not therefore say that the police never saved me from the fury of the mob, for

I never in my life needed their interference. I may say more, I believe no one, either European or Native, ever preached in Calcutta streets. I am sure the Police never had occasion to interfere. Such men are not aware of the contempt with which their flimsy and unprincipled statements are read here.

"Calcutta is no more the seat of infidelity, as it was some years ago. It was then the fashion; and men whose minds were contracted, or too superficial to think, joined the multitude, were staunch infidels, and made sport of religion, and the Bible. Now there are some hundreds of praying persons in the city, and some in every department of life. The consequence is, that now a multitude who never attend any place of worship, are desirous of being included in the number of nominal Christians. Genuine religion, however, does prevail, and the cause of Truth is spread on every hand."

In 1817, about two years after the death of Andrew Fuller, the first secretary of the Society, a misunderstanding arose between the Serampore Missionaries and the parent Society in England, which ultimately, after ten years' discussion, led to the dissolution of the connexion which had hitherto subsisted between them. It is impossible, within the limits of this Memoir, to enter fully into the nature of the dispute; suffice it to say that various considerations led the Society to recommend a new, and, as they believed, a more satisfactory investment of the Mission property, and that a number of gentlemen in England should be associated in the trust with the Missionaries themselves. To this arrangement Dr. Carey and his brethren declined to accede; and, sustained by the Danish government, to which Serampore belonged, they invested the property in a way more agreeable to their own wishes. This disagreement, however, did not, in the slightest degree, interrupt the labors of the Missionaries; nor did it at all destroy their friendship with the junior brethren, who took a different view of the matter from themselves. All continued instant in prayer and in every good work. It is pleasant to add, that, many years since, all the difficulties in the way of reunion vanished away, and the two bands again became one.

For several years but few events suitable for the pages of the Biographer occurred in the history of the venerable Carey. His preaching, pastoral, and translating labors were all continued as usual; all pleasant; and all successful. It will probably gratify the reader to have introduced in this place a Fac-Simile of a letter written by Dr. Carey, and of the signatures of the Pastors and Deacons of the church at Serampore, in 1817:—

To the Baptists of the United States no apology can be needed for the introduction of even a long letter, written by Carey, and addressed by him and his colleagues to the Board of the American Baptist General Convention, under date of June 25, 1816:—

"Dear Brethren,

"We have seen, with peculiar joy, the attention of our dear brethren throughout the whole continent of America, excited to the state of the heathen, who have indeed been given, in the Divine covenant, to the Redeemer, for an everlasting possession. The indifference formerly felt respecting the extension of that kingdom, which is the subject of all prophecy, of all dispensations, and for the universal spread of which the world itself is kept in existence, is a reflection which ought to cover every one whose song is 'Crown him Lord of all,' with confusion of face. We were too long absorbed in the affairs of individual societies, when all the prophecies, and all the promises, as well as attachment to Him who is to be called 'the God of the whole earth,' should have led our devotions to the salvation of the whole world, and filled our contemplations with the delightful scenes on which the mind of Isaiah dwelt with so much rapture.

"We rejoice to see the American churches making this a common cause, and that means have been taken to unite all their energies in the hands of so venerable a body of pious ministers. We now send our congratulations and most fervent wishes for the success of your efforts. May many thousand souls, each more precious than the whole material system, recovered to a state of endless blessedness, be your certain, ample, and imperishable reward.

"Should Divine Providence give you favor in the eyes of the Burman Government, as we hope it will, that empire stands in great and pressing need of many more Missionaries; and we would recommend you to send, as soon as possible, to other places, as to Siam, Bassein, Ummurapore, Ava, Martaban, etc. By thus confining your present efforts to this empire, the languages of which have, no doubt, a strong affinity, your agents will form a united phalanx. Having an immense people of the same manners, prejudices, religion, and government, as their object; and being near each other, and engaged in the same country, the experience and acquirements of each will come into the common stock, and bear an ample interest. They will be able eventually to give solid and matured advice; and in cases of removal by death, to supply the loss of those gone to receive their great reward. We would strongly recommend, that *one or more*, who may hereafter come out, obtain a competent knowledge of medicine. Perhaps Missions in no Eastern country need so much all the wisdom, and advice, and mutual help, which Missionaries can supply to each other, as, from the despotic and capricious character of its Government, that in the Burman empire does.

"The attempts of our Society in this empire, have ended in the transfer of the Mission to brother Judson, and those from you who may join him; brother Felix Carey, our last Missionary at Rangoon, having gone into the service of his Burman Majesty. Something, however, has been done. A Mission-house has been built; the language has been opened; a grammar printed; materials for a Dictionary formed; a small part of the New Testament printed, and a number of copies put into the hands of the natives.

"We know not what your immediate expectations are relative to the Burman empire, but we hope your views are not confined to the immediate conversion of the natives by the preaching of the word. Could a church of converted natives be obtained at Rangoon, it might exist for a while, and be scattered, or perish for want of additions. From all we have seen hitherto, we are ready to think that the dispensations of Providence point to labors that may operate, indeed, more slowly on the population, but more effectually in the end; as knowledge, once put into fermentation, will not only influence the part where it is first deposited, but leaven the whole lump. The slow progress of conversion in such a mode of teaching the natives, may not be so encouraging, and may require, in all, more faith and patience; but it appears to have been the process of things, in the progress of the Reformation, during the reigns of Henry, Edward, Elizabeth, James, and Charles. And should the work of evangelizing India be thus slow and silently progressive, which, however, considering the age of the world, is not perhaps very likely, still the grand result will amply recompense us, and you, for all our toils. We are sure to take the fortress, if we can but persuade ourselves to sit down long enough before it. 'We shall reap if we faint not.'

"And then, very dear brethren, when it shall be said of the seat of our labors, the infamous swinging post is no longer erected; the widow burns no more on the funeral pile; the obscene dances and songs are seen and heard no more; the gods are thrown to the moles and to the bats, and Jesus is known as the God of the whole land; the poor Hindoo goes no more to the Ganges to be washed from his filthiness, but to the fountain opened for sin and uncleanness; the temples are forsaken; the crowds say, 'Let us go up to the house of the Lord, and he shall teach us of his ways, and we will walk in his statutes;' the anxious Hindoos no more consume their property, their strength and their lives, in vain pilgrimages, but they come at once to Him who can save to 'the uttermost;' the sick and the dying are no more dragged to the Ganges, but look to the Lamb of God, and commit their souls into his faithful hands; the children, no more sacrificed to idols, are become 'the seed of the Lord, that he may be glorified;' the public morals are improved; the language of Canaan is learnt; benevolent societies are formed; civilization and salvation walk arm in arm together; the desert blossoms; the earth yields her increase; angels and glorified spirits hover with joy over India, and carry ten thousand messages of love from the Lamb in the midst of the throne; and redeemed souls from the different villages, towns, and cities of this immense country, constantly add to the number, and swell the chorus of the redeemed, 'Unto Him that loved us, and washed us from our sins in his own blood, unto HIM be the glory;'—when this grand result of the labors of God's servants in India shall be realized, shall we then think that we have labored in vain, and spent our strength for nought? Surely not. Well, the decree is gone forth! 'My word shall prosper in the thing whereunto I sent it.'

"We shall be glad to render you, and our brethren in the Burman empire, every assistance in our power. We have always met the drafts of brother Judson, and have sent repeated supplies, various articles of food, etc., to meet the wants of our dear brother and sister there.

"Hoping to hear from you by every opportunity, we are, very dear brethren, your affectionate brethren and fellow-laborers in the kingdom of Christ.

W. CAREY,
J. MARSHMAN,
W. WARD."

An extract from another letter, addressed to a minister in this country, December 6, in the same year, will not be unacceptable, especially as it is the last one sent by him to the United States, which we shall give:

"I am now recovering from a severe bilious fever, which brought me to the brink of the grave; and am still so weak as to be scarcely able to write. The Lord has had mercy on me, and I am enabled now again to engage in my beloved work, though close application is absolutely forbidden by the physicians. Yours, my dear brother, is the land of wonders. The great things which God, by his Spirit, is doing in the United States, are truly astonishing, and call at once for the most grateful praises, and the most entire confidence in all his gracious promises.

"Among these things must be reckoned the missionary exertions now making; and the Peace Society lately established at New York, and other places; a society with whose objects my heart most cordially coincides, and which must, through the Divine assistance, which will assuredly be granted, be finally successful in the accomplishment of its ultimate object.

"To me it is a matter of much joy, that the

churches in Kentucky, and other parts, insist on a Mission to the West. The American Indians are undoubtedly committed exclusively to the American churches; and I trust the work of publishing the gospel to them, setting up schools for their instruction, translating the word of God into their languages, and other things necessary to their faith, civilization, and comfort, will be engaged in with eagerness, and persevered in with tenacity, till the great object be accomplished. Faith cometh by hearing, and hearing by the word.

"We live in a land where every thing around us tends to freeze the warmest affections of the mind; and yet very much good has been done; many have been converted under the Word. There are many churches in India, and every year brings a considerable increase of laborers in the cause of God. Yet all that has been done, seems lost in the vast population who fear not God; and though our brethren, and even churches, are scattered all over India, yet a person, unacquainted with their local situation, might travel over India, and hear very little of them.

"One favorable circumstance in this country is, the very general attention which has lately been felt by most classes of Europeans, to the establishing of schools for the education of the children of the natives. We have a good number of these schools belonging to the Mission, and many are established by others, which promise to be of great utility. Brother Marshman has just drawn up a plan for these schools, which I think an excellent one. Upon that plan they may be extended to every part of India, if funds can be obtained, and ensure instruction in reading, writing, grammar, geography, astronomy, general philosophy, and morals, for the trifling sum of three rupees [less than two dollars] a year for each lad thus instructed. This plan includes a vigorous superintendence of the schools, which in every practicable instance will be performed by pious men, who will thereby have innumerable opportunities afforded them of recommending to the children, and the inhabitants of the villages and towns where the schools are situated, the Gospel of the grace of God."

While thus engaged in promoting the highest interests of mankind, the devoted CAREY was again visited with a most severe calamity in the death of his second wife. This was a bereavement of no ordinary kind. "My loss," says he, "is irreparable. If there ever was a true Christian in this world, she was one." To be thus deprived of one who was so admirably qualified, from her Christian character and attainments, to sympathize with him in all his joys and sorrows as a Missionary of the Cross, was a severe trial of his faith and patience. The stroke was a painful one; but he bore it with Christian resignation, feeling that she whom he loved and revered upon earth, had gone to be for ever with her Lord. How many are there, even of God's own people, who, when the desire of their eyes has been taken away from them, have been ready to weep as if they had lost their all! Such was not the feeling of this excellent man. He prized the precious gift of God while it was in his possession, and at the command of God he calmly surrendered it. The Lord had given, and the Lord now took away; and he felt that he could say from the heart, "Blessed be the name of the Lord." A short Memoir of this excellent lady may be found in the APPENDIX to this volume.

In the early part of 1821, it was deemed, by the London Missionary Society, composed of Pedobaptists, chiefly Dissenters, expedient to send a deputation to visit their different stations throughout the world. The appointment was accepted by the Rev. Daniel Tyerman, and George Bennet, Esq., both since deceased, the former at the Mauritius, on his way back to England. After speaking in their Journal, May 3, 1826, of an invitation they received from the Baptist brethren of Serampore, to pay them a visit, and of their boat being sent to convey them from Calcutta to that city, they add, "Here we were most cordially received and welcomed by that venerable man, Dr. CAREY, whose 'honor, name and praise,' are in all our churches, at home and abroad. Dr. Marshman being absent in England, Mrs. Marshman showed us every hospitable attention. We found Dr. CAREY in his study; and we were both pleased and struck with his primitive, and we may say, apostolical appearance. He is short of stature; his hair white; his countenance equally bland and benevolent in feature and expression. Two Hindoo men were sitting by, engaged in painting some small subjects in natural history, of which the doctor, a man of pure taste and highly intellectual cast of feeling, irrespective of his more learned pursuits, has a choice collection, both in specimens and pictorial representations. Botany is a favorite study with him, and his garden is curiously enriched with rarities. In the evening Mr. Tyerman was invited to preach, which he did from Acts viii. 5—8; the subject, *Philip at Samaria.* The congregation consisted chiefly of the Mission family; namely, a hundred and twenty children of both sexes, at Mrs. Marshman's school, and about thirty other persons." A couple of days were very pleasantly spent by these brethren with the worthy doctor, who with them visited the temple of Juggernaut, and other scenes of interest.

As our object in this Biography is to show Dr. CAREY as he was at home, no apology will be deemed necessary for giving an extract of a letter from Mr. Leslie, an excellent missionary at Calcutta, almost immediately after his arrival in India, in 1824:—"At Serampore, where we all were last week, much good appears to be done. Dr. CAREY, who has been very ill, is quite recovered, and bids fair to live many years;—and as for Dr. Marshman, he has never known what ill health is, during the whole period of his residence in India. They are both active to a degree which you would think impossible in such a country. Dr. CAREY is a very equable and cheerful old man, in countenance very like the engraving of him with his pundit, though not so robust as he appears to be there. Next to his translations, Botany is his grand study. He has collected every plant and tree in his garden that will possibly grow in India,—and is so scientific withal, that he calls every thing by its classical name. If, therefore, I should at any time blunder out the word *Geranium*, he would say *Pelargonium*, and perhaps accuse me of ignorance, or blame me for vulgarity. We had the pleasure of hearing him preach from Rom. vii. 13, when he gave us an excellent sermon. In manner he is very animated, and in style very methodical. Indeed he carries method into every thing he does; classification is his grand *hobby*, and wherever any thing can be classified, there you find Dr. CAREY; not only does he classify and arrange the roots of plants and words; but visit his dwelling, and you find he has fitted up and classified shelves full of minerals, stones, shells, etc., and cages full of birds. He is of very easy access, and great familiarity. His attachments are strong, and extend not merely to persons, but places. About a year ago, so much of the house in which he had lived ever since he had been at Serampore, fell down, so that he had to leave it;—at which he wept bitterly. One morning, at breakfast, he was relating to us an anecdote of the generosity of the late excellent John Thornton, at the remembrance of whom the big tear filled his eye. Though it is an affecting sight to see the venerable man weep; yet it is a sight which greatly interests you,—as there is a manliness in his tears—something far removed from the crying of a child."

It would be easy to give not a few similar pleasant accounts of happy interviews with CAREY and his colleagues. We will furnish but one more.

In the commencement of 1831 the family at

Serampore was visited by the excellent missionaries Mr. and Mrs. J. T. Jones, on their way from this country to Burmah. Of course, they, for the time being, found a home. The venerable Marshman said to them, "We think all the missionaries who come to this country belong to us." Speaking of CAREY, the excellent Mrs. Jones, in her interesting Memoir, sold by the AMERICAN BAPTIST PUBLICATION SOCIETY, says,—"We next went to pay a visit to the good old patriarch, whose dwelling is very near the College and Mission House. He gave us a hearty welcome, and showed us his extensive library, and collection of natural curiosities. After dining at brother Marshman's, we took an affectionate farewell of our kind friends, scarcely conscious that our acquaintance was that of a day. On my part, it really was not so, for the names of CAREY, and Marshman had been known, loved, and associated with all my ideas of India and missionary operations since the days of early childhood."

All these parties who then met and conferred together on the kingdom of grace, have since, we doubt not, met in that of glory; nor will they ever look back to their first interview with any other feeling than that of gratitude, that they had been thus called to labor for their adorable Master.

Not long after this account was given, Dr. CAREY met with an accident, by which he was considerably injured, but which soon gave way to the most rapid improvement; so that on the 1st of February following, he thus wrote to his estimable friend, Dr.

Ryland, not supposing that that most excellent man was then in his grave:—"I have now the pleasure of saying, that I am in a state of as good health as I ever enjoyed, except that I limp a little; it is, however, scarcely perceived by others, though sufficiently so by myself. The goodness of God has very far exceeded my expectations, and those of every one else. I cannot walk to any great distance; and seldom preach to the natives. This is, however, abundantly compensated, as it respects them, by the labors of Brother Mack and Brother Williamson, both of whom are truly excellent men, and much interested in the salvation of the heathen. As it respects myself, I am not so well satisfied; for though I have, for several years, been principally engaged in the translation of the Scriptures, still I frequently preached to them till I received the hurt. I take my turn in English preaching, as usual. Next week we have a Mission Association of the Baptist, Independent, [Congregational,] and Lutheran ministers employed by the Church [Episcopal] Mission Society. I am to preach the English sermon on Tuesday evening at the Circular Road Chapel. I think of taking the text, 'Let us not be weary in well doing, for in due season we shall reap if we faint not.' Gal. vi. 9. I, who have seen the work from the beginning, think that much fruit has been reaped already; but some, who came later to the work, cannot compare two periods so distant from each other, as I can, and therefore need encouragement in their work."

We will take yet another view of this excellent man, who thus apologizes to a friend for not writing to him:—"I rose this morning at a quarter before six, read a chapter in the Hebrew Bible, and spent the time till seven in private addresses to God. I then attended family prayer with the servants in Bengali. While tea was getting ready, I read a little in Persian with a Moonshi who was waiting when I left my bed room; read also before breakfast, a portion of the Scriptures in Hindostani. The moment breakfast was over, sat down to the translation of the Rámáyuna from Sanscrit, with a pundit, who was also waiting, and continued this translation till ten o'clock, at which hour I went to college, and attended the duties there till between one and two o'clock. When I returned home, I examined a proof sheet of the Bengali translation of Jeremiah, which took till dinner time. After dinner, translated, with the assistance of the chief pundit of the college, the greater part of the eighth chapter of Matthew into Sanscrit. This employed me till six o'clock. After six sat down with a Telinga pundit, who is translating from the Sanscrit in the language of his country, to learn that language. At seven I began to collect a few previous thoughts into the form of a sermon, and preached in English at half past seven. About forty persons present, and among them one of the puisne judges of the Sudder Dewany 'dawlut. After sermon I got a subscription from him of five hundred rupees, towards erecting our new place of worship; he is an exceedingly friendly man. Preaching was over, and the congregation gone by nine o'clock.

I then sat down, and translated the eleventh chapter of Ezekiel into Bengali, and this lasted till near eleven; and now I sit down to write to you. After this, I conclude the evening by reading a chapter in the Greek Testament, and commending myself to God. I have never more time in the day than this, though the exercises vary."

From the pen of the excellent John Dyer, we take our last view of the results of Dr. CAREY'S labors:—"By steady perseverance in a course of exertion like this, Dr. CAREY was enabled to accomplish a vast amount of philological labor, all more or less subservient to the great design of transferring the inspired oracles into as many of the Oriental tongues as possible. His Mahratta Grammar was followed by a Sanscrit Grammar, extending to more than a thousand quarto pages, in 1806; a Mahratta Dictionary, in 8vo., in 1810; a Punjabi Grammar, 8vo., in 1812; a Telinga Grammar, 8vo., in 1814; besides the Rámáyuna, in the original text, carefully collated with the most authentic manuscripts, in three volumes, quarto, which appeared between the years 1806 and 1810. His philological works of a later date, were, a Bengali Dictionary, in three volumes, quarto, 1818, of which a second edition was published in 1825, and another, in 8vo., in 1827–30; a Bhotanta Dictionary, quarto, 1826; also a Grammar of the same language, edited by him and Dr. Marshman. A Dictionary of the Sanscrit, nearly ready for press, was consumed in the fire of 1812. It is not known that this work was ever resumed; nor did he complete a more extensive undertaking for all, which he had not only projected, but for which he had collected materials—this was—"*An Universal Dictionary of the Oriental Languages derived from the Sanscrit,*" on the plan of Johnson's Lexicon, with the Synonyms in the different affiliated tongues, with the Hebrew and Greek terms of a corresponding meaning.

"Great as were these achievements in the field of Oriental Literature, they were entirely subordinate to, and surpassed by Dr. Carey, in the province of Biblical translation. The versions of the sacred Scriptures, in the preparations of which he took an active and laborious part, include the Sanscrit, Hindu, Brijbbhassa, Mahratta, Bengali, Oriya, Telinga, Karnata, Maldivian, Gurajattee, Bulooshe, Pushtoo, Punjabi, or Shikh, Kashmeer, Assam, Burman, Pali, or Magudha, Tamul, Cingalese, Armenian, Malay, Hindostani, and Persian. In six of these tongues, the whole Scriptures of the Old and New Testament have been printed and circulated; the New Testament has appeared in twenty-three languages; besides various dialects, in which smaller portions of the Sacred text, have been printed. In thirty years, CAREY and his brethren rendered the Word of God accessible to one-third of the world."

No one can be surprised that a man like this should be the admiration of the most dignified personages, especially when we learn that he always remained the humble Christian and the devoted Missionary. Hence we are ready to believe the statement that the Governor General of India once asked him what the Government could do to serve the Missionaries, and we cannot but exult in his noble reply,—"My Lord, the only favor we ask is to be let alone."

About the time that Mrs. CAREY died, the King of Denmark sent to the Doctor and his brethren Marshman and Ward, each a letter, signed with his own hand, expressing his full approbation of their labors, accompanied with a gold medal for each; and shortly after arrived an order from the same quarter to convey a house and grounds, the property of his Majesty, to the Missionaries for the use of the college. He says also in a letter to Dr. Ryland, "I have just received from England information of my being elected a Fellow of the Linnean Society of London; and a member of the Geological Society; and a diploma constituting me a corresponding member of the Horticultural Society of London;" and then, as though turning to his higher engagements, he adds, "I bless God, that, though nearly sixty-two years of age, I enjoy nearly as good health, and get through as much work as ever."

In 1824 he says to the same correspondent: "I think I informed you in my last, of my third marriage. I can add, that my present wife is a person who fears God, and that I have as great a share of domestic happiness, perhaps, as those who are most favored in that respect." Shortly before this he had buried his beloved son Felix, of whom he had spoken, in a letter to this country, as having engaged in the service of the emperor of Burmah. When that event occurred, he asked the prayers and sympathies of his friend Dr. Ryland, because his "poor son had descended from the office of a Missionary of the Cross to be an ambassador of an earthly court."

The Rev. John Leechman, after his arrival in India as a Missionary, wrote in April 1833, a pleasing description of the proceedings at Serampore :—

"Our venerable Dr. CAREY is in excellent health, and takes his turn in all our public exercises. Just forty years ago, the first of this month, he administered the Lord's supper to the church at Leicester, and started on the morrow to embark for India. Through this long period of honorable toil, the Lord has mercifully preserved him ; and at our missionary prayer meeting, held on the first of this month, he delivered an interesting address to encourage us to persevere in the work of the Lord. We have also a private monthly prayer meeting held in Dr. CAREY'S study, which is to me a meeting of uncommon interest. On these occasions we particularly spread before the Lord our public and private trials, both those which come upon us from the cause of Christ, with which it is our honor and privilege to be connected, and those also which we as individuals are called to bear. At our last meeting, Dr. CAREY read part of the history of Gideon, and commented with deep feeling on the encouragement which that history affords, that the cause of God can be carried on to victory and triumph, by feeble and apparently inefficient means."

CHAPTER X.

Decline of Dr. Carey's health—Continued devotedness to his work—Spirit of patience and humility manifested by him—Death—Funeral—Will—Tombstone and inscription—Resolutions of respect to his Memory by Baptist Missionary Society—British and Foreign Bible Society—Asiatic Society of Bengal—Agricultural and Horticultural Society of India—Notice in the Asiatic Journal.

INTENSELY interested in his various engagements, and feeling the importance of pressing on to perform his "one thing," CAREY and his friends were long unwilling to believe that his strength was really failing; but it soon became too evident that he had never fully recovered from the effects of the accident to whieh we have already referred. He was at no time afterwards in sound or even tolerable health for any lengthened period. Besides which, he had more than completed his seventy years, and who could expect, especially when it was remembered that he had labored nearly forty years, in India, that he would again be strong? Attacks of fever, sometimes slighter, at other periods stronger, soon convinced him that the end of his course was fast approaching. But he must, if possible, die in the midst of his engagements, and therefore as soon as he could, he assiduously re-commenced his beloved work of Biblical translation. The only difference he made in his plan was, that he somewhat contracted the circle of his labors, that he might render his work more effective. He now began to concentrate his efforts upon a few of the more important dialects, in order to bring them nearer perfection. His special labor was bestowed upon the Bengali version. Upon the New Testament in this language, his work as a translator commenced; and with the final revision of it, which he completed a little before his death, it closed.

None of my readers will expect to find any thing very marvellous in the circumstances of the death of Dr. CAREY. He had never been a noisy man, nor had he the habit of speaking very much about his feelings. He rested on the atoning sacrifice of Christ for salvation, and labored in the cause of Him who died for sinners like himself, humbly expecting mercy —sovereign and free mercy,—when he came to die. Nor was he disappointed. When he had fully completed the translation to which we have just referred, he remarked, that his work was done, and that he had nothing more to do than to wait the will of his Lord. He would speak of the missionary enterprize in India, and say, "What hath the Lord wrought?" But of his own labors he spoke with much humility, and viewed himself as an unprofitable servant, continually needing the grace of his Saviour. Though he was exceedingly weak, he was pleased to sit as heretofore at his desk, and though he could do very little, he corrected now and then a proof for the press, and spent most of his time in reading. During his illness, he often lamented what he considered his unprofitableness, and always seemed fearful lest he should prove a burden to his friends.

While in this state, daily increasing in debility, he was visited by many who knew and esteemed his character, and came to show him their tender regard. On one occasion, a visiting minister of his acquaintance, asked him how he felt as to his hopes respecting a future world; his reply was very characteristic, "I cannot say I have any very rapturous feelings; but I am confident in the promises of the Lord, and wish to leave my eternal interests in his hands —to place my hands in his, as a child would in his father's, to be led where and how he please." In this frame of mind he continued during the whole of his illness. He suffered from extreme debility, but was nearly free from pain for six months before his decease. On more than one occasion during that period, his end was momentarily expected, but again he revived. So much was he at length reduced, that he could not turn himself on his bed; and for several weeks nearly all he could articulate was "yes," or "no," to questions proposed to him. Nine days only before his death, the brethren at Serampore wrote:—"He is now reduced to the greatest possible debility, and often seems scarcely possessed of conscious existence. But when the letters [from some of his brethren in Europe,] were read, by brother Mack, as he was able to hear them, his spirit seemed to revive, and all his remaining strength was summoned up to bless God, and to pray for blessings on those who were thus inclined to help the Redeemer's cause. Even in the wanderings of his mind, once so masculine and strong, he seems to dwell on this delightful subject. Often in his delirium has he asked to be taken to his desk, that he might write a letter of thanks to the friends at home for all their kindness."

Two days before the death of the venerable saint, the Rev. John Mack wrote to the late Rev. Christopher Anderson, of Edinburgh;—"Respecting the great change before him, a single shade of anxiety has not crossed his mind ever since the beginning of his decay, so far as I am aware. His Christian experience partakes of that guileless integrity which has been the grand characteristic of his whole life. Often when he was yet able to converse, has he said to his friends,—'I am sure that Christ will save all that come unto him; and if I know any thing of myself, I think I know that I have come to him.' The ascertaining of that all-important fact had been his object in much honest self-examination, and the result was a peaceful assurance that his hopes were well-grounded. Having pursued the enquiry to this result, when in the prospect of death, he seems to have been enabled to dismiss all further anxiety on the subject from his mind, and to have committed all that concerned his life and death to the gracious care of God in perfect resignation to his will. We wonder much that he is yet alive, and should not be surprised were he taken off in an hour. Nor could such an occurrence be regretted. It would only be weakness in us to wish to retain him. He is ripe for glory, and already dead to all that belongs to life."

The Rev. John Leechman says:—"When last able to speak on the subject, he told us he had no raptures, but he had no fears. The cross of Christ, the atonement of the Redeemer was the only and all-sufficient ground of his joy."

His removal was now at hand. On June 8, the night before his death, he breathed very hard, and was exceedingly restless, but there appeared no particular symptoms of dissolution. Very early in the morning, as the day dawned, it was evident that he was sinking. He remained in this state till about half past five o'clock, when his spirit took its flight to its eternal home.

The funeral took place on the following morning at five o'clock, and was followed to the Missionary burial ground by a long train of mourners. Several gentlemen from Calcutta attended the mournful solemnity; as did also two officers and the chaplain of the Governor General, sent by the lady of that distinguished personage, to pay the last tribute of respect to the memory of a great and good man. The shortness of the time, the state of the weather, the prevalence of sickness, and other causes prevented many from being present, who sent their kindest assurances of sympathy, and of reverence, and regard for the deceased. The Rev. Micaiah Hill, Congregationalist, then of Calcutta, now of London, offered prayer before they left the house. The procession then slowly moved to the burying ground, the road being lined by the poor natives for whom he had labored so long, and so successfully; among whom there were many of the native brethren and sisters, who joined the procession, and accompanied their friend and pastor to the tomb. After singing the hymn beginning:—

"Why do we mourn departing friends?" etc.

Dr. Marshman delivered an address, and the venerable Missionary Robinson closed with prayer. On the following Sabbath, according to Dr. CAREY'S appointment, Dr. Marshman preached, from a text also chosen by him, for his funeral sermon. The text was, "By grace ye are saved." Eph. ii. 8.

For more than one reason, a copy of the last Will of Dr. CAREY will be acceptable to the reader:—

"I, William CAREY, Doctor of Divinity, residing at Serampore, in the province of Bengal, being in good health, and of sonnd mind, do make this my last Will and Testament in manner and form following:—

"First—I utterly disclaim all or any right or title to the premises at Serampore, called the Mission Premises, and every part and parcel thereof; and do hereby declare that I never had, or supposed myself to have, any such right or title.

"Secondly—I disclaim all right and title to the property belonging to my present wife, Grace Carey, amounting to twenty-five thousand rupees, more or less, which was settled upon her by a particular deed, executed previously to my marriage with her.

"Thirdly—I give and bequeath to the college of Serampore, the whole of my museum, consisting of minerals, shells, corals, insects, and other natural curiosities, and a Hortus Siccus. Also the folio edition of Hortus Woburnensis, which was presented to me by Lord Hastings; Taylor's Hebrew Concordance, my collection of Bibles in foreign languages, and all my books in the Italian and German languages.

"Fourthly—I desire that my wife, Grace Carey, will collect from my library whatever books in the English language she wishes for, and keep them for her own use.

"Fifthly—From the failure of funds to carry my former intentions into effect, I direct that my library, with the exceptions above made, be sold by public auction, unless it, or any part of it, can be advantageously disposed of by private sale; and that from the proceeds, fifteen hundred rupees be paid as a legacy to my son, Jabez Carey, a like sum having heretofore been paid to my sons Felix and William.

"Sixthly—It was my intention to have bequeathed a similar sum to my son Jonathan Carey; but God has so prospered him that he is in no immediate want of it. I direct that if any thing remains, it be given to my wife, Grace Carey, to whom I also bequeath all my household furniture, wearing apparel, and whatever other effects I may possess, for her proper use and behoof.

"Seventhly—I direct that, before every other thing, all my lawful debts may be paid; that my funeral be as plain as possible; that I may be buried by the side of my second wife, Charlotte Emilia Carey; and that the following inscription, and nothing more, may be cut on the stone which commemorates her, either above or below, as there may be room, viz.:—

"'William Carey, born August 17th, 1761; died ——.

> "'A wretched, poor, and helpless worm,
> On thy kind arms I fall.'

"Eighthly—I hereby constitute and appoint my dear friends, the Rev. William Robinson, of Calcutta, and the Rev. John Mack, of Serampore, executors to this my last will and testament, and request them to perform all therein desired and ordered by me, to the utmost of their power.

"Ninthly—I hereby declare this to be my last will and testament, and revoke all other wills and testaments of a date prior to this.

WILLIAM CAREY."

It will be seen by these testamentary arrangements that Dr. CAREY finally terminated the controversy to which we have referred on the question of the property connected with the Mission; and it is gratifying to add that in the end all parties became entirely satisfied, and that, too, without any appeal to courts of law or equity.

It was one of the last injunctions of Dr. CAREY that no marble monument should mark the spot where his remains might rest. His request has been literally complied with, and a little to the north of Serampore, in a calm and retired spot, in the mission grave yard, is deposited all that was once mortal of the great and good man. On a plain cenotaph, his epitaph, by his express direction, is merely this:—

WILLIAM CAREY,
Born 17*th August*, 1761, *Died* 9*th June*, 1834.

> "A wretched, poor, and helpless worm,
> On thy kind arms I fall."

This burial ground contains about an acre, enclosed with a good brick wall; its beautiful gravel walks are lined at proper distances with mahogany trees, and the whole is surrounded with palm groves. Here lie also Ward and Marshman, Krishna Pal, the first Hindoo convert, and a large number of other members of the Mission, till the glorious morning of the resurrection.

Perhaps the divine declaration, "Them that honor me, I will honor," never had a more full accomplishment than in the case of WILLIAM CAREY. The perusal of the following extracts from the Records of some of the most important societies in Europe and Asia will show a very striking contrast between the estimate which that truly great man formed of himself, and that formed by others:—

BAPTIST MISSIONARY SOCIETY.

"The Secretary having reported that intelligence had arrived of the death of Dr. Carey, at Serampore, on Monday, the 9th of June last, it was

"Resolved,

"That this Committee cordially sympathize, on this mournful occasion, with the intimate connexions of Dr. CAREY, by whose death, not merely the Missionary circle with which he was most intimately associated, but the Christian world at large, has sustained no common loss. The Committee gratefully record, that this venerable and highly-esteemed servant of God had a principal share in the formation of the Baptist Missionary Society; and devoted himself, at its very commencement, to the service of the heathen, amidst complicated difficulties and discouragements, with an ardor and perseverance which nothing but Christian benevolence could inspire, and which only a strong and lively faith in God could sustain. Endowed with extraordinary talents for the acquisition of foreign languages, he delighted to consecrate them to the noble purpose of unfolding to the nations of the East the Holy Scriptures in their own tongue: a department of sacred labor in which it pleased God to honor him far beyond any predecessor or contemporary in the Missionary field. Nor was Dr. CAREY less eminent in the holiness of his personal character. Throughout life he adorned the gospel of God his Saviour by the spirituality of his mind and the uprightness of his conduct; and especially by the deep and unaffected humility which proved how largely he had imbibed the spirit of his blessed Master.

"In paying this brief and imperfect tribute to the memory of this great and good man, who was long their associate in Missionary exertion, and whom they have never ceased to regard with feelings of the utmost veneration and respect, it is the anxious desire of the Committee to glorify God in him. May a review of what divine grace accomplished in and by this faithful servant of the Redeemer, awaken lively gratitude, and strengthen the devout expectation that He, with whom is the residue of the Spirit, will favor his church with renewed proofs of his love and care, by thrusting forth many such laborers into the harvest!"

BRITISH AND FOREIGN BIBLE SOCIETY.

The following Memorial was adopted by the Committee of this important Society, on hearing of Dr. CAREY's death:—

"The Committee cannot receive the intelligence of the death of their venerable friend, Dr. CAREY, without expressing their long-cherished admiration of his talents, his labors, and his ardent piety. At a period antecedent to the formation of the British and Foreign Bible Society, Dr. CAREY, and his earliest colleagues, were found occupying the field of biblical translation; not as the amusement of literary leisure, but as subservient to the work to which they had consecrated themselves,—that of teaching Christianity to heathen and other unenlightened nations.

"Following in the track pointed out by the excellent Danish missionaries, they set sail for British India, intending there to commence their enterprize of zeal and mercy; and there, notwithstanding impediments which at first threatened to disappoint all their hopes, but which were afterwards succeeded by the highest patronage of Government—there, for forty years, did CAREY employ himself, amid the numerous dialects of the East; first, in surmounting their difficulties, and compelling them to speak of the true God, and of Jesus Christ whom He hath sent; and then presenting them in a printed form to the people.

"For this arduous undertaking he was qualified in an extraordinary degree, by a singular facility in acquiring languages—a facility which he had first shown and cultivated, and amidst many disadvan tages, in the retirement of humble life. The subsequent extent of his talent, as well as of his diligence and zeal, may be judged of by the fact, that, in conjunction with his colleagues, he has been instrumental in giving to the tribes of Asia the sacred Scriptures, in whole or in part, in between thirty and forty different languages.

"For many years, it was the privilege of this Society to assist him in his labors; he was among its earliest correspondents. If, for the last few years, the intercourse has been less regular, and direct assistance suspended in consequence of difficulties arising out of conscientious scruples on the part of himself and his brethren, still the Committee have not less appreciated his zeal, his devotedness, his humility; and they feel, while they bow with submission to the will of God, that they have lost a valuable coadjutor, and the Church of Christ at large a distinguished ornament and friend."

THE ASIATIC SOCIETY OF BENGAL

held a meeting on Wednesday evening, July 2, 1834, The Right Reverend the Lord Bishop of Calcutta, Vice President, in the chair. The Bishop addressing the meeting, said, it had been suggested to him that the death of the Rev. Dr. CAREY, one of the oldest and warmest supporters of the Asiatic Society, was an occasion which called for some testimonial of the sense entertained by all its members of the value of his services to the literature and science of India, and of their sincere respect for his memory. He had himself enjoyed but two short interviews with that eminent and good man; but a note from Dr. Wallich, who was prevented from attending to propose the resolution, supplied his own want of information:—'Dr. CAREY had been twenty-eight years a member of the Society, and, with the exception of the last year or two of his life, when protracted illness forced him to relinquish his Calcutta duties, a regular attendant at its meetings, and an indefatigable and zealous member of the Committee of Papers since the year 1807. He had enriched the Society's Publications with several contributions. An interesting report on the Agriculture of Dinajpur, appeared in the tenth volume of the Researches; an account of the funeral ceremonies of a Burman Priest in the twelfth. The catalogue of Indian plants and drugs in the eleventh volume, bearing Dr. Fleming's name, was also known to have been principally derived from his information and research. As an ardent Botanist, indeed, he had done much for the science in India; and one of the last works upon which he had been engaged, was the publication, as editor, of his deceased friend Dr. Roxburgh's *Flora Indica*. His Bengali, Mahratta, Telinga, and Punjábé Dictionaries and Grammars, his translation of a portion of the Ramayuna and other works were on our shelves to testify the extent of his learning as an oriental scholar. It was well known that he had prepared, some time ago, an elaborate Dictionary of the Sanscrit language, the manuscript of which, and a considerable portion of the work already printed off, the result of many years intense labor and study, had been destroyed by the fire which burned down the Serampore premises. He had also been of great assistance, as the author testified, in the editing of Baboo Ram Comal Sen's Anglo-Bengali Dictionary. The memory of those members who had been longer associated with him than himself, would easily fill up this very imperfect estimate of his various services. During forty years of a laborious and useful life in India, dedicated to the highest objects which can engage the mind, indefatigable in his sacred vocation, active in benevolence, yet finding time to master the languages and the learning of the East, and to be the founder, as it were, of printing in these languages, he contributed by his researches and his publications, to exalt and promote the objects for which the Asiatic Society was instituted. The close of his venerable career, should not, therefore, pass without a suitable record of the worth and esteem in which his memory was held. His Lordship begged to move that the following minute be entered on the Journals of the Society—it was seconded by Col. Sir J. Bryant, and carried unanimously:—

"The Asiatic Society cannot note upon their proceedings the death of the Rev. WILLIAM CAREY, D. D., so long an active member and ornament of this Institution, distinguished alike for his high attainments in the original languages, for his eminent services in opening the stores of Indian literature to the knowledge of Europe, and for his extensive acquaintance with the sciences, the natural history, and botany of this country, and his useful contributions, in every branch, towards the promotion of the objects of the Society, without placing on record this expression of their high sense of his value and merits as a scholar and a man of science, their esteem for the sterling and surpassing religious and moral excellencies of his character, and their sincere grief for his irreparable loss."

And that it may be seen the feelings of affectionate esteem for the character and memory of Dr. CAREY, were not so far as India was concerned, temporary and evanescent, we may add to the memorials already given, that a large and highly important meeting of THE AGRICULTURAL AND HORTICULTURAL SOCIETY OF INDIA, was held on Wednesday, August 10th, 1842, more than eight years after the death of CAREY, which was presided over by the Honorable Sir John Peter Grant, President of the Society, at which the following motion, notice of which had been regularly given at the preceding meeting, was carried unanimously:—"That the Agricultural and Horticultural Society of India, duly estimating the great and important services rendered to the interests of British India, by the founder of the Institution, the late Rev. Dr. W. CAREY, who unceasingly applied his great talents, abilities, and influence, in advancing the happiness of India, more especially the spread of an improved system of industry and gardening, desire to mark by some permanent record, their transcendent worth, by placing a marble bust to his memory in the Society's new apartments at the Metcalf Hall, there to remain a lasting testimony to the pure and disinterested zeal and labor of so illustrious a character; that a subscription, accordingly from the members of the Society, be urgently recommended for the accomplishment of the above object."

Even at the risk of undue length, which in truth we do not very much fear, we shall transcribe the notice given of Dr. CAREY, in *The Asiatic Journal*, a work over which his personal friends, or his family had no control. The extract will be the more pleasing, because it presents CAREY'S sons, and co-laborers, in connection with himself:—

"Dr. WILLIAM CAREY, whose long, steady, and zealous labors, as a missionary, have gained for him that 'good name' which 'is better than precious ointment,' was one of those pleasing instances wherein humility of deportment is preserved, when acquirements, works, and high reputation might excuse some share of earthly vanity.

"Though of humble origin, the patronage acquired by his merits, so early after his arrival in India, did not elevate him too much, as in some other instances. Four-and-thirty years ago, this good Christian and exemplary Pastor, to his great credit, was selected for the honorable office of Professor of Sanscrit and Bengali in the College of Fort William. With that meekness and singleness of purpose which mark the good Christian, he for a long period was too diffident to avail himself of his distinction as 'Professor,' preferring the humble denomination of 'teacher;' and proving his sincerity of character by declining the acceptance of the full allowance assigned to the more eminent rank. The enlarged income thus derived, was invested in the common fund for the support of the Baptist Mission at Serampore; each 'brother' of the Baptists, as they term each other, drawing therefrom the means for his personal support. Nothing could exceed the harmony in which the brothers Carey, Marshman, and Ward lived together at Serampore. Marshman alone survives. Happily for the interests of Literature, their powers have been so judiciously employed in kindred pursuits, yet sufficiently distinct, as to produce results in which each is an example of excellence of its own kind, and which, at the same time, forms an essential branch of inquiry in those several departments, wherein local circumstances admitted of their rendering themselves most useful to science. Ward, for instance, excelled in a knowledge of Hindoo life; of which he must be accounted to have been a thorough master. From a continual study of the subject, he had insensibly acquired no inconsiderable share of the outward habits of the Hindoos; not the less, however, did he unceasingly pursue, under the banner of the Cross, his attacks upon the strong holds of Hindoo idolatry, as may be seen in his '*View of the History, Literature, and Mythology of the Hindoos.*' His address to the ladies of Liverpool, against the burning of widows, first brought him conspicuously before the eye of the public in England. Dr. Marshman shines as a Chinese philologist, and has shown considerable ability in polemical Divinity. He assisted Dr. CAREY in his translation of the '*Ramayana*' from the Sanscrit, the second great epic poem of the Hindoos. '*The*

Friend of India,' a periodical established by these missionaries, and conducted chiefly by Dr. Marshman,* contains much valuable information regarding the Hindoo civil polity, and of a statistical, local, and commercial nature.

"Dr. CAREY taught Mahratta, as well as Sanscrit and Bengali. A school for instruction in Christian knowledge, English literature and composition, and other branches of European science, is established at Serampore, under the immediate management of Dr. Marshman. The first native newspaper in the Bengali language, called the '*Sumachar Durpun*,' or 'Mirror of News,' was issued from the Serampore Mission press about fifteen years ago; and for the last three years it has been published in the two languages, English and Bengali. The regulations and advertisements of the Bengal Government, which were translated officially into Bengali by Dr. CAREY, are published in this paper, which is edited by Mr. John C. Marshman, son of the Rev. Dr. Marshman

"Dr. CAREY'S productions as a linguist were various and remarkable. His profound knowledge of Sanscrit, aided as he was throughout his long career by the constant attendance of his pundit; and which knowledge we have heard spoken of in terms of the highest admiration by the learned Brahmins of the presidency of Fort William, en-

* This admirable paper, is now conducted by John C. Marshman, Esq., entirely separate from the Mission; and exerts on the whole of India, a salutary influence beyond all estimate.

abled him to acquire the derivative dialects of this original language with astonishing facility. These observations may be verified by reference to his Grammars of the Sanscrit, Bengali, Mahratta, Telinga, and Sikh languages, and by the able manner in which he edited, with a chivalrous devotion to the interests of science, the first Grammar of the Bhotan language, originally prepared by the late Mr. Schroder. Dr. CAREY'S works are distinguished for their practical character, as may be imagined from the opportunities he possessed of drawing his materials from living authorities ; advantages which he did not fail zealously and efficiently to improve, to the great benefit, be it spoken, of Eastern letters. His Grammars of the Pracrita dialects are compendious and easy. In these, he has wisely avoided the evil of great books, and kept difficulties out of sight; a remark, however, which can hardly be extended to his Sanscrit Grammar, nor to that ponderous production, completed with astonishing perseverance, his Bengali Dictionary. It was the opinion of his son, the late Felix Carey, at the earliest stage of this work, as he told us at Serampore, that the first letter of the alphabet, forming the Sanscrit and Greek privative prefix, had been injudiciously multiplied by examples, the positive forms of which were to be found in the subsequent pages. The Doctor, however, acted from the best motive,—an anxiety to supply his pupils with a ready resolution of primary difficulties. As evincing the practical tendency of his works, we may notice a very useful performance, his Bengali and English Colloquies. These were composed in the original Bengali, probably by a clever native, and may be compared, in respect to the graphic power they discover of showing life as it is,—in its rustic and familiar, as well as more polite forms,—to the detached scenes of a good play, exhibiting correct transcripts of nature. But can we avoid noticing here the multiform and able works for the spread of a knowledge of Bengali which have issued of late years from the Calcutta press? Their utility consists in their idiomatic excellence; some of the translations of standard English works into Bengali are speaking instances of success. This language has been widely diffused under the fostering influence of that patron of learning and merit, esteemed for his zealous exertions in the promotion of Oriental literature, and his indefatigable labors as the President of the Calcutta School Book Society.

"It is really wonderful how well these men have succeeded, considering the appalling difficulties of their task. The Bengali style of writing has been considerably improved since the labors of CAREY commenced. This may be seen to high advantage in the published controversies of Ram Mohun Roy with the Missionaries. Not only did CAREY put the wheels in motion by which this result has been produced, but his children and their children are following up the same pursuits. The grand-son of Dr. CAREY studied Hebrew under the late Mr. Greenfield,* with the view of rendering it auxiliary to

* For a brief sketch of this very extraordinary man see APPENDIX.

Missionary efforts. The late Felix Carey, the Doctor's son, who was ten years in Ava, during which period he assiduously studied the Burman language, was as surprising a man as his father. He had the merit of writing and publishing with his own types, the first Burmese and English Grammar. Though the examples selected in this work are not suited to the beginner, being taken from compositions too elaborately worked up, and far removed from the natural colloquial style, to a degree which renders them unintelligible to common people; yet the work, as a whole, has high and singular merit: it is the production of a man of learning, thoroughly versed in the language he expounds. This is clearly evident in the translations, and particularly in the appendix of verbal roots, the most valuable portion of the work; every monosyllabic root has been explained in its several senses, in Burmese and English. By this plan, all the synonymous verbs can be readily found; about ten, for instance, having the sense of 'helps,' may be collected with little trouble. This is a great facility to both the tyro and the advanced student. The critical accuracy with which this section of the work has been executed, is beyond all praise; and indicates a *bona fides* which is perfectly gratifying. Felix Carey was likewise an excellent Sanscrit scholar. We have an abridged *Mugh 'dha Vod 'ha*, arranged for his own convenience and that of the English student, which he printed at the Serampore press. The *Mugh 'dha Vod 'ha* may be rendered 'the charm of wit,' and is a Grammar extensively used in Bengal and the adjacent countries: the pundits of Assam use no other. Felix Carey translated '*The Pilgrim's Progress*' into Bengali, as well as '*Goldsmith's Abridgement of the History of England*,' and other pieces; and at the period of his death he was engaged in several useful undertakings.

* * * * *

"That Dr. CAREY was a successful teacher, we have proofs in men who have risen to the highest dignities in their service, even to be Governors of India. Adverting to the invaluable exertions of the Calcutta School Book Society, of the Committee of Public Instruction in Bengal, and of the Baptist Mission Press, let us not overlook the grand work. CAREY may be said to have translated the Bible into three languages—Sanscrit, Bengali, and Mahratta.

"We may say of the venerable scholar to whom we have dedicated this brief notice, 'Mark the good and perfect man, for the end of that man is peace.'"

CHAPTER XI.

Importance of Christian Independence—General character of Carey's mind—Decision—Constancy—Opinion of Dr. Wayland —Anecdote of his Pundit—Conscientiousness—Aversion to judicial oaths—Benevolence—Simplicity—Shown in his Preaching—An excess of it in social life—Its eminent beauty in connexion with his piety.

THE reader, who has with ordinary care, read the preceding part of this volume, will have perceived that, by the native force of his own mind, and the providential circumstances through which he passed, the principal features of Dr. CAREY'S CHARACTER have stood out with so much prominence, that it is scarcely necessary for the biographer to present any final review. Yet a few brief reflections may not be deemed improper, especially as the volume is more especially designed to portray a sound, vigorous, and simple Christian mind yielding itself to the light of truth, and obeying without reserve certain great principles. We have shown to what religious eminence a man of no original pretension, and with many adverse influences to resist, under the guidance of such light and principles may attain, as well as the good he may accomplish. We may see, too, the importance of investigating the sacred volume for ourselves, and of paying but a measured deference to the opinions of others. Like CAREY, we should, under some circumstances, be content for awhile to follow our convictions of duty, without enjoying the concurrent judgment of others. If we are patient in the prosecution of judicious plans, we shall, in due time, conciliate to ourselves the wise and the good, and secure their patronage; and even the timid may at length commend both our wisdom and our zeal. When the subject of this Memoir first mentioned to his father his purpose of becoming a missionary to the heathen, the good man asked, "William, are you mad?" and when he endeavored to impress the importance and practicability of Missionary efforts upon some of the more enlightened of his brethren, of his own age and standing, the answer was, "If the Lord open windows in heaven, then may this thing be." His life indeed was so long protracted, and his labors were so successful, that he won the good opinion of all whose principles and moral worth deserved regard; but had he died at an early period, before so full a developement of the results of labor had been given, he might have been far less esteemed. "Let every man, therefore, prove his own work, and then shall he have rejoicing in himself alone, and not in another."

In Dr. CAREY'S mind and habits of life there was nothing of the marvellous; no great and original transcendency of intellect; no enthusiasm and impetuosity of feeling; nothing to dazzle or surprise. Whatever of usefulness, and of consequent reputation he attained to, was the result of an entire and patient devotion of a single heart and clear intelligence to a well-defined, great, and practicable object;—an object which demanded great labor, but which presented great attraction, and ultimate success. He had nothing of the sentimental, the tasteful, the speculative, or the curious in his mental constitution. He had, therefore, no help from the warmth of feeling, or the glow of spirits, from the fervor or the fire which actuate painters and poets, and by which even some zealots in religion and morals show themselves to have an existence. To this want of excitement may be traced many of those upbraidings of himself for his imagined inactivity and want of zeal. He was often heard to say, "I think no man living ever felt inertia to so great a degree as I do." He was a man of principle, not of impulse.

Every thing narrated in this volume shows that CAREY'S characteristics were those of decision, constancy, conscientiousness, benevolence, and simplicity. A more marked man for *decision* is scarcely to be found on the scroll of history. There was about him nothing doubtful or vacillating, so that none of his strength was lost in pursuits irrelevant to his purpose. He could clearly discover, and fully grasp, and well define to others, what fixed his attention and commanded his pursuit. The force of his character in this view was seen in the earliest developments of his mental powers. When at school, under the tuition of his father, he never failed in the acquirement of whatever came before him, and would always have time to help his less successful companions. His father, who was singularly averse to the practice of eulogizing the members of his own family, never hesitated to bear testimony to the assiduity, good conduct, and proficiency of William. In his engagements, even in childhood, such as climbing, or collecting objects of natural history, he was always adventurous and persevering. He had used to say, that if there was a tree, the height and difficulty of ascending which daunted the courage of all others, he would never rest till he had reached its topmost bough. If in endeavoring to attain his object he failed, notwithstanding the pain and the peril he had incurred, as soon as he could again leave his home, his object was to climb that same tree, and to take that same nest.

His religious life no sooner commenced, than his true character began to be clearly developed. He threw into religion his whole soul. He investigated truth with his utmost ardor, and when he had found it, "he rejoiced as one who had attained great spoil." He sought to ascertain the will of God, with the simple purpose of obeying it, no matter to what it conducted him. He always maintained that every discovery of divine truth was to be held precious, and that every conviction of duty should be promptly complied with; saying, that the judgment would speedily warp, if its decisions should be found unwelcome; and the conscience soon cease to importune, if its calls were slighted. Commencing thus a diligent and ingenuous enquirer after truth, and holding himself to an uncompromising submission to its dictates, his mind was never thwarted in its purposes, nor weakened by its own criminal indecision; nor were his intellectual and moral powers thrown into conflict. Every impression being justly entertained, it was corrected or confirmed by each succeeding one; so that the soul gathered new vigor with every step of its advancement, and undeviatingly maintained an ascending progress.

In pursuing his scriptural enquiries, the infinite benevolence of the Gospel, and the duty of universally diffusing its blessings indelibly impressed his mind. He clearly saw, that as God's own command lay at the foundation of this duty, so his promise secured the success of those who obeyed it. To engage unreservedly in the work of extending this Gospel he felt was to be the work of his life, and the time when success should be given, together with its degree, and the difficulties to be surmounted in its progress, he could confidently leave with God. He was assured that a dispensation was committed to him, and in fulfilling it he was entirely willing to risk his life. The trials he endured on his first arrival in India, in the neighborhood of Calcutta, at Bandell, and Deharta, the peculiar severity of his domestic affliction at these places, the increased distress this sorrow gave him during his residence at Mudnabatty, above all, the long-continued disappointment of his hopes as to the conversion of the heathen,—will all recur to the recollection of the reader, but when, amidst these vicissitudes and discouragements did he, even for a moment, swerve from his purpose, or falter in his course?

When, in process of time, other brethren joined him in the work, and the requisite facilities were at his command, he chose from the general objects of Missionary life, one, the most appropriate to his talents, and congenial with his taste, we see a still greater concentration of his energies, and are furnished with a still greater help to the just appreciation of his character. To supply the Holy Scriptures to the millions of the East, was the master-purpose of his life. With this, nothing in his esteem was of sufficient importance to justify even a comparison. After he had fully entered upon this labor, the writing of an unnecessary letter, or the diversion of his attention from it for a single hour, he deemed to be sacrilege. To read "a proof" on the Lord's day, he considered to be as holy an act as to study and preach a sermon, or to engage in any of the solemnities of worship; and indeed, in its consequences of far higher importance. In pursuing this work, he was scarcely aware of any obstacles which he had to surmount. Grammars or Dictionaries he generally had none. He learned different languages in the use of them; and then furnished such elementary works as the digests of his own acquirements, for the help of his successors.

It scarcely need here to be said that Dr. CAREY'S character was marked by *constancy*. He was perseveringly steady, and imperturbably regular in all his engagements. This, indeed, this was the great secret of his surprising success. No novelty, either in speculation or practice, ever seduced him from the plain line of duty or labor. He had a calm and dignified satisfaction in the paramount interest of his work, which, arduous as it was, converted it into rest and pleasure. Hence, his mind could submit to the same unvaried routine every day, for thirty years in succession, without relaxation, and without uneasiness. He was subject to many interruptions, had many unexpected and often unprofitable calls, but he would suspend his engagement, whatever it might be, and would attend to them with ease and courtesy. So long as any thing remained to be shown them, or any question for them to propose, he was as much the gentleman of perfect leisure, as though to form his museum and display its subjects, and to plant his garden and describe its productions were the sole employments of his life. But on the moment of their departure, he resumed his chair; for that same moment ended the interruption. There was no alienation of mind to be corrected; for he and the proper object of his attention had never been separated; nor was any mental effort necessary to recover either words or thoughts—except, perhaps, through the dozing of his pundit, who had remained firm to his seat, a statue-like fixture, during the absence of his employer; but he himself had forgotten nothing, and was therefore ready at once to resume his work at the point at which his attention had been suspended. His collegiate engagements, his distant and extensive correspondence, the claims preferred by scientific, literary, and other useful institutions, in the origination and management of which he bore so prominent a part, were enough to absorb the capabilities of an ordinary man, but to him they formed a refreshment rather than a task.

It will be readily believed that he was a very strict economist of time. By regularly apportioning to specific objects, and rigidly adhering to the division, he could keep a number of works advancing together, without seeming to hinder the progress of any, transferring his attention from one to another, without distraction or inconvenience. By devoting to them, without intermission, mere fractions of time, he brought several massive works to a successful issue. Hence his Sanscrit grammar of a thousand pages. Hence, too, his Bengali Dictionary of three quarto volumes, designed and executed on a painfully elaborate plan. And hence, also, his translation of the celebrated Sanscrit poem, the Ramayana; which last work, to the extent of several volumes, he effected by dictating to an amanuensis about two hours only once in seven days. By this means his scriptural translations advanced by slow, but regular degrees, until, in the course of years, the work arrived at so prodigious an aggregate, as to require no ordinary effort to believe it possible that any one man, let his advantages be what they might, could accomplish so vast an achievement. But invincible patience in labor, and unceasing constancy, secured his triumph over every obstruction. He once said to his nephew and first biographer, "Eustace, if after my removal, any one should think it worth his while to write my life, I will give you a criterion by which you may judge of its correctness. If he give me credit for being a plodder, he will describe me justly. Any thing beyond this will be too much. I can plod. I can persevere in any definite pursuit. To this I owe every thing." But how few can *plod!* Many can devise a magnificant scheme, but the plodder is the man who will rise to eminence and respect; and should he live long will make the world his insolvent debtor. It is indeed a true witness which is borne by Dr. Wayland, "The secret of his power resided in energy of will, in indomitable perseverance, and in unconquerable resolution. Hence, whatever he possessed, he used to the uttermost; and by so using, he every day made it greater. In this, more than in any thing else, he differed from other men. Without this, he would have sunk into the common level, and have been scarcely known out of his native village. By means of it, he made himself one of the first men of his age, and has sent abroad an influence which will continue to increase with every year of our world's duration."

This may be a suitable place in which to relate an anecdote of Dr. CAREY from the pen of his son Jonathan. So scrupulous was he of his time, when overcome by sleep, he would double his vigilance to regain what he had lost. In Calcutta he formerly attended three days in the week in the discharge of his duty as professor; and such was his constant attention to his studies, that three pundits were obliged to attend him alternately through the day; one in the morning before breakfast, who was relieved by another after breakfast, occupying his time till his college duties required his attendance. Upon his return from college, another attended him for the afternoon. It was his practice during the hot months to rest half an hour in the afternoon; and on one of these occasions, on a sultry day, some pressing business being on his hands, he requested his pundit to wake him in a quarter of an hour, and leaving his watch on the table to direct the pundit, he retired to his room. It is well known that

Hindoos have a particular aversion to disturb a person in sleep; but the Doctor being strict in his direction, the pundit, when the appointed time was nearly expired, approached softly to the room to awake him; but the door being a little open, he could see him in bed, and hearing him breathe hard, as if in a sound sleep, he could not take the resolution of disturbing him, and came back to the table. Five minutes after the appointed time, the pundit again approached, making a noise with his feet as he walked, in order to arouse him; but this did not succeed, and the pundit's resolution again failed. In about ten minutes after the appointed time the good Doctor awoke; and finding he had overslept the time, he upbraided the pundit for his neglect; when he informed him of what he had done; and pleaded, as his excuse, the custom of the natives, not to disturb a person in sound slumber.

Conscientiousness, it will have been clearly seen, was a very prominent feature in the character of Dr. CAREY. His principles were regular and firm; they were adopted after examination, and never could be departed from; nor did he ever shrink from avowing his sentiments. He had conscientious scruples against taking an oath; severely condemned the manner in which oaths were administered, and urged the propriety of altogether dispensing with them. Several instances may be given in which he took a conspicuous part on this subject, highly characteristic of the man. On one occasion, when a respectable Hindoo servant of the college of Fort William, attached to Dr. CAREY's department, was early one morning proceeding to the Ganges to bathe, he perceived a dead body lying near the road; but it being dark, and no person being present, he passed on, taking no further notice of the circumstance. As he returned from the Ganges after sunrise, he saw a crowd near the body, and then happened to say to one of the watchmen present, that in the morning he saw the body on the other side of the road. The watchman took him in custody as a witness before the coroner; but when brought before that officer, he refused to take an oath, and was, consequently, committed to prison for contempt. The Hindoo, being a respectable person, and never having taken an oath, refused to take any nourishment in the prison. In this condition he continued a day and a half, Dr. CAREY being then at Serampore. On his return, the circumstances were mentioned to him, and the fact that the man had refused to take an oath was enough to make him feel an interest on his behalf. He was delighted with the resolution which the man had taken—rather to go to prison than to take an oath; and determined to do all he could to procure his liberation. He first applied to the coroner; but was directed by him to the sheriff. To that functionary he instantly proceeded; who informed him that he could make no order on the subject. He then sought an interview with the chief Judge, by whose interference the man was set at liberty.

Another instance related to himself personally. On the occasion of his last marriage, the day was fixed on which the ceremony was to take place—

friends were invited—and all necessary arrangements made; but, three or four days before the one fixed, he was informed that it would be necessary for him to obtain a license, in doing which, he must either take an oath, or have banns published. To taking an oath he at once objected, and applied to the senior Judge, who informed him that, as he was not a Quaker, his oath was indispensable; but rather than take an oath, he applied to have the banns published, and postponed the arrangements for the marriage for another three weeks.

The third instance in which he showed this dislike to taking an oath was still different. It was necessary to prove a will in court, in which the name of Dr. CAREY was mentioned, in connexion with the Serampore Missionaries, as executor. An application was made by one of his colleagues, which was refused by the court, on account of the vagueness of the terms "Serampore Missionaries;" but, as Dr. CAREY'S name was specifically mentioned, the court intimated they would grant the application if made by him. The communication was made; but when he was informed that an oath was necessary, he shrunk with abhorrence from the idea; but after much persuasion, he consented to make the application, if taking an oath would be dispensed with. He did attend, and stated his objection to the chief Judge, which being allowed, his affirmation was received and recorded by the court.

Assuredly Dr. CAREY was not less distinguished for *Benevolence* than for any other excellence. The highest authorities in India bore testimony to the mighty influence he had in abolishing some of its most cruel superstitions. So long ago as during the government of the Marquis Wellesley, he presented to that able Governor General three memorials; the first relating to the exposure of infants, chiefly in the northern parts of Bengal, and he saw the entire abolition of infanticide, by government prohibiting the offering of children to the Ganges at Saugor, where a guard was for many years sent to prevent the performance of the horrid rite.

He was also among the number of those who first urged government to abolish *Suttee*, or the burning of widows with the corpses of their husbands; and his assistance was afforded under different administrations, in throwing light on the Hindoo writings on the subject, in order to induce the Government to abolish the rite; and he lived to see his hopes realized in the destruction of it throughout the East India Company's dominions. He likewise interested himself very deeply in endeavoring to remove the pilgrim tax, and the aid afforded to idolatrous worship, and rejoiced in seeing others take up these subjects in a way more energetic than he now could.

The same spirit of benevolence was shown in all his intercourse with his servants, and in his closing years he paid them their wages with his own hands, that none of them might by any possibility be neglected. Their attachment to him was almost boundless. To the poor, especially to those of "the household of faith," he was exceedingly mild and tender; being always ready to relieve them, as far as he was able from the small sum he reserved to himself; and when this failed, he always made them feel the extent of his sympathy.

In remarking on benevolence as one of the leading features of CAREY'S character, Dr. Baron Stow has well remarked that "he deserves a place by the side of Clarkson and Wilberforce," and then goes on to say, with equal truth and beauty, "Every enterprize that could contribute to the advantage of the people, found in him an active and conscientious patron; and long before his course was finished, he had the felicity to see the various forms of agency which he had either originated or strengthened, working out their legitimate results in the improvement of society. And if the spirits of those who rest from their labors are ever permitted to return and watch the progress of their favorite enterprises, and thence derive accessions to their exalted enjoyments, how large must be his income of blessedness, as he shall observe the majestic influence of the moral eauses to which he gave the earliest impulse!—causes whose utility is already felt around the circumference of the globe, and which promise to clothe all lands with

'The beauteous tints of Eden's bloom.'

When that scene, the consummation of his wishes, the end of his toils, and the answer of his devout petitions, shall open upon his gratified vision, what bosom in all heaven, will throb like his, with benevolent triumph?"

But most of all was Dr. CAREY distinguished for his *simplicity*. Here, indeed, lay the great charm of his character;—its main element—its moral beauty, and its mighty strength. Simplicity, indeed, was not in him so much a distinct attribute of character, distinguishable among many others, as the modifying, controlling principle of them all, giving transparency and force to every sentiment, affection, and motive. It guided his whole conduct and intercourse with men, and made him both venerable and lovely. This simplicity, as guided by Divine wisdom, influenced CAREY in the fear of God to *expect great things, and to attempt great things;* his spirit was that of self-annihilation, and firm trust in God. Here was simplicity from which he could never be moved.

It must have been owing to this simplicity of character, that in science he would hear of nothing bnt facts, and pure rigid induction. The great Linnæus was pre-eminently admired by him; and the Count de Buffon almost contemned. So in religious life and principle, no matter who theorized, who speculated and refined; he read the Scriptures, from the beginning of his religious career till its close, simply as a disciple; to learn and to obey; being ever anxious in their exposition, for the edification of others, as well as in his own practice, to maintain the very letter of divine truth.

In his preaching, he was very remarkable for his choice of plain and elementary truths; because he found them to be the life of his own spirit, and never imagined that they could be exhausted, or become trite in the estimation of others. In his visits of later years to Calcutta, he was always expected to preach, and few of the leading persons in society would willingly stay away; yet it was observed by some who had but little relish for his theology, that he had but one statement to make,—that God had done right, and that man had done wrong, and that unless man became reconciled to God he would be punished for ever. Let the unregenerated man smile as he may, here is the grand scope of Christian preaching, excepting that these persons should have gone on to say, that the gratuitous justification of a sinner before God, for the sake of Jesus Christ, with the motives and the duties which it originates formed the grand basis of his ministry, and suggested almost every topic upon which he dwelt. His manner of discussion was always easy and natural. His introduction would be clearly expressed, usually explanatory of the sense of the sacred writer, and of the precise portion of Scripture then under discussion; and by a very few simple sentences, and the easiest possible division, he would approach his subject, and lay open its principal doctrine so clearly, that none could mistake it. Here is a specimen, in a letter to Mr. Anderson, of Edinburgh, two or three years before his death:—"I intend to preach my next sermon from Psa. cxxii. 6. '*Pray for the peace of Jerusalem,*' and to show:—

I. That all the best men in the world belong to Jerusalem, or the church of God.

1. That the inhabitants of Jerusalem are influenced by the highest principles of justice and benevolence.

2. That their actions are calculated to make others happy, and to set forth the glory of God.

3. That the word and all the means of grace are constantly used in the church.

II. That notwithstanding these things there are contentions in the church. They arise from :—

1. The different parties which divide the Christian world.

2. Local disputes and ungenerous rivalries.

3. The associating of the members of Christ with the world in any shape. "Every plant which my heavenly Father hath not planted shall be rooted up." Therefore, pray for the peace of Jerusalem. 1. Sincerely. 2. Earnestly. 3. Perseveringly.

In Dr. CAREY'S preaching, it will be acknowledged there was little excursiveness, no great variety and range in his illustrations, nor, as might be inferred from the character of his mind, was there the least approach to the imaginative or the poetic. There was no *style* about him in any thing; he never even seemed to think of such a thing. The things which he said and did must intrinsically recommend themselves, or fall away. His diction was contracted, his voice inharmonious, and his manner rustic and without ease, yet never offensive. He commended "the truth to every man's conscience in the sight of God;" but it was always by its naked exhibition. The superficial, therefore, and the unthinking, would be very unlikely to receive much impression; and all who heard him must be aware of the absence of those melting and sweet attractions with which Christ himself so commonly invested the doctrines he preached, and which caused his hearers to "wonder at the gracious words which proceeded out of his mouth." This absence of pleasing illustration called forth the quaint remark of the senior Hall, of Arnsby, of which Carey himself used to speak, when criticizing one of his early pulpit exercises:—"Brother CAREY, you have no *likes* in your sermons. Christ taught us that the kingdom of heaven was *like* to leaven hid in meal, *like* to a grain of mustard, etc. You tell us what things *are;* but never what they are *like.*"

Yet none who attended his ministry ever complained that he was tedious; but, on the contrary, it was refreshing and profitable in proportion to the piety of his hearers. There was little enough in the congregation of the Mission house at Serampore to excite, it being composed rarely of few others than the members of the family, the children of the school, and a few insolvent and superannuated settlers. Yet he seemed as lively and as deeply in earnest, as though he had before him an audience of a thousand people. He often told his brethren that he never wrote a sermon in his life, and that he should feel quite unable to set about such an exercise. And when it is recollected, that from an hour to an hour and a half was the utmost he ever gave to the meditation of a sermon, the wonder will be that he could preach so instructively, and with so much precision and acceptance as he usually did. But he had gone through the sacred books so often, and with so much critical attention, and in so many languages, that there was scarcely a passage with the insulated or connected sense of which he was not perfectly familiar. Then, too, he was always reading; so that his mental resources were never exhausted, nor become obsolete. His information was incessantly augmenting, or undergoing correction; while the regular and vigorous exercise of his powers made him capable of commanding, at any time, whatever he knew, for the purpose for which it was available. And though he paid little or no attention to composition, yet he could express a very clear judgment of what constituted its real excellence. "Never," he would say, "have recourse to a figure, unless it renders the idea in connection with which you use it, more clear or more forcible than it would be without it. Let your figures, also, be congruous and agreeable." His own illustrations, when he did happen to use one, were generally derived from some great object in nature; as the sun, the air, the light, or some grand law in the economy of the material universe; and very seldom, indeed, descended to any thing feeble and common-place.

In general conversation Dr. CAREY never excelled. Of this he was entirely conscious, and often complained of himself for what he called his misanthropy. Though, if the subject happened to turn on early friendships, or on Missions, no one's sympathies would sooner kindle, nor could any one exceed him in spirit and energy. To the unpretending, to the poor, and to young persons he was always affable and communicative. But to the inferior social accomplishments, the talking much to little purpose, the sitting patiently and being at ease, or seeming to be bland or complaisant when the topic or spirit of remark was not strictly in accordance with his principles or feelings,—to all this he was unequal. And without at all lessening his excellencies, it must be confessed that somewhat more of ease and elasticity, and a greater readiness to assimilate to the manners of others would have added greatly to the pleasures of his society. But he thought promptly, and always frankly uttered the first impressions of his mind. To flattery he was utterly and inherently averse. Compliments and commendations he used but seldom, and very measuredly. And when he once deviated from his own manner, he met with so decided a repulse that he never again felt disposed to renew the attempt. A nephew of the distinguished President Edwards once called upon him in Calcutta, from this country, and was congratulated by the Doctor on his relationship to so great a man; but the blunt American stopt him short with the remark:—"True, sir, but every tub must stand upon its own bottom."

Excellent, however, as was the simplicity of Dr. CAREY in point of morals, and as adding to the essential worth of his character, we cannot but think that in some economical details of life it was excessive, and injurious both to his own comfort, and the interests of his own department of the Mission. It sometimes left his mind too little his own property; rendering it defenceless, and too accessible to influence from persons of very different mental habits, who could control his practical decisions. The Rev. Thomas Swan, now of Birmingham, in a Missionary address thus adverted to him:—"Dr. CAREY was meek, humble, benevolent, kind, unassuming, undesigning; without what some persons call *tact*. You never felt as though he had some object in view, in rendering you subservient to him or his interests. If he had any defect in his character, I think it was that he was too easy. He once said to me,— 'Brother Swan, I am not fitted for discipline. I never could say—no. I began to preach at Moulton, because I could not say—no. I went to Leicester, because I could not say—no. I became a Missionary because I could not say—no.'" This defect is often intimately associated with great virtue.

But in his religious feelings and experience, his simplicity was most to be admired, and was worthy of entire imitation. The plain, substantial, doctrines of the Gospel were the basis of his hope for eternity; the stay of his soul. "I see no one thing in all my past life," he observed to his friend Dr. Ryland, after recovering from illness, "upon which I can rest; and am persuaded of the hourly necessity of trusting my perishing soul in the hands of my Redeemer. Should you outlive me, and have any influence to prevent it, I most earnesty request that no epithets of praise may ever accompany my name; such as 'the faithful servant of God,' etc. May I but be accepted at last, I am sure all the glory must be given to divine grace from first to last. To me belongeth shame and confusion of face." In this spirit he lived, and thus he died, "looking for the mercy of our Lord Jesus Christ unto eternal life."

APPENDIX

NO. I.

MEMOIR OF MRS. CAREY.

In my judgment there are three things which entitle this brief Memoir to a place in this volume:—The *first* is, that it contains internal evidence of having been written by Dr. Carey; the *second*, that it is an account of a very pious and interesting lady; and the *third*, so far as my knowledge extends, it is at present altogether unknown in this country:—

On Wednesday, the 30th of May, 1821, a little before one in the morning, died at Serampore, Charlotte Emelia, the wife of Dr. Carey, in her 61st year, after an illness of about five days, in which her mind was so graciously supported that death seemed to be disarmed of all its terrors.

Mrs. Carey was born at Rundhof, in the duchy of Sleswick, March 11th, 1761. Her father was the Chevalier de Rumohr, who married the Countess of Alfeldt, the descendant of an ancient family of that name, for several centuries resident in that duchy, and which had now no heir male to inherit the title.

Miss Rumohr was from her childhood the subject of much bodily affliction, which was increased by the mistaken tenderness of her parents, in debarring her, through her weakness of body, that exercise which might possibly have proved its cure. About the age of fifteen, the accidental burning of their family house, in which the lives of her whole family were saved by her waking, almost suffocated with the smoke, and awaking her mother and the other branches of the family, so affected her health, as to render her incapable of walking up or down a staircase to the end of her life.

As she advanced in years, Miss Rumohr found her constitution so greatly improved, that at the earnest persuasion of her parents she left her native country, and sought that health in the South of France and various parts of Italy, which she found it impossible to enjoy at home. In the South of Europe, therefore, she resided some years, till at length her health appeared so much improved, that she thought she might venture again to return to her native land. She had no sooner reached her native shores, however, than she relapsed into her former state of weakness; and a residence there of a few months convinced her friends that it was in vain for her to hope for the enjoyment of health in the north of Europe. Thus debarred the comfort arising from the enjoyment of her family connexions, she felt constrained to look out for some climate better suited to her debilitated constitution. Among other countries pointed out to her, one of her friends suggested India, as likely from the mildness of its climate to agree with her best. She immediately made up her mind to the voyage, intending to settle at Tranquebar, his Danish Majesty's chief settlement in India; and Mr. Anker, one of the Directors of the Danish East India Company, who had been long acquainted with the family, recommended her in a particular manner to the care and kindness of his brother, General Anker, then Governor at Tranquebar. That gentleman also, during her stay at Copenhagen, put "*Pascal's Thoughts*" into her hands, from reading which she received her first genuine religious convictions.

While Tranquebar was her object, however, Divine Providence, who had in reserve for her a blessing infinitely superior to bodily health, was pleased so to order things, that she came in a ship bound to the Danish settlement of Serampore, where she arrived early in the year 1800. Here she was received with great respect by Colonel Bie the Governor, and other Danish gentlemen residing there, and no opportunity offering of her immediately going to Tranquebar, she made up her mind to settle there. It happened that about three months before this, Messrs. Marshman, Ward, Brunsdon, and Grant, (of whom the last was then dead,) had arrived at Serampore from England, and had been persuaded by the good old Governor to settle at Serampore themselves, and invite their brethren Carey and Fountain, to join them, which they did early in January 1800. In these circumstances, Colonel Bie introduced Miss Rumohr to the Mission family, as a lady from her retired habits desirous of having intercourse with them, and who, from her ill state of health, would feel happy in that sympathy and assistance to be expected from a family like theirs. This incident naturally led to an intercourse between Miss Rumohr and them, and to her attendance on Divine worship with them as often as her ill state of health would permit. To enable her to do this, she applied with such diligence to the study of English, that in a few months she was able both to converse with them, and to understand Divine worship in that language.

Brought thus within a religious circle, Miss Rumohr began closely to reflect on the meaning and import of those doctrines which constantly came before her. She had been accustomed from her childhood to read the Scriptures; but while she held them in general high estimation, she had admitted into her mind strong doubts respecting their leading doctrines, particularly those which relate to forgiveness through the death of the Redeemer. This led to much conversation on these subjects with various members of the Mission family, and to her searching the Scriptures with increased diligence. In doing this, she found to her astonishment, that those parts of the Scriptures which she had hitherto almost neglected, particularly Paul's Epistles, were those which most fully developed these doctrines. Although brought up in the Lutheran persuasion, she had never realized the importance of those doctrines which shine so prominently in the works of that illustrious reformer; but she now plainly saw, that the way of salvation laid down in the sacred writings, was evidently through faith in that atonement which Christ had made for sinners; and that genuine faith and repentance were the only means through which sinners could become interested in this salvation, and that the faith which brings it, is that alone which works by love, and changes the whole heart. In a word, they led her to the Friend of sinners, in whom she found one able to save to the uttermost.

Her searching the Scriptures also led her to different views of the ordinance of Baptism. She always thought it wrong to baptize infants, who could have no knowledge of the ordinance; but she now clearly saw that this ordinance was enjoined by the Saviour on all those who should believe on him, to the end of time, and on those alone. Convinced, therefore, that she had never obeyed this command, she was baptized June 13th, 1802.* The following is the account she then gave of her Christian experience:—

"I have been the greatest part of my life a sceptic, but often wished to be convinced of the truth of revelation. For some time past it has pleased God, in his great mercy, to bless to my soul the reading of the Scriptures, too often neglected by me in many parts of my life, and at other times I found them as a sealed book. I highly prized the morals of Scripture; but its evangelical doctrines did not reach my heart. I felt, however, a gradual conviction continually deepening in my mind; the holiness and mercy of God, displayed in the work of redemption, filled my heart with love and admiration, and made sin appear truly heinous, and more to be feared than any thing besides. God also appeared so lovely and glorious as to fill my whole soul. The first sin of which I was convinced, was the alienation of my heart from God. I felt, with grief and shame, that I had lived without God. My whole life now appeared in the most

* It is well known that the female branches of the families of the German nobility are placed in Chapters endowed for that purpose. Miss R. was in one of these Chapters, which admitted of her enjoying its emoluments without being obliged to reside in it. When the account of her baptism reached Germany, she received a letter from the officers of the Chapter, threatening her with the loss of her emoluments, unless she chose to subscribe to the Confession of Augsburgh. She replied, by informing them of her real sentiments, and at the same time denying that they had any right to enquire about her religious sentiments, the Chapters not being religious houses, but mere establishments for the temporal advantage of those who belonged to them. She informed them, that if they pressed the religious test upon her, she would relinquish her right in the Chapter, but that she considered the demand as unjust. It is probable that the matter was dropped; for she enjoyed the emoluments till her marriage, by which they were forfeited.

humbling light: yet I felt no terror. While seeing the infinite evil of sin, and all the aggravations of my crimes, I felt also the infinite value of that sacrifice, which is sufficient to atone for the sins of the whole world; and was led to hope that God would not have awakened my heart if he had not graciously intended to have mercy upon me, and perform his own work in me. I humbly hope for pardon and acceptance through the atonement of our dear Saviour, having no other hope. Every day and every moment afford me new proofs of the evil of my heart, and render him more necessary and precious to me. I experience daily that without him I can do nothing. My most ardent wish is to cleave to him, and to walk in his ways; and my continual wandering from him and his commands, fills me with grief and shame, and shows me how much I need continually to pray, 'Create in me a new heart, O God; and renew a right spirit within me!'"

On the ninth of May, 1808, Miss Rumohr was married to Dr. Carey, which brought her into closer connexion with the Mission family at Serampore, and gave them an opportunity of more fully witnessing her Christian walk and conversation. This connexion God was graciously pleased to continue thirteen years, although the precarious state of her health at its commencement seemed almost to forbid the hope of its continuing a single year. And although she was at no time able to take an active part in domestic concerns, her love to the cause of God, and her esteem for the various members of the family, were sufficiently manifested. Immediately after her marriage, the house she had previously built for her own residence, she gave to the brethren of the Mission, that they might constantly apply the rent of it to the support of native preachers. Towards the native converts she manifested a spirit of Christian affection, rejoicing in their godly walk, and encouraging them by conversing with them in their own language as she had opportunity, which language she had acquired chiefly with this view. In whatever related to the extension of the Gospel, she constantly manifested a deep and lively interest. Whatever seemed encouraging relative to it filled her with pleasure; and she mourned the occurrence of any thing which threatened to retard its progress. In schools she felt a peculiar interest; and though little can as yet [1821] be done in female education, that little she endeavored to encourage to the utmost. Hence, when her daughter-in-law, Mrs. William Carey, had an opportunity at Cutwa, of raising and superintending a school for native girls, she immediately took the expense of that school on herself.

As her weak habit of body confined her much to the house, she devoted a large portion of her leisure to the reading of the Scriptures and of works on practical religion. Among these she much delighted in Saurin, De Moulin, and other French Protestant writers. She admired Massillon's language, his deep knowledge of the human heart, and his intrepidity in reproving sin; but felt the greatest dissatisfaction with his total neglect of his Saviour, except when he is introduced to give efficacy to works of human merit. These authors she read in their native language, that being more familiar to her than English.

She in general enjoyed much of the consolations of religion. Though so much afflicted, a pleasing cheerfulness generally pervaded her conversation. She indeed possessed great activity of mind. She was constantly out with the dawn of the morning when the weather permitted, in her little carriage, drawn by one bearer; and again in the evening, as soon as the sun was sufficiently low. She thus spent daily nearly three hours in the open air. It was, probably, this vigorous and regular course which, as the means, carried her beyond the age of three-score years, (twenty-one of them spent in India,) notwithstanding the weakness of her constitution.

About three weeks before her death, her sight, which had enabled her hitherto to read the smallest print without glasses, failed at once without any previous indisposition, and was afterwards restored only in a partial degree. This seemed to indicate the approaching dissolution of her mortal frame, and as such she appeared to regard it. She, however, still continued her morning and evening airings. But on May 25th, as she was returning in the evening, within a few hundred yards of her own house, she was seized with a fit, which deprived her of perception. From this spasm she recovered in about an hour; but her perception and memory were evidently impaired, of which, however, she seemed scarcely at all conscious. About five in the afternoon of the next day, as she was sitting and conversing cheerfully with her husband, she experienced another convulsive attack, but recovered in about the same time as before. On Lord's day, the 27th, she had no attack, and seemed so well as to give hopes of her recovery. But on Monday she had five attacks in about fifteen hours. Of these, however, while she suffered little pain in them, she retained no subsequent recollection; but they evidently left her memory and perception more and more impaired. During Monday night she had two more attacks, and one on Tuesday morning. This was followed by an ardent fever, which continued till her decease, between twelve and one on Wednesday morning.

On the Lord's day and Monday, she appeared quite sensible that this was the breaking up of her earthly tabernacle; but to her husband, who conversed with her on the probable issue, she strongly expressed her willingness to depart and be with Christ, and intimated that for her death had no terrors. In this serene and happy state she continued, sensation gradually lessening, without apparent pain, till it appeared wholly to depart, which it did some hours before her release from the body.

She was interred on Wednesday evening in the Mission burying ground, at Serampore. Besides her own and the Mission family, the Rev. Messrs. Hough, Bardwell, E. Carey, Yates, and Messrs. Penny and Pearce attended her funeral. The pall on this occasion was supported by Major Wickedie, Dr. Marshman, the Rev. Mr. Hough, R. Williams, Esq., Mr. J. C. Marshman, and a neighboring Armenian gentleman. At the grave Dr. Marshman gave out that hymn of Watts, "Why do we mourn departing friends?" and addressed the spectators; and the Rev. Mr. Hough concluded in prayer. On Wednesday evening, Dr. Marshman preached a funeral sermon for her from 2 Cor. v. 1, "For we know that if our earthly house of this tabernacle be dissolved, we have a building of God, a house not made with hands, eternal in the heavens," selected by Dr. Carey for the occasion. Most of the members of the Danish government attended, with other gentlemen of Serampore, to testify their respect for her memory.

During the thirteen years of her union with Dr. Carey, they had enjoyed the most entire oneness of mind, never having a single circumstance which either of them wished to conceal from the other. Her solicitude for her husband's health and comfort was unceasing. They prayed and conversed together on those things which form the life of personal religion, without the least reserve; and enjoyed a degree of conjugal happiness while thus continued to each other, which can only arise from a union of mind grounded on real religion. On the whole, her lot in India was altogether a scene of mercy. Here she was found of the Saviour, gradually ripened for glory, and after having her life prolonged beyond the expectation of herself and all who knew her, she was released from this mortal state almost without the consciousness of pain, and as we most assuredly believe, had "an abundant entrance ministered unto her into the kingdom of our Lord and Saviour Jesus Christ."

NO. II

MEMOIR OF MR. WILLIAM GREENFIELD.

Probably no thoughtful reader, when he has carefully examined this Memoir, will doubt the propriety of its insertion in this place. Perhaps few men more closely resembled Carey in his humble origin, his acquirements as a linguist, and the application of his attainments to the preparation of the Scriptures. It is mournfully pleasant to the author of this volume to record the memory of one whom he knew and esteemed in life, and whose works will long contribute to make his name fragrant. "When," says the able editor of the English Baptist Magazine—"When we mention the editor of '*The Comprehensive Bible*,'* it will be perceived that we refer to one to whom many of our readers are indebted for a work of great utility, the compilation of which required extensive knowledge and sound judgment; but when we add that, in the service of the British and Foreign Bible Society, his varied talents were brought into exercise in no fewer than twelve European, five Asiatic, one African, and three American languages, and that the committee of that institution believed themselves justified in ascribing to him in all the works in which he had been engaged as editor, 'sound learning and a critical judgment—a constant perception of the duty of a faithful adherence to the very letter of the sacred original—and minute and unwearied diligence,' it will be seen at once that he was a philological prodigy, and that the history of his intellectual rise and progress deserves attention." For the materials of this narrative we are indebted to the late Samuel Bagster, Esq., a deacon of a Baptist church in London.

* This best of all editions of the sacred volume for the pulpit or the pastor's study, has been beautifully reprinted in this country, by Messrs. Lippincott, Grambo & Co. of Philadelphia.

William Greenfield was born in London, April 1st, 1799. His parents were of Scotch extraction; his father was a seaman, and at the recommendation of his pastor, the Rev. Dr. Waugh, of the Scottish Secession church, he was employed as a foremast-man on board the Duff, in her second missionary voyage, from which he returned in safety, but was subsequently drowned. William thus became fatherless when he had scarcely reached his third year. His mother, who was a pious woman, having relatives in Scotland, removed from London in 1802, to Roxburghshire, where she obtained her livelihood in service; placing her little boy under the care of a relative, in the vicinity of her employer's residence, by whom William was treated as one of the family, sharing in the education of his young cousins. When he had reached his tenth year, his mother, finding him averse to agricultural employments, determined on quitting her situation, and removing with him to London, where she entered the service of another family; and through the kind patronage of the venerable Dr. Waugh, her son was, in 1812, bound apprentice to Mr. Rennie, a respectable bookbinder, in whose family strict religious discipline was maintained.

In the interval which elapsed between his removal to London, in 1810, and the date of this engagement, William was confided to the care of his two maternal uncles. These young men, being of a studious and devout turn of mind, had formed a strong desire to read the holy Scriptures in the original languages; and their nephew, finding them employed in these studies, expressed an ardent desire to be taught the Hebrew. This desire, as far as their slender means afforded, was gratified; and to this circumstance, unimportant as it seemed at the time, may be traced the first development of young Greenfield's unsuspected faculty for acquiring languages, and the direction given to his future literary pursuits.

After his removal to Mr. Rennie's, his progress in the study of the Hebrew was advanced by a circumstance, which afterwards he could not but regard as providentially arranged. In the house in which his employer occupied workshops, there dwelt a Jewish Rabbi, who was a reader of the law in the synagogue at Denmark Court, Strand. This gentleman was in the practice of urging among the apprentices and journeymen, his objections against the Christian interpretations of the prophecies relating to the advent of the Messiah, and the truth of Christianity itself. Young Greenfield had frequent disputations with him on these points, as he subsequently had with several other Jews; and being pressed closely with objections, built on the alleged defectiveness or inaccuracy of the authorized version of the Old Testament, he offered to give up his opinions, if, upon being thoroughly taught the Hebrew language by his opponent, he should find his assertions to be founded in truth. The Jew took him at his word; and, though fully and laboriously employed at his master's business during the day, Greenfield employed himself with so much assiduity and enthusiasm to his studies after working-hours, that he soon became so well versed in the language as to surpass his teacher, and to subvert his learned arguments against the Christian faith; notwithstanding which, the Rabbi became warmly attached to his young pupil, and ever afterwards expressed a high sense of his extraordinary talents, and moral worth. In these discussions, which were always conducted with good temper, young Greenfield displayed his native shrewdness, as well as his familiar acquaintance with the Bible; and anxious to avoid committing the cause of truth by inconclusive reasonings, whenever he found himself at a loss, or foiled in dispute, he modestly applied to his venerable pastor, Dr. Waugh, for advice and assistance. The Doctor, however, like the Jewish Rabbi, soon found himself surpassed as a linguist by his young disciple, and is reported to have said to him, on one occasion, "Hout, mon; ye ken depths of criticism that I na meddle with: ye are gone over me." For a considerable time, Greenfield enjoyed the privilege of meeting Dr. Waugh, in the evenings, two or three times a week; and so well satisfied was the venerable pastor, from these interviews, of the piety and theological attainments of his amiable *protege*, that he admitted him at the early age of sixteen, as a communicant in the church over which he presided, and of which Mr. Greenfield continued a beloved and consistent member till the decease of his honored friend and spiritual father.

During his study of the Hebrew, young Greenfield, to facilitate his own acquirements, compiled a complete Lexicon of that language, of which he became passionately fond. Having made great advancement in this branch of sacred literature, he next applied himself to the study of Chaldee, and some other cognate dialects. The language of the Christian Scriptures now engaged his attention, and he prosecuted the study of the Greek, as well as afterwards of the Latin, in a class with several other young men connected with him in business, and in the Fitzroy chapel Sunday Schools, in which he had become a gratuitous teacher. The extraordinary facility with which he acquired a knowledge of these languages, apparently without labor or effort, and the ease with which he overcame difficulties, that to his classmates seemed almost insurmountable, are stated to have been truly astonishing. Their fellow-student soon became their instructor. Yet his acknowledged superiority was unattended by any of that conceit, or self-complacency, which too frequently characterizes the self-taught scholar; and those who knew him at this period, bear witness to his amiable and unassuming manners, which engaged the love of all his associates. From Latin he proceeded to the French; and thenceforward he thought nothing of encountering the difficulties of a strange language, even when enveloped in a peculiar character.

During this time he is said to have labored very hard in his master's business, working, with the intervals of meal-hours, from six in the morning till eight in the evening, in summer, and from seven to nine in winter. After the expiration of his apprenticeship, at twenty-one, he worked for two or three years, at his trade, as a journeyman; nor did he ever suffer his favorite studies to divert him from his business, or to break in upon the time which he considered as his employer's. By bringing his dinner with him in the morning, and despatching his frugal meal in a quarter of an hour, he had three-quarters of an hour left, during the absence of his fellow-workmen, which he was at liberty to devote to studious recreation. In this way he accumulated a fund of general information, as well as improved his knowledge of the learned languages.

Having purchased a copy of the edition of the Hebrew Bible belonging to Mr. Bagster's Polyglott, Mr. Greenfield addressed a letter to the Publisher, suggesting some improvements, and pointing out the desirableness of a Hebrew Lexicon, as a companion volume. This led to interviews, and subsequently to Mr. Greenfield's employment by Mr. Bagster as a reader of proofs in various learned and foreign languages ; in which capacity he distinguished himself by his literal accuracy, as well as by his higher qualifications as a linguist.

In the years 1828 and 1829, Mr. Greenfield conducted through the press an edition of the Syriac New Testament, for the Polyglott series, and the preface to that publication was furnished by himself in Syriac. In 1830, he undertook, at Mr. Bagster's request, a new edition, or rather a new version of the New Testament in Hebrew. About the same time, he edited the Greek Testament of the Polymicrian edition ; compiled, as a companion volume, the Polymicrian Greek Lexicon of the New Testament; and prepared the corresponding edition of Schmidt's Greek Concordance.

The Comprehensive Bible was first published in the year 1826. The title was adopted, as explained in the prospectus, on account of the extensive and multifarious nature of the contents; comprising four thousand illustrative and critical notes, and five thousand marginal references, a general introduction to the study of the Scriptures, introductory and concluding remarks to each of the sacred books, and several different tables of contents and indexes. So valuable a mass of biblical information was never before condensed into a single volume.

In 1830, the concerns of the British and Foreign Bible Society had become so extensive and varied in their character, that it was deemed necessary to select a gentleman whose special duty it should be, to exercise a superintendence over the versions and editions prepared and printed, with the aid of the society. The extraordinary acquirements and habits of Mr. Greenfield, pointed him out as a suitable person to occupy the post; and in consequence, the superintending of the editions printed in foreign languages, whether in England or abroad, was committed to his charge; the correspondence with the translators, revisors, and editors of translations, was confided to him: and he was rendered responsible for the accuracy and conformity with the rules of the Society of all editions of the Scriptures coming under his revision. In this important office he labored with great diligence, and exhibited enterprizing powers. The perusal of his Quarterly Reports fills the mind with astonishment. A faculty of discovering the genius of a new language, almost intuitive, seems to have been accompanied in him with a memory so retentive that it parted with nothing, and an appetite for labor which constant exertion could never satisfy.

"The most astonishing proof, however," says Mr. Bagster, "that he gave of his facility in mastering a new language, and of his talents for philological criticism, is to be found in his published 'Defence of the Serampore Mahratta Version of the New Testament; in Reply to the Animadversions of an Anonymous Writer in the Asiatic Journal for September, 1829.' In this pamphlet of about eighty pages, which procured for its author the honor of being chosen a member of the Royal Asiatic Society, no fewer than two and twenty languages are brought to bear successfully on the argument; each cited in its proper character. It is quite a typographical curiosity, and the expense of printing it would have been enormous, had I not been provided with a polyglott apparatus. The subject I first introduced to him, and the whole expense of the printing I took upon myself. The most remarkable feature of the pamphlet, however, is the accurate acquaintance which the writer appears to have attained of the Mahratta itself,—a language of which, but a few weeks before his undertaking to enter the lists with one of the first Mahratta scholars of the day, he was utterly ignorant,—never having had his attention drawn towards it, or having even learned the character. The acquisition of a new alphabet was, however, the work of only twenty-four hours; and in this instance it was strikingly evinced, how soon his aptitude for philological investigations, aided by his previous acquisitions, enabled him to master any language to which he turned his mind." The origin of this publication is described in its preface, and as it goes to show much of the character of its author's mind, no apology need be made for quoting the passage :—

"The present pamphlet owes its origin to a friend. Aware of my attachment to critical literature, he put into my hands, about the commencement of December last, the Asiatic Journal, containing the critique on 'The Oriental Versions of the Scriptures,' accompanied by a request that I would freely and impartially state my opinion on the subject. I accordingly sat down to its perusal, and was struck with the bitter spirit which it betrayed, and the manifest inconsistencies which every where appeared. This naturally aroused my suspicions of the accuracy of the writer's statements, and the truth of the assertions which he so confidently made. I therefore made notes of every thing which appeared inaccurate or unfounded, in order to assist me in my proposed communication. In the meanwhile, however, having accidentally met my friend, I expressed my conviction of the untenable nature of the charges against the Mahratta version, and read a few observations in support of my statement. Encouraged by his approbation, and that of another friend who was present, and in compliance with their united request to make public the facts of the case, I threw my remarks into their present form. The result of this examination is now before the reader ; from which he will perceive the utter falsehood of the accusation, and the consequent accuracy of the Mahratta version. Never was there, perhaps, a case of more complete failure. Every charge has melted away before the rays of truth ; and nothing remains apparent but the gross errors and misrepresentations of the accuser."

It was this masterly production which first directed the attention of the Committee of the British and Foreign Bible Society to Mr. Greenfield. In the Resolutions which they passed on occasion of his death, they say, "They remember with delight, that it was his valuable defence of the Mahratta version of the New Testament, against the criticisms advanced in the Asiatic Journal for September, 1829, that first brought him under the notice of the Committee." This defence was regarded by Oriental scholars as triumphant, and the Royal Asiatic Society showed their judgment of its merits by electing him a member of their body.

Cordially attached as Mr. Greenfield was to the doctrines of Revelation, he did not escape those imputations which men of contracted minds too often delight to throw on all those whose views of truth are more enlarged than their own. The knowledge of what opponents urge, and of the only ways in which they can be successfully met, often exposes an advocate of truth to the suspicion of those who see but one side of any subject, and are only acquainted with the arguments which pass current in their own circle. Mr. Greenfield's appointment to office in the Bible Society, was the signal for a sudden, unmeasured, and most disingenuous attack, chiefly by some violent and bigoted ministers of the Established Church. This cruel conduct, there can be no doubt, hastened his end.

The first symptoms of serious indisposition manifested themselves October 22, 1831; but they did not prevent his attendance on the morning service on the following day at Jewin street Chapel, where, since the death of the Rev. Dr. Waugh, he had been a constant attendant, under the ministry of the late Rev. Thomas Wood. As the week advanced, his bodily illness increased, and his spirits became greatly depressed. The effects of intense and constant application, together with the anxiety and mental distress which he had suffered from the unjust aspersions cast upon his character by his polemical assailants, now made themselves unequivocally apparent, when it was too late to repair the mischief which had been wrought. For some time his health had been undermined; and there was, perhaps, something morbid in the acuteness with which he felt attacks, that he ought to have despised. A friend, to whom he paid a short visit in September, was so much struck with these indications of the overwrought and unhealthy state of his bodily frame, as to urge upon him, very earnestly, the imperious necessity of his taking more exercise, and paying strict attention to his regimen. At that time, a temporary relaxation from study, and a little medicine, might have averted the fatal attack, which, under other circumstances, would scarcely have put on so serious a form. On the 28th, nearly a week after the first symptoms appeared, the Rev. Mr. Wood visited him, and found him in a composed and happy state of mind; but he seems to have been not without some presentiment of the issue. In this interview, he expressed his confident trust in Jesus Christ as his Redeemer. On the following day, his pastor again visited him, when Mr. Greenfield expressed himself in the following terms:—" Since I have been here, I have learned more of the depravity of my heart, than I knew before; but, blessed be God, I have also had the inward witnessing of the Spirit, that I feel myself to be a pardoned sinner through the blood of Jesus Christ. *For worlds I would not have been without this illness.* I have had most delightful intercourse with my heavenly Father. I have enjoyed that nearness of access, which prevents my doubting my interest in the precious blood of a crucified Redeemer; and I am ready and willing, if it be the Lord's will, to depart and to be with Christ." Even under the influence of delirium, he gave indications of what was uppermost in his thoughts and feelings. Frequently would he exclaim, " They are piercing me through and through. I am not a Neologian." But so far was he from cherishing any angry feeling towards his calumniators, that in a mild interval, he earnestly entreated that no step might be taken in his vindication during his illness, desirous that, if he should not survive, all animosity might be buried in his grave; and he expressed the most cordial forgiveness towards all who had injured him. His dying breath fully attested the noble and striking confession of his faith which, a short time before he had made, addressed to the editor of the " *Christian Observer*," an organ of the Evangelical party in the established church.

On the event of his death being communicated to them,

the Secretaries and Editorial Committee of the British and Foreign Bible Society expressed their wish to testify their high regard for their deceased colleague by attending the funeral. Other gentlemen, esteemed for their literary attainments, united in this desire; and arrangements were made accordingly. His remains were interred in the burial ground of the chapel of Ease, at Holloway, a northern suburb of London, November 14th, the funeral being attended by not less than forty clergymen of different denominations, besides very many professional and literary gentlemen and private friends. The following inscription may be found on the stone which covers the spot:—

> "This stone records the Burial place of that devoted and amiable Servant of the Lord Jesus Christ, WILLIAM GREENFIELD, M. R. A. S., Superintendent of the Editorial Department of the British and Foreign Bible Society, Author of several important Works, and an eminent Linguist,
>
> *Multæ Terricolis Linguæ, Celestibus una,*
> ΠΟΛΛΑΙ ΜΕΝ ΘΝΗΤΟΙΣ ΓΛΩΤΤΑΙ,
> ΜΙΑ Δ'ΑΘΑΝΑΤΟΙΣΙΝ.
> Born April 1, 1799.—Died Nov. 5, 1831."

At a meeting of the Committee of the British and Foreign Bible Society, held at their house in Earl Street, November 21, 1831, a series of Resolutions was adopted, in which it is stated, "That this Committee feel it a duty to record their persuasion, that nothing has occurred during his brief connection with the Society, to invalidate those satisfactory assurances of the unexceptionable moral and religious character of Mr. Greenfield, which were received at the time of his appointment; while in the transaction of business, he has uniformly conducted himself with such skill, diligence, and urbanity, as fully to realize the expectations which the Committee had entertained."

In the subsequent Annual Report, the Committee express

their deep regret, at the loss which the Society had sustained by the decease of Mr. Greenfield, whose "extraordinary talents, combined with his habits of business, rendered his services peculiarly valuable." His removal, it is added, "has made the committee more and more sensible of the importance of the office which he held. They can hardly expect to meet in any single individual such extraordinary powers as were possessed by Mr. Greenfield;" but "they have felt how necessary it is, with as little delay as possible, to fill up the vacancy." The examination and printing of the Persian Version, and several others, was for some time suspended altogether, on account of his removal.

But the crown of his character was his fervent piety. In illustration of this fact, it ought to be mentioned, that he approached all his biblical labors in a devotional spirit. It is said, that he never sat down to the translation of the New Testament into Hebrew, his last great work, without first imploring the assistance of the Holy Spirit, by whose inspiration the sacred volume was given. Religion was in him an ever active principle, the source of his happiness, as well as the main-spring of his conduct. In conversation he was always the instructive and cheerful companion, ever ready to impart, without ostentation, the information he possessed, and, by the charm of his manners, interesting all who came into communication with him.

One additional fact shall close this brief sketch, which we hope will encourage many a young man in our land in "the pursuit of knowledge under difficulties." He was once in company at the house of a friend, with a gentleman of deistical principles, a stranger, who proposed to him the following among many similar questions:—"Can you give me the reason why Jesus Christ is called THE WORD? What is meant by THE WORD? It is a curious term." Mr. Greenfield, unconscious of the motive, or the sceptical principles of the inquirer, replied, with the mild simplicity and decision by which his character was marked, "I suppose, as words are the medium of communication between us, the term is used in the Sacred Scriptures to demonstrate that HE is the only medium between God and man. I know no other reason." The lips of the deist were closed, for no answer could be made to such a reply; and the friend in whose presence this passed, could not but admire the meekness of wisdom with which a reply was returned, so well adapted to silence the gainsayers.

NO. III.

THE LITERARY CHARACTER OF DR. CAREY.

By H. H. Wilson, Esq., M. A., F. R. S., Boden Professor of Sanscrit in the University of Oxford, Member of the Royal Asiatic Society, and of the Asiatic Societies of Bengal, Paris, etc.

[Written in 1836.]

The labors of Dr. Carey in Oriental literature were subordinate to the great object of his sojourn in India, and were devoted especially to the great purpose, especially of facilitating the acquirement of various Indian languages, with a view to their employment in the translation of the Holy Scriptures, and in maintaining with the natives that colloquial intercourse which is the readiest and surest mode of influencing their feelings and opinions.

At the time when Dr. Carey commenced his career of Oriental study, the facilities that have since accumulated were wholly wanting, and the student was destitute of all elementary aid. With the exception of those languages which are regarded by the natives of India as sacred and classical, such as the Arabic and Sanscrit, few of the Indian dialects have ever been reduced to their elements by original writers. The principles of their construction are preserved by practice alone, and a grammar or a vocabulary forms no part of such scanty literature as they may happen to possess. Accustomed from infancy to the familiar use of their vernacular inflexions and idioms, the natives of India never thought it necessary to lay down rules for their application; and even in the present day they cannot, without difficulty be prevailed upon to study systematically the dialects which they daily and hourly speak. Europeans, however, are differently cir cumstanced. With them the precepts must precede the practice, if they wish to attain a critical knowledge of a foreign tongue. But when the Oriental languages first became the objects of investigation, those precepts were yet to be developed, and the early students had therefore, as they gathered words and phrases, to investigate the principles upon which they were constructed, and to frame, as they proceeded, a grammar for themselves. The talents of. Dr. Carey were eminently adapted to such an undertaking, and, combining with the necessities of himself and of others, engaged him, at various periods, in the compilation of original and valuable elementary works. His Sanscrit grammar was the first complete grammar that was published; his Telinga grammar was the first printed in English; his Karnata and Mahratta grammars were the first published works developing the structure of those languages; his Mahratta Dictionary was also one of his first attempts in the lexicography of that dialect; his Punjabi grammer is still the only authority that exists for the language of the Shikh nation; and, although he must concede to Halhed the credit of first reducing to rule the construction of the Bengali tongue, yet, by his own grammar and dictionary, and other rudimental publications, Dr. Carey may claim the merit of having raised it from the condition of a rude and unsettled dialect, to the character of a regular and permanent form of speech, possessing something of a literature, aad capable, through its intimate relation to the Sanscrit, of becoming a refined and comprehensive vehicle for the diffusion of sound knowledge and religious truth.

The first of the Indian tongues to which the attention of Dr. Carey was directed, was naturally that of the province which was the scene of his Missionary duties—Bengal. He soon found, however, that a thorough knowledge of Bengali was unattainable without a conversancy with Sanscrit, which he always regarded as "the parent of nearly all the colloquial dialects of India," and "the current medium of conversation amongst the Hindoos, until gradually corrupted by a number of local causes, so as to form the languages at present spoken in the various parts of Hindostan, and perhaps those of some of the neighboring countries." He commenced the study of the Sanscrit, therefore, at an early period of his residence, and his labors in it have placed him high amongst the most distinguished of our Sanscrit scholars. It appears also that he was early induced to acquire a knowledge of Mahratta.

Upon the first establishment of the college at Fort William, by Marquis Wellesley, in 1800, the known attainments of Dr. Carey pointed him out to the government of India as a fit person to be attached to the new institution, and he was accordingly engaged to give tuition in the Sanscrit, Bengali, and Mahratta languages, with the title of teacher; his own humility disclaiming the more ambitious designation of professor, at least till the year 1807, when he submitted to be so entitled. He continued to occupy this situation until the virtual abolition of the college by the discontinuance of European professors in 1830—31. He then retired upon a pension, far from adequate to the length and value of his services, and the character for ability, industry, regularity, and judgment which he had uniformly maintained.

One of the first works published by Dr. Carey was his Grammar of the Sanscrit language. In his dedication to Lord Wellesley, dated in 1806, he terms it "the first elementary work in the Sanscrit language yet published."* The first and only volume of Mr. Colebrooke's Grammar was printed in 1805, and would be entitled to the merit of priority; but, in point of fact, it was preceded by a more than equal portion of Dr. Carey's work, a part of which, containing the first three books, was published in 1804, although the whole did not appear until a later date. The contemporaneous appearance of the two works is evidence that they were compiled separately and independently, and that the later could not in any way have been indebted to the earlier of the two. This is also manifest from the difference that prevails in the plan of them, and their resting upon the authorities of various schools. Dr. Carey may be considered,

* "A Grammar of the Sanscrit Language, composed from the works of the most esteemed Grammarians; to which are added Examples for the exercise of the Student, and a complete list of the Dhatoos or Roots. By W. CAREY, Teacher of the Sanscrit, Bengali, and Mahratta Languages in the College of Fort William. Serampore Mission Press, 1806."

therefore, correct in calling his the first complete Grammar of the Sanscrit language; and it was undoubtedly an original work, which made its appearance in the very infancy of Sanscrit study.

The Sanscrit Grammar of Dr. Carey is a work of immense extent and labor. It forms a quarto volume of more than a thousand pages. It is divided into five books; the first treats of the letters and of their euphonic combinations; the second, of declension; the third, of conjugation; the fourth, of the formation of derivative nouns; and the fifth, of syntax. Attached to the syntax is a translation of the first three chapters of the Gospel of St. Matthew, and the text of one of the Upanishads, or theological sections of the Yajur Veda, with an English version. There is also a very useful appendix, consisting of a list of all the radicals of the Sanscrit language, alphabetically arranged, with the indicatory letter of their respective conjugations, and their meaning both in Sanscrit and English. A copious index concludes the Grammar. The general plan of the work is to collect the principal rules of each subject into separate sections, and then to subjoin the examples, connected with the foregoing precepts by appropriate numbers. This is particularly the case in the books on declension and conjugation: in the others, the rules and exemplifications are more nearly approximated. The rules are given in the technical language of the authorities followed, which are especially the works current in the lower Gangetic provinces, or those of Vopadéva, Kramadeswara, Durgadása, etc. To a mere English student, the rules are of a somewhat unusual, and therefore unintelligible character; and to make a satisfactory use of this Grammar, a native Grammar, particularly the Mugdhabodha, of Vopadéva, should be read at the same time with it. All that is strange and perplexing will then disappear, and the work of the English Grammarian will be found a most serviceable illustration and interpreter of the brief and technical compilation of the Indian philologist. It is some disadvantage, however, to Dr. Carey's work, that the system which he followed, and which the circumstances of his situation recommended, is that which is peculiar to Bengal, and is of comparatively local and limited currency. The unwieldy size of the volume, arising, not only from the abundance of the materials, but from the unnecessary size given to the Sanscrit types in the early stages of Hindoo typography, is another venial imperfection. But, notwithstanding these drawbacks, Carey's Sanscrit Grammar is a work of very great merit; and in the immense accumulation of useful examples and illustrations which it affords, especially in the paradigmas of the verbs, and in the development of derivative nouns, it is of invaluable assistance, both to the beginner and to the more advanced student.

Dr. Carey never engaged to any considerable extent in the prosecution of Hindoo literature unconnected with philological research. The only published work in which he is known to have been concerned, is the text of the epic poem, the Rámáyana, which he edited, and to which he subjoined a translation, in concert with Mr. Marshman.* This publication originated with the Asiatic Society of Bengal, and the Council of the College of Fort William, and was the first of an intended series of translations from Sanscrit, "designed to disseminate a just idea of the religion and literature, the manners and customs of the Hindoos." The Rámáyana was the work first selected by a Committee of the Asiatic Society and the College Council, and the translators were employed under their patronage and instructions. The work, which was begun in 1806, had advanced, in 1810, as far as to three volumes, comprising only two out of the seven books of the original. It was either then or shortly afterwards discontinued; the patronage, it is believed, being withdrawn, and the means of its prosecution having therefore ceased. The task, in truth, was not very congenial to the talents and pursuits of the translators. A mytho-epic

* "The Ramayana of Valmeeki, in the original Sanscrit, with a Prose Translation and Explanatory Notes. By DR. CAREY and JOSHUA MARSHMAN. Serampore." Vol. I., 1806; Vol. II., 1808; Vol. III., 1810. The latest lists of Serampore translations announce four volumes of Ramayana, but it is not known when the fourth was published.

poem was scarcely within the scope of missionary study, except as subsidiary to the acquirement of the language, or to an acquaintance with the belief of the Hindoos. The text is printed with considerable care; but the translation, in which the translators avow that " elegance of expression, and even perspicuity, has been sacrificed to a strict conformity to the original," does not adequately or truly represent the original, although it is written in a style of exceeding simplicity. The book was also printed in an injudicious form, and would, if the work had been completed, have extended to a very inconvenient and expensive multiplication of volumes.

The remaining contributions of Dr. Carey to Sanscrit literature are less easy to be defined. Mr. Colebrooke has acknowledged his assistance in conducting the Amara Kosha through the press at Serampore; and the same gentleman, in his introductory remarks to the condition of the Hitopadesa, ascribes to Dr. Carey the office of editor.* In this publication, the text of the Hitopadesa, the original of Pilpay's Fables, was printed upon a collation of six manuscript copies; and although many errors require correction, yet they are not more than might have been expected from the variations and defects of the manuscripts, and the novelty of the task, it being the first Sanscrit book ever printed in the Devanagari character. The same volume comprehends an epitome of a collection of Tales, called the Dasa Kumára, and the three Satakas, or Poetical Centos of Bhartri Hari. Besides this acknowledged aid to the cultivation of Sanscrit, it seems probable that Dr. Carey assisted Mr. Ward in his Account of the Hindoos, especially in the Abstracts and Translations of the Philosophical Works there given. It was understood, also, that he had prepared for press some translations of treatises on the metaphysical system called Sánkhya; but these were never published. It was not in Dr. Carey's nature to volunteer a display of his erudition, and the literary labors already adverted to arose in a great mea-

* " The editor, Mr. Carey, undertook the publication on a suggestion from the Council of the College of Fort William, and under the patronage of Govern ment."

sure out of his connexion with the College of Calcutta, or were suggested to him by those whose authority he respected, and to whose wishes he thought it incumbent upon him to attend. It may be added, that Dr. Carey spoke Sanscrit with fluency and correctness.

The department of Oriental literature which may be considered in an especial manner as that over which Dr. Carey presided, was, however, the language and literature of Bengal. The situation of the capital of British India; the extent and importance of the province, comprehending a population, it has been computed, of 25,000,000; and the multiplied and intimate relations which have grown out of its long-continued connexion with British rule, have always rendered it advisable to rear a body of public functionaries, competent to discharge in Bengal the duties of their appointments for themselves, and without the intermediation of native agents. Hence a considerable proportion of the junior members of the Bengal civil service were enjoined, or induced to acquire a knowledge of Bengali, during their early career as students in the College of Fort William; and the tuition of a permanently numerous class devolved therefore upon the Bengali Professor. When Mr. Carey commenced his lectures, there were scarce any but *viva voce* means of communicating instruction. There were no printed books. Manuscripts were rare; and the style or tendency of the few that were procurable, precluded their employment as class-books. It was necessary, therefore, to prepare works that should be available for this purpose; and so assiduously and zealously did Dr. Carey apply himself to this object, that, either by his own exertions, or those of others, which he instigated and superintended, he left not only the students of the language well provided with elementary books, but supplied standard compositions to the natives of Bengal, and laid the foundation of a cultivated tongue and flourishing literature throughout the country.

According to a highly competent authority, Baboo Ram Comol Shen, the compiler of a valuable Dictionary, English and Bengali, which has recently arrived in England, it appears, that no book was ever written in the language of Bengal prior to the sixteenth century. From that date, to the commencement of the nineteenth, a few legendary tales were composed, and some Sanscrit compositions were translated, but no elementary books were written; and the cultivation of the language, insignificant as it had been, was on the decline when the College of Fort William was founded. "From this time forward," says our author, "writing Bengali correctly may be said to have begun in Calcutta, and a number of books were supplied by the Serampore press, which set the example of printing works in this and other eastern languages. The college pundits, following up the plan, produced many excellent works; amongst them the late Mrityunjaya Vidyalankara, the head pundit of the college, was the most eminent.* I must acknowledge here, that whatever has been done towards the revival of the Bengali language, its improvement, and, in fact, the establishment of it as a language, must be attributed to that excellent man, Dr. Carey, and his colleagues, by whose liberality and great exertions many works have been carried through the press, and the general tone of the language of this province has been so greatly raised." No individual is better qualified than the talented native whose words are here cited, to appreciate accurately the share taken by Dr. Carey in the improvement of the language and literature of his country.

The first Grammar of the language of Bengal was compiled by Mr. Halhed, of the East India Company's civil service, and printed at Hoogly in 1783. It is a work of merit; but in the interval that had elapsed between its appearance and the institution of public lectures in Bengali, it had probably become scarce, and was no longer available for the wants of the students of the College. Dr. Carey printed the first edition of his Grammar in 1801; and whilst acknowledging the aid he had derived from Halhed, observes, "I

* Mrityunjaya Pundit was especially attached to the service of Dr. Carey, as professor in the college, and was held by him in high and deserved estimation. His portrait is included in the picture taken by Mr. Home of Dr. Carey, and which has been engraved for this volume. He continued until his death associated with his master and friend in useful literary occupations.

have made some distinctions and observations not noticed by him, particularly on the declension of nouns and verbs, and the use of particles." In the preface to his second edition, printed in 1805, he remarks, "Since the first edition of this work was published, the writer has had an opportunity of obtaining a more accurate knowledge of this language. The result of his application to it he has endeavored to give in the following pages, which, on account of the variations from the former edition, may be esteemed a new work." The variations alluded to were chiefly of the nature of additions, particularly in the declensions and derivations of nouns, and in the conjugations of the verbs, extending the Grammar to nearly double its original size. Several editions have been subsequently printed, but they have not differed in any material respect from the second and more perfect form.

The Bengali Grammar of Dr. Carey, explains the peculiarities of the Bengali alphabet, and the combination of its letters; the declension of substantives, and formation of derivative nouns; the inflexions of adjectives and pronouns; and the conjugations of the verbs: it gives copious lists and descriptions of the indeclinable verbs, adverbs, prepositions, etc., and closes with the syntax, and an appendix of numerals, and tables of weights and measures. The rules are comprehensive, though expressed with brevity and simplicity; and the examples are sufficiently numerous and well chosen. The syntax is the least satisfactorily illustrated; but this defect was fully remedied by a separate publication, printed also in 1801, of Dialogues in Bengali, with a translation into English, comprising a great variety of idioms and phrases. This work, also, has passed through several editions; and, independently of its merit as a help to the acquisition of the language, it presents in many respects, a curious and lively picture of the manners, feelings, and notions of the natives of Bengal.

A more laborious and important publication was effected at a later period by Dr. Carey, in his Bengali and English Dictionary. The first volume was printed in 1815: but the typographical form adopted, being found likely to extend the work to an inconvenient size, it was subsequently reprinted in 1818: a second and third volume appeared in 1825. These three volumes comprehend above two thousand quarto pages, and about eighty thousand words; a number that equally demonstrates the copiousness of the language, and the industry of the compiler. Besides the meaning of the words, their derivation is given wherever ascertainable. This is almost always the case, as the great mass of the words are Sanscrit. Mr. Halhed long since maintained "the impossibility of learning the Bengali dialect without a general and comprehensive idea of the Sanscrit, from the close and intimate connexion between the two;" and Dr. Carey observes with regard to the materials of his Dictionary, "Considerably more than three fourths of the words are pure Sanscrit, and those composing the greater part of the remainder are so little corrupted that their origin may be traced without difficulty. Dr. Carey also states, that he endeavored to introduce into the Dictionary every simple word used in the language, and all the compound terms which are commonly current, or which are to be found in Bengali works, whether published or unpublished. It may be thought, indeed, that in the latter respect he has been more scrupulous than was absolutely necessary, and has inserted compounds which might have been dispensed with, their analogies being obvious, and their elements being explained in their appropriate places. The Dictionary also includes many derivative terms, and privative, attributive and abstract names, which, though of legitimate construction, may rarely occur in composition, and are of palpable signification. The insertion of such words, however, is no otherwise objectionable, than that it tends to swell the Dictionary to an inconvenient and costly bulk, and must have added materially to the trouble of the compiler; at the same time it evinces his careful research, his conscientious exactitude, and his unwearied industry. The English equivalents of the Bengali words are well chosen, and of unquestionable accuracy. Local terms are rendered with that correctness which Dr. Carey's knowledge of the manners of the natives, and his long domestication amongst them, enabled him to attain; and his scientific acquirements and conversancy with the subjects of natural history, qualified him to employ, and not unfrequently to devise, characteristic denominations for the products of the animal and vegetable world peculiar to the East. The objection taken to this Dictionary, on account of its bulk, was subsequently obviated by the publication of an abridgement, prepared under Dr. Carey's own superintedence, by Mr. J. Marshman, printed in 1827. Most of the compound and derivative terms were omitted, and the publication was reduced to a thick octavo volume. Although, however, this has the advantage of being more readily consulted, it by no means obviates the necessity of the original, to all who seek to acquire any thing beyond the rudiments of the Bengali language, in which the Dictionary of Dr. Carey must ever be regarded as a standard authority.

In addition to these elementary works, which were especially his own, Dr. Carey took an early and active part in the promotion and preparation of works intended to facilitate the acquisition of the Bengali language. This duty was most urgent in the early part of his career, when Bengali works, as we have seen, had scarcely any existence, even in manuscript, and printing was utterly unknown to the natives of Bengal. A press was speedily established by Dr. Carey and his colleagues at Serampore, and in subordination to its especial purpose of multiplying copies of the translations of the Scriptures, it was devoted to the printing of the first efforts of native literary talent. Various translations from Sanscrit into Bengali, as the Hitopadesa, the Buttees, Sinhasan, and others, were prepared and printed in 1801. In 1802 the early translations of the Ramayana and Mahabharat were published; and from that time to the present day many useful works in Bengali, as well as in other languages, have issued from the Serampore press, to most of which Dr. Carey contributed encouragement or aid. The indirect promotion of Bengali literature, effected by the example and impulse of the press of Serampore, has been still more important, and of late years has rendered it less necessary for the directors of that establishment to originate compositions in the language of Bengal. Calcutta now abounds with printing presses, belonging either to Europeans or to natives, which are kept actively at work upon the productions of indigenous talent and attainment; a striking contrast with the state of things thirty years ago, when the means of promulgating knowledge was as defective as the disposition to seek or the ability to impart it, and an alteration for which Bengal is mainly indebted to Dr. Carey and the missionaries of Serampore.

Of a less prominent, but equally useful character, were the labors of Dr. Carey in other Indian dialects. The political relations that arose between the British government and the Mahratta States, about the date of the institution of the college of Fort William, recommended the introduction of the study of the Mahratta tongue, and to Dr. Carey was assigned the office of teaching it. In this, as in the other dialects, elementary books were wanting, and Dr. Carey, to use his own expressions, "thought it his duty to do the utmost in his power towards facilitating its acquisition by attempting a grammar." A Mahratta grammar, he states, had been written many years before in the Portuguese tongue, but he was not able to procure a copy, and was therefore obliged to reduce the language to its rudiments for himself. This work was published in 1805, and five years afterwards he printed a Mahratta Dictionary, containing about ten thousand words. Of late years, considerable attention has been paid to the cultivation of Mahratta in the Presidency of Bombay, and more perfect and elaborate grammars and dictionaries have been given to the public. To Dr. Carey, however, belongs the merit of having set the example, and of having under the most unpropitious circumstances, first rendered the language attainable by European students.

The same merit applies to his grammars of the Telinga, Karnata, and Punjabi dialects. The Telinga was the first published grammar of that tongue in English. For the Karnata grammar, also, no model existed, nor was there any for the Punjabi. The two former have been succeeded by works prepared in the countries where these languages are spoken, and with the benefit of more protracted and regular cultivation; but the Punjabi grammar of Dr. Carey is still the only medium through which a conversancy with the dialect spoken between the Indus and the Sutlej, is to be obtained. These works are all characterized by the same features—succinctness and perspicuity; and are excellently adapted to the wants of young students. The intentions of this author, and the modest estimate he formed of the value of his productions are thus stated in the preface to his Telinga grammar:—"A wish to contribute to the more extensive cultivation of the Indian languages, has induced the writer to undertake this work. Should this object be in any measure accomplished hereby, he will feel gratified, and still more so, should it induce any one who has opportunity and leisure to execute any of these elementary works which are necessary to render us familiar with the languages of India, so brightly deserving of cultivation." The wish here expressed has been, of late years, satisfactorily complied with; and its fulfillment is, in a great degree, owing to the example set by the venerable scholar by whom it was entertained.

In addition to the works which were intended to facilitate the acquirement of the vernacular languages, Dr. Carey took an active interest in every attempt to make India familiarly known, both to its rulers and its people. He was an early associate of the Asiatic Society of Bengal, and furnished one or two instructive papers to the Researches; and he was a diligent contributor to the Agricultural Society of Calcutta, of which he was one of the founders, and for some time president. Besides a valuable catalogue of the plants of the Company's Botanical Garden at Calcutta, which he printed in 1814, Dr. Carey was engaged for several years, in the publication of a Flora Indica, in concert with Dr. Wallich: two volumes only of this work have appeared. He had contemplated other works on the natural history of India, and particularly on its ornithology, with which view he had at one time formed a collection of birds, that he might observe their living habits. But his public duties, his literary pursuits, and the task to which his best energies were dedicated, prevented him from accomplishing this desirable object. There can be no doubt that he also bore a part in the periodical publications of the Serampore press, particularly in the journal denominated "*The Friend of India,*" which was published monthly or quarterly for several years at Serampore, and in which questions of high importance to the moral and political improvement of British India were discussed with ability, experience, and judgment.

These various pursuits were, however, all secondary to the main end of multiplying and disseminating translations of the Holy Scriptures, which has been steadily pursued by the Society of which he was the chief ornament, for about forty years. It appears that Dr. Carey commenced his labors in this department before 1794, and that he had completed a version into Bengali of the whole of the New Testament, and of part of the Old, by 1796. The former was printed and circulated in 1801, and a translation of the Psalms and of the prophecies of Isaiah was printed in 1803. His next undertaking was a Sanscrit translation, in which the New Testament was printed in 1808, the Pentateuch in 1811, the Historical Books in 1815, and the Hagiography in 1816. Subsequently, improved editions of both versions were taken in hand by the original translator, and a revised version of the Bengali was prepared and published in 1832.* Considerable advance had been made also in the revisal of the Sanscrit translation, and the Pentateuch and Historical Books had been printed. It is to be hoped, therefore, that Dr. Carey may have been spared to put the finishing hand to the work, at least in manuscript, and thus wound up his pious labors and his well-spent life together.

The revised edition of Dr. Carey's Sanscrit translation will, no doubt, be exempt from many of those imperfections which its preparation at so early a period of Sanscrit study ren-

* This formed the third edition of part of the Old Testament; and the fourth of the rest, the sixth edition of the New Testament, and the seventh of the Gospels.

dered unavoidable. These defects were neither incorrectness nor obscurity; but inelegance of expression and harshness of construction. The latter was, in a great measure, inseparable from the principle which appears to have influenced all the Serampore versions—that of translating as closely to the letter of the text as practicable; a rigor of fidelity that cannot fail to cramp and distort the style of the translation. The novelty of the subject, also, and the necessity of employing words to designate meanings which, although admissible, were unusual and unknown, contributed to disfigure the composition; and the Sanscrit version has, accordingly, never been popular with the learned natives of India, for whose use, more particularly, it was designed.

The intimate and long-continued intercourse maintained by Dr. Carey with all classes of the natives of Bengal, and the repeated opportunities of revision afforded by the multiplied editions of his Bengali translations, have very naturally improved their character, and rendered them generally intelligible, and acceptable to the population of the Province. The latest editions, however, still retain something of the newness of the first; and the style is less easy and idiomatic than might have been expected. They are, however, performances of real merit, and have been very extensively serviceable in diffusing accurate notions of Gospel truth amongst the millions of Bengal.

Shortly after the establishment of Dr. Carey and his brethren at Serampore, they devised and carried into execution a comprehensive scheme for the translation of the Scriptures into all the languages of India. Accordingly, they published, in the course of about five and twenty years, translations of portions of the Old and New Testaments, more or less considerable, in forty different dialects. It was not to be supposed, nor did they pretend, that they were conversant with all these forms of speech. The mode they adopted has been explained by the Missionaries in several of their reports. Each version was made by a competent native, to whom the language of the translation was vernacular, and who was also conversant with one or more of the languages into which the original had been previously translated. The individuals usually employed on the task usually sat and wrote in the same room; and, when any difficulty arose, had thus an opportunity of referring to some one or other of their associates, who was qualified to give them information and assistance. Their performances were also superintended and finally revised by their European employers. The language of the version might not, it is true, be familiar to the reviser; but a knowledge of Sanscrit, and of one or two vernacular dialects, was usually sufficient to enable him to appreciate the general character of the translation. "Above three fourths," say the Missionaries, "of the words in most of the secondary cognate languages, were understood in all their bearings, through the Sanscrit,, the Bengali, and Hindee, before those secondary languages were begun; and in some of them, even seven eighths of the words, to say nothing of the construction, the idiom, and the usual figures of speech, in which there is little variation throughout the whole of the Indian family." There can be no question of the general accuracy of this statement; and a conversancy with Sanscrit affords a highly useful key to all the dialects spoken in India. A knowledge of it, and of one or two of its principal derivations, would, no doubt, enable the possessor to follow a pundit in his explanation of the version in a form of Indian speech not regularly studied, and to ascertain its general conformity with a given original. It may be doubted, however, if such preparation is sufficient to estimate the precise force even of simple terms in all cases; and still less can it appreciate idiomatic phraseology. It is to be apprehended, therefore, that many of these versions are written in too scholastic a style, and partake too much of the nature of Sanscrit composition, to be universally understood by the unlettered population of the districts in which they were designed to circulate. At the same timo, it must be acknowledged that this difficulty is insuperable in the actual state of most of the dialects of India. They are inadequate to the expression of new ideas; terms for these must, therefore, be borrowed from the kindred or parent tongues, with a cer tainty that these equivalents are as unfamiliar to the people at large as the notions which they are employed to convey. It was scarcely possible, therefore, to have published versions essentially dissimilar from those which have been printed; and the only question is, Whether the time was ripe for such translations at all? Admitting their expedience, it cannot be denied that the plan devised for their preparation was judicious; and it is equally indisputable, that surprising industry and uncommon attainments were displayed in its execution. In this department, Dr. Carey took a leading part; and it was in connexion, especially, with his duty of revising the different translations, that he added, to his great proficiency in Sanscrit and Bengali, a knowledge of those dialects whose elements he first investigated. Possessed, in this way, of at least six different dialects, and of Sanscrit, the parent of the whole family, and endowed with a genius for philological investigation, Dr. Carey was peculiarly qualified to superintend the translation of the Scriptures into a number of cognate languages; and it may be granted that, in combination with his colleagues, he carried the project to as successful an issue as could have been expected from the bounded faculties of man.

The review which has thus been attempted of Dr. Carey's labors in Oriental literature, whether for purposes of general utility, or the special objects of his Mission, is necessarily brief and imperfect. The books referred to are not all in the writer's possession, and they are not procurable, perhaps, in this country. Had they been at hand, however, a more detailed examination would have been of interest only to the few Orientalists who have already formed their opinion of the works in question. Enough has, perhaps, been said to show that Dr. Carey was a man of no ordinary powers of mind; that he was endowed with prompt and acute apprehension; that he must have been capable of vigorous and enduring application; that his tastes were varied, and his attainments vast; and that he perseveringly and zealously devoted all his faculties and acquirements to the intellectual and spiritual improvement of his fellow creatures in the East.

INDEX.

INDEX.

A.

B.

C.

D.

E.

F.

G.

H.

J.

K.

L.

M.

N.

O.

P.

Q.

R.

S.

T.

U.

V.

W.

THE END.

www.ingramcontent.com/pod-product-compliance
Lightning Source LLC
LaVergne TN
LVHW020246110826
845151LV00003B/1028

* 9 7 8 1 4 2 5 5 3 2 2 1 5 *